SEVENTY YEARS ON A MOTORCYCLE

October 3 2009

dear Kate —

Herb would love it (only a suggestion) if this book helps to encourage you towards the delights possible!

A pleasure to have met you
Best Joan Gunnison

ii

SEVENTY YEARS

ON A

MOTORCYCLE

*An Up-to-the-Hilt Reminiscense
by a College Literature Professor*

Herbert Foster Gunnison

To order additional copies of this book, contact:
Xlibris Corporation
1-888-795-4274
www.Xlibris.com
Orders@Xlibris.com
15141

CONTENTS

PART I
The Endless Delights
of Being Freshly Alive

PART II
Education is not What
it is Cracked up to be:
it is just Cracked up

PART III
7,500 Miles
of Looking Back—Through Rear View Mirrors

PART IV
Options for People Who Hate to go to Work

PART V
Lordy How I'm Going to Hate It When the Music Stops

viii

This book is dedicated
to the memory of
Henry Adams
1838-1918

No honest historian can take part with—or against—
the forces he has to study.
To him even the extinction of the human race
should be merely a fact to be grouped
with other vital statistics.
Henry Adams

'Sublime on radiant spires he rode'
—From Dryden's text for Handel's
"Alexander's Feast"

And to
Joan
my Eternally Feminine
wife and editor

PREFACE

Way back in the twentieth century when the *fin de siecle* ritual of combining wishful thinking with numerology was approaching its climax and the illusion of permanence was languishing in intuitive minds, I celebrated my seventy-fifth birthday by riding my 1978 BMW motorcycle, which in mechanical terms was at that time roughly equal to my living vintage, 7,500 miles—one hundred miles for every year of my life. The year was 1994, the trip was a month-long celebration of the happiness of being alive and my beemer was the perfect traveling companion because whizzing like a projectile across a static roadway adds supernatural dimensions to landscapes, fantasies and sensations.

This book is also a celebration of the pleasures of the intellect and imagination, and while my ballpoint pen may not be the perfect vehicle in a word-processed society for this soul-searching odyssey, let's hope that strolling arm in arm and linked by mutual good will we can at least manage to journey across the street. If nothing else we may discover where we once were, which side of the street we prefer, and above all the pleasure to be had from crossing against the light whenever we catch the fuzz picking his teeth.

At various stages of my calculated rebirth I was given four parties and established an unofficial world record by blowing out three hundred birthday candles. This wasn't because I'm such a lovable guy, but rather because when you get to be seventy-five you become a living metaphor for everyone's hope for immortality. All the laughter, candlelight and frostings on cakes were reminders to me, at least, that the minute you try to go beyond such moments the fun goes down the drain. I worship at the shrine of the silly birthday cake because you only have to devote a few minutes a year to it and because for most of my life it has seemed obvious that if God had truly revealed the secret of immortality to us there would be only one religion.

On an even merrier note my whimsical friend John Duthie presented my 1978 beemer with a surprise birthday cake with sixteen flickering candles on it. We disconnected the spark plug wires, and, while John held the cake under the muffler, I hit the starter: the bike blew its candles out fumelessly in a humongous, 1,000 cc puff. Not bad for an engine with over 200 thou on its lungs, eh? This was a touching moment for the three of us, because you rarely see technology used playfully these days. For the life of me I can't see why everyone takes electronics so seriously. Not all that long ago an unsung genius gave us the unforgettable drawing of Christ laughing, but we still don't get it: we keep trying to make the Computer think when our goal should be to make It laugh.

What we are about to share is the story of my near tragic trip and the events which led up to it, including all the education the law allows in any one discipline, which in my case happened to be American Literature.

It is also, along with other life-related themes, a dramatized yet lighthearted account of how my love/hate relationship with formal education and technology evolved and how I learned to live in a state of beatitude while the world I loved was crumbling under my feet.

INTRODUCTION

Two Perspectives on the Bridge

to a World of Your Own

From Mozart I learned to say important things in a
conversational way.

—George Bernard Shaw

Before I begin to tell you about what I have always considered to be the most exciting life I ever expect to live I'd like to fill you in on how it got that way because, believe me, it was no accident.

For this job we only need a smattering of philosophy, so the purpose of these preliminary remarks is simply to sketch in the intellectual sources of my excitement.

Because we are conditioned to think of philosophy in grandiose terms and because motorcycles play a thematic role in this book, I ask you please to give me a break and not assume that my references to bikes have complex metaphorical purposes, because they don't.

In my book the motorcycle is nothing more profound than an occasional symbol for the imperishable joy of being alive and able-bodied—in Part I as a callow experimenting adolescent, in Parts II-IV as an adult systematically looking for answers and in Part V as a completely fulfilled old man about to face the greatest challenge of his life.

» » » » »

Before getting down to the nitty-gritties an important caveat is necessary for readers who, through no fault of their own, do not have a clear idea of the difference between the world of books and the world of living social intercourse. This can be a serious problem, especially in a deliberately informal memoir such as this one, because unless a distinction is made between a written account of the truth as it occurred in the author's life and the same truth as it might be expressed in a conversation, the author can easily wind up as a victim because descriptions of his or her little successes may be interpreted as boasting when the writer was merely attempting to push the reader's envelope by means of experiences described as artfully as the motivating talent will allow.

My writing credo is that good writing is the business of telling the truth. Every author I respect has this credo, and, like my colleagues, I also believe that readers of seriously conceived books are people who seek out and appreciate this kind of information because, whether it turns out to be *actually* true or not in their case, it nevertheless helps them get a handle on who they really are.

My living credo is similar to my writing credo: I view life as a game of solitaire in which the only rule that matters is that you don't cheat. The same principle must apply to a game of double solitaire.

In view of the above, whether it turns out that my parents were rich or poor or that I was a success or a failure by your frames of reference, what matters is the account of my solitary struggle for self-fulfillment which follows—and more importantly, by extension, your struggle, dear reader—a sobriquet I am using for what will surely be the first of many times, since we're in this together.

» » » » »

If you are a non-biker and are curious about what it feels like to ride one, let me at least tell you how to simulate the experience, because as we both know all the greatest moments in life, almost by definition, transcend words.

The next time you're on a super slab and have occasion to walk across one of those glass-enclosed bridges from the parking lot on your Southbound lane to the culinary consummations of contemporary culture on the Northbound lane, take time out from your fast-moving life to check out the following drill: as you walk above the roadway you just exited, the traffic will be moving beneath you from left to right. Disengage yourself from the crowd, walk over to the right window and, standing as close to it as possible, look as straight down as you can on the road below.

The chances are all you will see will be concrete.

Then,

without warning,

you will experience

a visceral

ZAP!!! as an automobile emerges into full view in 1/11th of a second.

For that 1/11th of a second the car is the equivalent of a motorcycle, but it instantly becomes just a car again as it seemingly moves slower and grows smaller and less significant until the underlying truth of what you have just witnessed disappears in the distance and is quickly forgotten.

For the motorcyclist, however, that incredible 1/11th of a second doesn't stop until the bike stops or slows down.

Motorcycles are the truth about speed. They exist purely for human exultation—like opera, like literature—like any major art-of-living resource.

All this is the opposite of truth as most people experience it. The human beings in the cars which ZAP out from under the overwalk in 1/11th of a second are not aware how fast they are really going. Even the fact that they're moving 114 feet per second doesn't mean anything. That's just arithmetic. But hell begins with arithmetic, as Wagner, I think correctly, said.

Our culture doesn't want us to know the truth that life at its best is a matter of sensations, or that the best ones are often dirty and dangerous. That's why everyone in that other world behind you walks in the middle of the glass-enclosed overwalk in a bemused trance, with eyes desperate for logos, oblivious to the opportunity for a fresh perspective on their existence which exists virtually under their feet.

This book, as intimated earlier, is about several of the most exciting of those worlds.

Motorcycles are the 2% antithesis of the dominant mind-set—a cultural disaster which a friend of mine once unwittingly summed up when describing the delights of his new car—"It's so smooth and quiet," he said proudly, "you hardly know you're moving."

ZAP!!!—you're dead.

That was years ago; alas, he is actually dead now and his chance to recoup lost for ever.

» » » » »

Let me now introduce the second perspective to a world of your own with a poem pilfered from Vladimir Nabokov's novel *The Gift*. (If you suspect you have a gift for writing and would like to join this rat race *The Gift* is a must-read.)

In order to appreciate the poem you will shortly be privileged to read, you should know that its creation was the result of a woman's death at an early age whom the poet had loved when he was sixteen. It was written in the Spirit of Romanticism—which thrived in various forms for centuries before the Age of Data klacked its onomatopoetic way via the Internet into what was once a human-dominated culture.

» » » » »

One night between sunset and river
On the old bridge we stood, you and I.
Will you ever forget it, I queried,
—that particular swift that flew by?
And you answered so earnestly: Never!

And what sobs made us suddenly shiver,
What a cry life emitted in flight!
Till we die, till tomorrow, for ever
You and I on the old bridge one night.

» » » » »

Now, just for the fun of it, imagine you are walking across an old wooden bridge over the Green River in Kentucky on a summer day. Go to the downriver side and look as straight down at the water as you can.

Drink in the beauty and serenity
for a few minutes
or perhaps a few hours
during which
(if you are lucky)
a single swift [hummingbird]
may fly by
and
if your luck still holds
without warning
AH!

A wood and canvas canoe, laden with camping stuff, will move slowly into view with paddles flashing wetly in the sun.
For the indeterminate time the canoe takes to reveal itself fully

it is the symbol of life lived within the embrace of art, rather than the clutch of computer-generated fiberglass or Kevlar. A fine hand-crafted wood and canvas canoe is transportation reduced to its simplest and most endearing terms. It is the string quartet of journeys which lie most intimately around the heart. Adventuring by canoe is one of the purest continuous states of aliveness I know. It provides great life-sustaining aerobic exercise—the results of which I enjoy keenly, today, at 83—and has the important bonus, which is getting rarer by the moment, of being comprised of satiety-proof satisfactions. A canoe trip is an eternity of endless first happenings during which our gratitude for life wells up and obliterates the inevitable cosmic betrayal lurking around an unremembered bend on a river of condensed clouds.

When I lived in Louisville I often took three and four day canoe trips on the Green River, which meanders intimately through the idly rolling hills of Kentucky. It was where I went whenever I needed to disengage myself from the perpetual motion of the latest technological frenzy and re-establish the perspective of protean forces. The Green River was my private Walden Pond, and I preferred it to my friend Henry's because a river is a pond with a past and a future. In this connection Heraclitus once commented that the same person can never enter the same stream twice, which strikes me as an unforgettable appreciation of the variety built into all *natural* phenomena.

Because Heraclitus is one of my heroes the following brief sketch will cue you in on what makes me tick and what you can expect in these pages during the next few days.

» » » » »

Heraclitus was a Greek philosopher who lived in the 6th-5th century B.C. To maintain the spirit of this section, which is after all just an introduction, let's simply say that he believed change and the tension created by contrasts were what made the world go 'round. Please note my use of the abbreviation: the world only goes *around* for astronomers, who have no business in this book because it has always been obvious to me from their formal language, preoccupation with math and choice of a profession which demands that they turn their back on the only world they will ever really experience, that they are not fun people, and by God I intend to make this a fun book even at the risk of slumping dead while agonizing over it. In any event, the reason Heraclitus is one of my heroes is because I have found his concept to be true: *change and contrast have always been the sources of my deepest satisfactions.*

Unfortunately, not long after Heraclitus died Zeno came along and set out to prove him wrong. To this end he created eight paradoxes. Some of them have survived in the writing of Aristotle. Their purpose was to disprove Heraclitus by means of contradictory evidence.

Here is the shortest and most approachable example of a Zeno paradox:

> 7. So long as anything is in a space equal to itself it is at rest. An arrow is in a space equal to itself at every moment of its flight and therefore also during the whole of its flight. Thus the flying arrow is at rest.

Don't laugh. Considering the enormous respect which historians of the development of intellectual thought have for Zeno's paradoxes and their pivotal role in the development of logic and rational thought, the eight paradoxes cannot be dismissed as silly for reasons too complex to go into here. The truth is that the Zeno paradoxes were embryonic forms of logic and reason which after 2500 years of increasingly sophisticated development made the creation of the nuclear bomb possible.

The purpose of this sketch, therefore, is to point out that where I part company with the overwhelming number of contemporary thinkers is in questioning the validity of logic and reason. I feel this way for two reasons, and each of them can be illustrated by referring to all-too-rare lightning bolt insights in our strobe-lighted culture.

The first is by Paul Valéry, who wrote: ". . . after all, what is logic but a speculation on the permanence of notations?" Note with relish his satiric use of super precise and sterile language to make his point, which suggests that while logic proved to be infallible in the development of such things as the nuclear bomb, it has yet to be *permanently* established that methodically creating the means of our personal annihilation was a "logical" move on mankind's part.

The second lightning bolt quote, from a widely differing source, comes from *Bird by Bird,* a delightfully gutsy book on the art of writing by Anne Lamott:

> The rational mind doesn't nourish you. You assume it gives
> you the truth, because the rational mind is the golden calf
> that this culture worships, but this is not true. Rationality
> squeezes out much that is rich and juicy and fascinating.

Ms. Lamott's point is in a way more profound than Paul Valéry's because it goes beyond a generalized comment on possible upcoming disasters I can do nothing about, and is a constant reminder (I have her quote over my desk) that when I succumb to the ever-present temptation to take the heavy duty aspects of life too seriously my writing becomes so stilted and academic the ink congeals in my ballpoint pen. It was little consolation to learn that Mark Twain had the same problem.

If you thrive on sweat-producing intellectual workouts, take a decade or two out of your busy life to digest Plato and Aristotle and Kant and Hegel while studiously avoiding Aristotle's *Poetics,* which may unnecessarily confuse and perplex anyone who equates complexity with profundity in order to establish a hard-earned aura of intellectual superiority.

Anyway, to summarize this introductory sketch, I think we have reached a point in formal education where we no longer even know how to ask vitally pertinent questions, such as (in our present context) should we get excited about who thinks motion moves and who thinks it doesn't, or should we knock it off and go fishing?

My game plan is to opt for the latter choice and you can be sure I'll be fishing with Heraclitus using our personally hand-tied dry flies and, with gossamer leaders, we will be dimpling the placid silvery streaks of sweetly-flowing streams.

Zeno? Let him dig for his own damn worms.

» » » » »

Since I was usually alone on my Green River canoe trips, I handled the shuttle problem caused by putting in upriver and taking out downriver by cartopping my canoe and hauling my dirt bike on a trailer. I would off-load my canoe and camping equipment at the put-in location, leave my car and trailer at the take-out point, and then, Heraclitus be damned, I would then ride, on the same unnatural asphalt road I had ridden many times on the same motorcycle, the same forty-odd miles back to my canoe, where I stashed my bike in a friendly farmer's barn.

Not only was I not confused and anxiety-ridden by these sharp juxtapositions, but I enjoyed each antithetical world for its own sake.

My quests for life's greatest moments all zero in on taking advantage of golden opportunities for variety and contrast. Technologists and drug pushers are always enticing us to live our lives in climax, but if we live our lives in climax, where do we go for great moments?

For me, two of life's finest contrasts are getting off a motorcycle and stepping into a canoe, or stepping out of a canoe and getting on a motorcycle, and although I never can remember which is the greater pleasure, it really doesn't matter. Redundancy, just a fancy word for excess, never enters the picture, because whichever way I spring, long experience has taught me I am rarely able to quit either of these sublime recreations without wanting more.

Early on I discovered that how to quit when you still want more is the most vital aspect of the art of sustaining the sharp-edge of life in a technological culture that keeps insisting this isn't necessary, that we can have it all, and more and more and blind, never-ending more.

Parlaying myself into wildly contrasting adventures has been a lifelong obsession, and if this book has unleashed your curiosity thus far, we may be kindred spirits. Perhaps the ultimate contrast for each of us is between mind and body, or spirit and sensation, or being a free spirit and waiting in line, and what we are able to make of these opportunities depends on who advised us when we were too young to question authority or perhaps how painfully the bondage cuts into our flesh as we grow up.

Come, dear reader—let's read and write together—and oh how I sometimes wish—when my pen is filled with white ashes instead of the black magic I bought and paid for—that we could take turns at the two obligations which make our joint adventure possible.

PART I

The Endless Delights of Being Freshly Alive

A happy childhood is always within reach

CHAPTER 1

Birth and Rebirth

There are two great riddles in this world: how was I born? I
don't remember. How shall I die? I don't know.

from *Matryona's House*
—Alexander Solzhenitsyn

November 11, 1918 was, in the supreme sense of the word,
an incredible day in my life.

As my mother and father separately told me many years later,
I was conceived at the very beginning of what school authorities
soon told me with perfectly straight faces was to be the war-free
millennium which started the day the "war to end wars" ended. To
be specific, the zygot that eventually turned out to be me was
conceived at the climax of the bacchanalian armistice hysteria which
celebrated mankind's release from the first World War's four
anguished years of multi-millioned deaths as the result of deliberate
technological mayhem.

Nine months to the day later, with uncharacteristic punctuality,
I had somehow managed to transform myself into a mature but
flawed, unviable fetus. As the obstetrician dangled what was on
the verge of being me upside down by the ankles, I simultaneously
felt the pain of a sharp slap on my buttocks and took my first gulp
of the earth's ambrosial atmosphere, which instantly changed me
from soulless flesh into a living, thinking, blinking human being.

The show that is this book was on the road!

In my role as a newborn entering the August 11, 1919, spawn of newcomers conceived in the days of uncaring frivolity which accompanied the winding down of a flat-out man-made inferno, I was not "trailing clouds of glory from heaven" as Wordsworth so beautifully expressed his bias, but instead simply emerged—after inflicting terrible expulsion pains on my mother—tangled in an umbilical skein of blood and nastiness.

In the early morning hours of the day I was born there were occasional spatterings of rain in Brooklyn, New York. I like to think the window was open and that hearing and enjoying their splashings was my first real-life encounter with mother earth—such natural joys have always clobbered recollections of the long-stilled hand that slapped me into life in the security of a hospital long ago razed by a wrecker's ball.

» » » » »

At the Peck Memorial Hospital in Brooklyn an obstetrician was having a heart-to-heart talk with a thirty-two-year-old man about his minutes-old son. There was trouble. Big trouble. The child had been born with two strikes against it: its blood was RH negative—a life-threatening condition which was aggravated by being its mother's third child. The doctor explained that unless the infant received massive blood transfusions—very shortly—it would not live through the night.

At that epoch in medical history these transfusions could only be administered to newborns by means of a recent technological breakthrough—a new type of syringe that enabled a doctor to transfuse blood through a large vein in the top of the infant's head, but unfortunately the Peck Hospital's purchase order for the newfangled syringes had been back ordered.

After several phone calls a suitable syringe was located in a hospital all the way across town, and since taxis would be scarce because the spatterings of rain had collected themselves into an out-and-out downpour, my father decided to run the errand of mercy in his own car.

As he crossed the parking lot huge sheets of rain were being blown against the glistening street-lighted asphalt with such great angled force that the drops appeared in fantasy as myriads of silvery flower children who sprouted bloomed kneeled in fear and died all in a wink—only to dissolve and gurgle into the sewer just in time for the next generation of sheeted raindrops to gust on the scene out of nowhere for their dark instant of shimmering glory.

I know this is not how my father responded to that glorious midnight storm, but that is how I would have fantasized about the ephemeral cavalcade of human life had I been, at that instant, my present eighty years, rather than my past eighty minutes old.

My family's 1913 Pierce Arrow cloth-topped touring car was drenched inside and out. Too desperate to trouble with snapping the isinglass curtains in place, my father reached behind the front seat, removed the lap robe from its lovely brass railing, folded the drier side up and placed it on the driver's seat.

The magnificent old Pierce engine roared into life at the third frantic tug on the crank handle and my father took off across town haunted by the fear that the son he wanted so badly would be dead before he returned—but why am I telling you all these details?

Surely the alert reader has kept all his common senses despite the age-old fascination of storytelling and already knows that the cause of my father's dread survived his birth night as well as the next eighty years and who knows—perhaps many more.

From the perspective of this accomplished fact I like to think I inherited whatever writing talent I have from my mother, who once said, "You looked like a freshly-made snowman with coal-black eyes instead of the rosy cherub I was expecting"—and from my father, who later told me that when I was being transfused through the top of my head, "You looked as if you were being filled down instead of up with pink paint and when you were full you smiled and wiggled your toes."

I was conceived at the climax of one of technology's bloodiest disasters but on the other hand was born dead and raised from the grave because mankind had invented the telephone, motor car and a newfangled nickel-plated syringe.

If you were me what would you be—a technophobe or a technophile?

Remember, before you jump to a conclusion, that in our culture you must go with the flow or become a nonentity.

If you were a writer, how could you best serve the latest rain-sheeted generations who know nothing of pandemic horror except by hearsay and everything about the well-advertised scientific marvels due in the next millennium or so?

Would you begin your book with the question Thackeray asked at the end of Vanity Fair—"Which of us is happy in this world? Which of us has his desire, or, having it, is satisfied?"

This, God help us, is what you and I are here to find out.

CHAPTER 2

The Big Day: 7,500 Miles to Go!

When I was a kid I used to love the "Dodgems"—you know—those stubby electric cars at carnivals with the stalk sticking up out of their rear end and a wiper sparking at the top as it sizzles you into a jillion electric units of steel-plated, ozone-laden excitement. You pressed the foot pedal to go and you twisted the steering wheel either to avoid getting centerpunched by a bruiser bent on mayhem, or to deftly nudge a pretty girl for the crude adolescent joy of seeing her tits flop, which incidentally was my first experience with Instant Enlightenment.

The trouble was that you got more for your two-bits than just the whirring sounds of dynamos, the screaming of virgins and the visceral impact of colliding worlds.

Your two-bits also bought you X amount of time, so I was always running out of quarters. X was never enough. The whole alphabet was not enough. Language was not enough. Shakespeare was not enough.

I was not enough.

When I grew up I realized that what I needed was a vehicle that began where "Dodgems" ran out of juice—something that didn't play money games with time but attacked the living problem head on. I desperately needed help that went beyond the constraints of language, which tends to cowardice and is fearful of censorship. I needed something tangible, intensely mobile, and perhaps in a way even brutal—something priceless that could carve time up

and serve it to me for supper and throw in the blackness of
night with a cherry on top for dessert.

For my past seventy years the fantastic contraptions known as
motorcycles have filled that bill to perfection.

» » » » »

The big day had arrived at long last.

I sat on my bike for five delicious minutes, savoring each unit
of time as its engine throbbed in perfect tune beneath me.

My odometer read 200,000.

When I returned it would read 207,500 miles.

I planned it that way.

Meticulously.

I hadn't ridden my bike for a week, so that the pleasure to
come would be a release from denial and therefore greater. There
was nothing in my owner's manual to this effect but why should
there be? When did a technologist ever include in his instructions
so much as a footnote on the art of living?

Here are the keys, kid, go have a blast!

I sometimes think I'm not like other people, and in fact might
be downright peculiar, but damned if I don't think it is a lack of
feeling for the momentousness of life that allows us to use
technological resources trivially.

Using a 90 H.P. touring bike to go to the corner grocery for a
pack of cigarettes is a lethal misuse of two major life resources—
lungs and bikes. You can't decently ride from a New York grocery
store yesterday to the Black Hills of South Dakota tomorrow any
more than you can make decent love without foreplay.

But the hell with philosophy. I was a happy *motorcyclist*—
what more did I want? What more did I need?

Besides, I'd paid my dues: I was raring to go: wild horses
couldn't stop me.

I snicked my personal Dodgem into first gear and rode out
into the wee hours of morning, still an adolescent to the core, with
an endless supply of quarters in my leathers.

I hadn't ridden my dynamo more than a hundred yards before I realized I was having a better time than I ever imagined in my carefully structured anticipations. Laughing out loud and rubbing my gloved hands together without taking them off the handlebars, I toed the golden foot-shift lever through the gates leading to the paradise of high and thus became one with my rig, my world and everything worthwhile that ever was.

The only clock I had was on the instrument panel and I checked to make sure it wasn't running. I had disconnected both of its wires the night before because you can't be too sure about time.

The clock had stopped at something dumb, like 11:48.

11:48 is not time.

The only time worth mentioning is time that is yet to be. Time was 75 miles before rosy-fingered dawn. Time was 100 miles of anticipation before my perfect cup of coffee with Eggs Benedict on the way. Time was 600 miles before pitching my one man tent beside a lonesome lake that begged me to adore it.

With heaven between my legs and under my tires as well as over my helmet, I could not have been happier if I had been twenty-five instead of seventy-five. There wasn't anyone on earth happier than I was at that moment. Especially millionaires, spaced-out scientists, movie stars and heads of state—especially heads of state.

As soon as the sun came up I stopped and after carefully wiping my lenses clean, I enveloped my eyes in rose-colored glasses. Thus protected forever from fate, I opened the throttle a hefty smidgen beyond wisdom and experienced the phantasmagorical rush that cuts in when the mill is on the cam and hot engine parts, stressed to the limit of their metallurgy, infiltrate my id by means of their high-tech alchemy and thus transmute mud puddles into duck ponds, clumps of spindly trees into climax forests and the ever-elusive horizon into a cozy private infinity where parallel lines get together for a family reunion. Such experiences leave me no choice but to oh! and ah! Oh!—whether you are a realist, a reader, a writer or a rider, let me be preachy just this once—turn it on, man, turn it on—whatever, whoever you are—TURN THE FUCKER ON!

The greatest non-spiritual contrast I know is the one between life and the very real possibility of death.

But all too soon I had to back off because if a highway life lived over 80 doesn't kill you outright, it inevitably kills your aspirations. I feathered the throttle and floated down to the speed at which the mellow sound of my tuned exhaust echoed most sweetly in my earplugged ears.

I love echoes.

Ever since pastoral poetry began with Theocritus in the 3rd century B.C. the echo has been a moving symbol of the reciprocity of man and nature.

The bark of unmuffled motorcycle exhausts, however, is—if you want to get classical about it—pure Cerberus, the watch dog guarding the entrance to Purgatory for his master Charon.

It is scary to realize that a large segment of the motorcycling fraternity honestly believes, as their bumper stickers claim, that "loud pipes save lives."

Cerberus would roll over in his grave.

When I am in the saddle my way of combatting such noisome threats to my right to ride a motorcycle is to "shake my head with my bike," that is, to bank it repeatedly from side to side in defiance of what physics professors will tell you is happening.

Those guys deal only with life in its most stilted form.

What *really* happens is that the bike remains vertical, while the sky tilts and the earth then has to move to accommodate it, and once you glom on to this mystical topsy-turvy world you will, if you learn from new experiences, lose all interest in conventional physics or traveling to outer space.

Why would anyone want to go to the moon when they could travel to lakes they had never seen before, camp out beneath the stars and be everywhere at home within the generous 24,000 mile circumference of the loveliest playground in our universe?

I set the throttle on beatitude and left nothing behind me but whirlwinds.

CHAPTER 3

Growing up the Hard Way

The game plan for my trip was to use odometer readings to help me recall corresponding epochs in my life for development in this book, but as the first few hundred miles rolled around I kept drawing blanks because I have no memory of what life was like for the first few hundred miles—or first few years, if you like. In an attempt to get a narrative line going I recalled a photograph of my mother taken when she was eight months pregnant with me but immediately rejected it. This is not that kind of a book—I was appalled at the snapshot's bizarre connotation of utter incest.

At mile 200,800 I hit the jackpot: my earliest significant memory occurred when I was about eight years old.

» » » » »

I was raised in the western tradition of rational thought. As a kid I subscribed to "Popular Science." I thought new things were the nuts. I wanted to be a scientist and learned, just for the fun of it, the symbols for all ninety-two elements in the periodic table because as I understood it they were the fundamental, irreducible substances which in various combinations made up everything in the world, heavens and my electric trains.

Learning the symbols for everything that comprised my world seemed like a good place to start and I was proud of my knowledge.

The symbol for mercury was my favorite—Hg—because those were my initials, and the other Hg, my namesake, so to speak, was the fascinating heavy lethal liquid metal plaything that I used to carry around in a tiny bottle just for the fun of it.

Thus subtly, without my being aware of it, I began to live two antithetical lives. One was me, Hg, walking around with a fun bottle of Hg in my pocket, and the other was the poisonous Hg in the bottle, which symbolically controlled my mind because of its fundamental, irreducible fascination.

If all this confuses you, don't worry about it. After all, I was only eight years old.

What did I know?

One night while I was asleep there was a terrible snowstorm. I swear, there must have been two feet of snow.

The question my two sisters and I asked, of course, was whether the schools would be closed.

We gathered around the radio. They would be. No, wait, they wouldn't. The city was doing its official best. Snowplows had been working all night. A highway supervisor came up with the brilliant idea of having the snowplows concentrate on the trolley tracks so kids could be hauled to school in trolley cars.

The radio messages all added up to the conclusion that unless all the kids in Brooklyn went to school *that day* the entire Western Tradition of Rational Thought, which began three hundred years earlier with Descartes, would go down the drain.

The radio had recently been invented and we had only had ours a few months. It was supposed to be transforming our lives, but it was obvious from what I was hearing that the radio was not going to transform the attitudes of rational minds who were trying to make a community of wide-eyed kids go to school on such a tremendous natural day and perhaps turn a few of them against education for the rest of their lives. This was my first inkling that using my brain rationally did not nourish me. I had been assuming it did because that was what I had been taught in school since day one. But a single phenomenon as substanceless as two ephemeral feet of snow convinced me on the spot that rationality, for the most part, tends to squeeze the joy out of life.

And by extension, I began to consider the possibility that there was no meaningful relationship between scientific progress and human progress, and that this might be the fundamental flaw in the law that said I had to go to school if the collective rational minds in Brooklyn could contrive to get me there.

I went to my room and shut the door, hoping, against all logic, that my mother might forget me when and if she had to walk her kids to the trolley.

I sat by my window for an eternity studying the snowfall. My initial reaction was purely physical. I felt a catch—a lump in my throat, as if I were coming down with something wonderful—like the maturation of youth. That indelible morning released something I didn't know was in me which was the capacity to appreciate the hypnotic beauty of the silence of deep snow. My world had been filled overnight with an immaculate whiteness tinged on the open areas with lovely pink membranes of frozen sunrays, while the shadowed blue-ice edges gave me my first ever jolt of loveliness enriched to the point where a tremendously exciting but scary ache became the mirror image of beauty.

Meanwhile scientific progress was making dismal attempts to assert itself. The sounds of motor cars were singularly muffled and about every third one had a broken snow-chain link that banged against the fender at every revolution of the rear wheel as if loudly proclaiming the right of even imperfect civilization to lord it over all the poofy white stuff the God of weather could toss at it.

That total morning—snow, radio, authority—was by far the most stimulating teacher I have ever had and this was not just because the snow was beautiful beyond belief: it would enable me to do things I had never done before. I could, if I dared, fall face down in it, straight as a stick, without hurting myself. Because steep hills could not be plowed they would be closed to traffic so I could probably, if I dared, rocket down them on my American Flyer sled faster than I had ever traveled alone in my whole entire eight years of life.

That snowstorm was my first significant memory.

Human beings like to ask each other what their earliest recollections were. It is a fun game, but not without a certain poignancy for those who like me, and surely some of my readers, live amidst time rather than amongst things. Henry James expressed this difference in outlook perfectly when he characterized one of his fictional women by writing "She didn't seem to be aware of being alive."

Because formal education assumes being alive is a given, not worth mentioning, early in life I decided that if I wanted an education I'd have to get it myself.

Self-education begins by asking yourself all the usual troublesome questions and getting honest answers, and the first question I asked myself was not merely what my first recollection was, but rather when I first became aware of how exciting a human life and the world it is lived in are.

Brooklyn, shimmering with snow on a school day in 1927, was my first day as a student in the school of my own making. I believed everything I told myself and wouldn't be writing this book if these lessons hadn't, despite my occasional pig-headed setback, enriched my life far, far more than they degraded it.

Despite the above brave words a heavy penalty resulted from my mindset which has dogged me all my life: it wasn't easy to find school chums who agreed with my views about heavy snowfalls on school days. These diametrically opposed viewpoints have been vying for attention all my life.

As the decades rolled by I began to sense that my problem was exacerbated because I was unable to articulate my feelings in a world that was increasingly interested in what I considered to be mere data. For example I never felt more alienated from the popular culture than while writing this book because I could never reach my friends on the telephone: they were always on the Internet.

While our culture was turning into a non-stop busy signal, I became a functional illiterate while writing this book of obsolete notions about the once-good life.

Are you ready for the first red flag?

If all the data on the Internet were at my immediate disposal it would do me no more good, *in the context of the life I am about to describe,* than knowing the exact geographical center of the state of Iowa.

» » » » »

I became a spiritual adult at the age of nine when I graduated from the ho-hum safety of a tricycle to the chancy razzmatazz of a bicycle. That was when I discovered, in the tingling rush of my first precarious wobblings, that balance-in-motion is one of the most durable and underrated functions of the human nervous system. This was still another revelation that has persisted throughout my life and is shared by only a small percentage of the adult population: almost everyone prefers four rock-solid wheels and I have never been able to figure out why this is so since two wheels require the rider to be completely and delightfully absorbed.

As my teetertotterings on my green 1928 Fairy bicycle began to stabilize and the scary part of learning to balance myself in motion subsided, I experienced, for the first time, the fire-formed joy that comes through overcoming raw, unreasonable fear.

I was now not only invincible but my body felt more graceful when I rode the bike. What was even more amazing was that my bicycle felt livelier when I was riding it. I dearly loved to look down at the front wheel sparkling in its pivoting fork as the pavement whizzed indefinitely beneath it. I also enjoyed the sight of my bare legs pumping, pumping, pumping below my short pants.

All this grace and loveliness was especially noticeable in turns, so I was always looking for twisty paths to ride, especially ones with bushes or tree limbs that brushed against my legs and intensified the rush. They also brushed against my bicycle and were as hard on the paint as they were sweetly sensual on my bare legs, but I didn't care. I loved what was happening to me even more than I loved my bicycle.

Which is saying a lot.

Not long after, when I discovered there was a hell of a lot more to fear in this world than a fall from grace on a bicycle or crying over a skinned knee, hooking into the rapture that comes through overcoming fear of the unknown became a lifelong obsession. Although this process could cut both ways, in retrospect I cried out with ecstasy far more than I wept in agony, and if I had my life to live over I wouldn't change a thing except I'd probably take better care of my teeth and develop my back hand in tennis into an offensive weapon.

» » » » »

In principle, the experience of learning to balance myself in motion on my bicycle was identical to the time, fifteen years later, when I first soloed in a blood red, open cockpit, 1929 Fleet biplane. Using every dirty trick I could think of to put death in its place, I banked 90° over the Hanover, Pennsylvania countryside and forced myself to look 2000 scary feet straight down at the almost-too-beautiful earth in order to immortalize the all-too-brief, once-in-a-lifetime thrill of being alone in the sky for the first time.

But great as that thrill was, I wanted more. I figured I'd done enough homework on such technical subjects as the theory of flight, rules and regulations, meteorology and aircraft maintenance to have earned a romantic, ball-busting revelation: at the very least I expected to feel the earth move.

And then, just as I realized the absurdity of expecting to feel the earth move when I was 2,000 feet above it, I heard myself singing at the top of my lungs. I was singing with the music of the wind in the flying wires: I was a soloist in a tragic song cycle for a stringed instrument and the human voice.

"I know you're down there, you bastard!" I sang at the top of my lungs to death, who I knew was lurking down there somewhere.

I checked my seat belt to make sure it was tight.

"Come up and get me, you prick," I sang, tightening my neck muscles like an opera singer to create a taunting, insulting effect.

I glanced anxiously down and around, like a World War I aviator looking for the Red Baron: all was serene in Pennsylvania—ah!

That triggered my psychic release.

The sky moved.

I would have been a fool not to settle for that.

I reentered the traffic pattern and soon experienced, in the lesser but no less real context of my own goals and capabilities, the ecstasy Lindbergh must have felt as he chopped the throttle and began his long sweet glide to Le Bourget Airdrome outside Paris.

» » » » »

I began the motorcycle part of this memoir with my simple bicycle because it seems that just last week civilization became so impossibly complicated the only way an individual, thinking person can really and truly have a blast is by reducing life to simpler, more manageable, more human terms.

If ever there was an individual, thinking man, it was Henry Thoreau, and that was essentially what he said well over a century ago. "Simplify, simplify," he wrote. What could be simpler than that?

It was true then.

Today it may be our only hope for an individual paradise on earth, lone-eagle "orgasms" in the sky not withstanding.

CHAPTER 4

Two Early Loves:

Mom and the Harley Davidson "Enthusiast"

I rode my bicycle every chance I had.

I rode it for the same reason otters will repeatedly slide down a muddy bank into the water, or that ravens will play with a stick in the air, dropping and catching, catching and dropping it to one another as they fly. (This is true: I have observed it.)

Otters and ravens have been playing together like this for thousands of years without any problems.

Man's problems began when he started keeping score and the best specimens of the species started playing for money.

Love—40.

The $25,000 putt.

Sudden death overtime.

Dow Jones closed down.

The beginning of the end.

» » » » »

I was constantly looking for new ways to enjoy my bicycle.

One day I got up before dawn, stuffed a sandwich and an apple inside my shirt and rode from our house in Scarsdale to Tuckahoe, using the trail along the Bronx River Parkway. It was eleven miles one way. I took my time, stopping to skip stones in the Bronx River, play hide and seek with squirrels around tree trunks, discuss my philosophy of life with stray dogs, and in general to enjoy being utterly alone in the woods, yet mobile in a way unheard of in the technical progress of man up until the invention of the bicycle, which really wasn't all that long ago.

At lunch time I was riding down the main street in Tuckahoe, steering with one hand in heavy traffic while eating my apple with the other, when I heard a startled voice call out "HERBERT! WHAT ON EARTH ARE YOU DOING IN TUCKAHOE?"

It was my mother, out shopping. She wasn't mad at all, just startled. She didn't ask me if I wanted a ride home or anything but just smiled and waved and then turned and walked away, but I could see her shaking her head. She was impressed, I could tell. She always shook her head when she was impressed.

When Don Bryan's mother caught him in Tuckahoe she brought him and his bike home in the station wagon and grounded him for a week.

» » » » »

In many respects my mother was like a hen Barrow's Goldeneye, a rare wild duck that nests so far north she has a serious problem getting her ducklings ready for migration before freeze-up wipes them out.

The mother duck swims out in the lake with her brood and then dives under the water and comes up beneath one of her baby ducks, grabs its webbed foot in her bill and pulls it under the water. She holds the poor thing under just long enough to scare the living bejeesus out of it. Then she releases her duckling, which pops to the surface, sputtering, and tries to swim away from whatever that awful thing was. The mother keeps doing this until her entire brood is scurrying across the lake, flapping wings like mad as it tries to get away from God-knows-what. This goes on day after day.

As the result of this seemingly cruel and unmotherly behavior, the ducklings develop their flying skills weeks sooner than ducks in less hostile climates. This enables them to migrate before freeze-up.

I was thinking about this obscure tid-bit of natural history recently while sitting in a duck blind. Whenever I recall it, I think of my mother, and for some reason it always follows that I remember her telling me that if it turned out that reincarnation was an option, she wanted to be recreated as a bird because she thought it would be fun to fly through the air and look down on everything.

Just then some birds pitched into our decoys and when we flushed them I shot, of all things, and for the first time in my life, a hen Barrow's Goldeneye.

As I returned to the blind with my bird I said to my friend Duthie, "Here, John, you take this duck. I don't want to eat it: I think I just shot my mother."

» » » » »

When I was nine years old I spent the summer at the Keewaydin Camp in Brandon, Vermont. Mothers were instructed to ship a footlocker of recommended clothes and supplies to camp before the campers arrived. When I opened mom's footlocker on the first full day of my life spent away from home there was an object in it that was not on the list of approved items for nine-year-old campers. It was right on top and in the exact center of the trunk.

It was a razor-sharp Case hunting knife in an oiled leather sheath.

Unlike many of my new acquaintances, I never got homesick. I figured that stuff was for children.

Me? I was an adult and had a Case hunting knife in an oiled leather sheath to prove it, though I kept it hidden under my pillow that first summer. My earliest recollections of the heightening of life through fantasy are keyed to that exciting knife: there's no telling how many attacking grizzly bears I knifed to death with it before drifting off to sleep that glorious first summer in the wilderness.

I've often wondered how my mother knew I was old enough to hide it instead of showing it off and having it confiscated by a counselor.

That was when mom and I began to conspire: that was when I realized how much I loved her.

Love is a conspiracy against the ordinary.

Mom was freelancing several vital lessons when she carefully placed that knife on top of, and in the exact center of, my camp duds. It was her way of teaching me the importance of adding drama to life, thus calling attention to highlights which otherwise might pass unappreciated. Her sharp knife act also taught me the value of bold strokes.

All of this happened seventy years ago, and at this moment the sight of that genuine bone handle and oiled sheath is even more vivid than it was before I started writing about it. It is also the benchmark by which I judge blister pack knives with skillfully imitated bone handles, and our culture generally, which is so proud of its ingenious artificialities.

My mother once remarked in an offhand way that the greatest sin you can commit is to be indifferent to life. She was a Barrow's Goldeneye through and through.

» » » » »

I developed a lifelong love of wilderness canoeing at Keewaydin Camp, which later extended to hunting, fishing, mountain climbing and camping, and all these intense pleasures probably were conceived when my mother fought back her misgivings and placed that Case knife in the exact center of everything. She probably reasoned that while underprotection might get me a cut finger, overprotection might bleed my heart dry.

I'm sure my mother would be gratified if she knew my life still has the razor-sharp edge she taught me how to hone and that I still have her knife and have field dressed deer, moose, elk, a Stone sheep, caribou and a grizzly bear with it.

» » » » »

A natural outgrowth of my love for bicycles was a fascination with motorcycles. A family story has it that when I was nine years old I told my father I "had something very important to ask him," and then asked him "in the most earnest way imaginable" if I could have a motorcycle when I grew up.

Harley Davidson used to run ads in "Popular Science" with coupons for a free subscription to The Harley Davidson "Enthusiast." The coupon had spaces for your name and address and a spooky little box where you were supposed to put your age. I proudly put my nine in the center of the box and then, after much anguish of the soul, put a two in front of it. Harley Davidson must have gotten a lot of coupon requests for the "Enthusiast" with the age numbers crowding the left side of that damned box, or with ones crudely shaped into twos, but I'm sure sending all those "Enthusiasts" to kids must have paid off over the years as I alone have owned at least a dozen Harleys and was enthusiastic about every one.

» » » » »

Sixty years ago I rode my Harley knucklehead up behind a school bus on a thruway. It was full of kids in baseball uniforms. They elbowed their way to the rear and looked at me.

I glanced right through them now and then as if they didn't exist in my world, but this was an act. I knew they were wondering what it was like to be a grownup riding a motorcycle because I'd been where they were, right down to my baseball uniform and catcher's mitt, so I put on a little show for them, being careful not to be obvious.

I shifted my position, rode with one hand, and dangled one boot an inch above the whizzing pavement. I carefully adjusted my rear view mirror. I looked at my watch. I waved more enthusiastically than usual as a bike zapped past going the other way. I picked up a damp sponge I kept in a little receptacle on the handlebars and wiped off my goggles. Then I dried them with a piece of chamois I had sewn on the back of my glove. I stood up on the footboards and stretched, then eased myself back on the seat with an air of deep satisfaction.

I completely ignored the future big leaguers while doing these things.

After several miles the bus slowed as it took an off ramp, and as our destinies split, all the kids moved to the left side of the bus to watch me go by.

I ignored them for a few seconds and then suddenly looked right at them and waved. They waved back so enthusiastically I swear I could see the bus rock from side to side.

When I told this story to my friend Keith Grant he laughed and said, "I'll bet you bit a minimum of two or three of those kids."

I sure hope so.

I like to think one of them is reading this.

» » » » »

Although I have spent an enormous amount of time reading serious works of literature, I do not attribute this to my education. Statistics show that middle-aged college graduates who majored in English rarely read the kind of books they were required to read as undergraduates. The reason, I believe, is because they were taught by professors who for the most part were unable or perhaps unwilling to make what they taught relevant to the lives the students were living. It is much easier to play guessing games with "hidden meanings" in literature than to come to terms with the meanings themselves, particularly when those meanings are generally out of synch with the status quo of any popular culture.

What excited me about the Harley-Davidson "Enthusiast" was that it was all about realizable goals. I knew that someday soon I would have my own Harley, and the good folks at Harley were enthusiastically urging me to come along for the ride. There were no "hidden meanings" in the Enthusiast nor were there any strings attached. The only purpose was pleasure and enthusiasm for life. It was as clear to me at the age of nine as it is today that this has to be the bottom line.

Imaginative literature never tries to define or prove a generalized notion of philosophy. It teaches by dramatizing examples. It doesn't lecture, but slips up on you and catches you by surprise. It assumes the only superlative that matters is happiness, which is readily accessible through simple, idiosyncratic trial and error.

The Harley-Davidson "Enthusiast" was, in the above sense, literature. It had a profound effect on my subsequent lifestyles, and if I had my way a collection of the best stories from the Harley-Davidson "Enthusiast" would become the final transcendent volume of the Harvard Classics.

CHAPTER 5

How I Became Anything but a Businessman

When I was an adolescent growing up in Scarsdale, New York, I discovered that I was different from the other boys in ways that had nothing to do with the beauty of heavy Brooklyn snowfalls. This was confusing and made me rebellious. I was a walking firecracker waiting to go off, and sure enough one fateful Halloween when I was eleven years old I blew my top and began my life of crime.

The only two close friends I had were also different from the other boys and I think our first serious brushes with the law resulted from a misconception of what Halloween was supposed to be.

We considered Halloween superior to Christmas because that was the night when all boys who were different from other boys could legally raise hell and attack the system set up by good, normal boys who had become adults and were throwing their dead weight around.

Like all rebels worthy of the name we were well armed. Among the three of us we had seven bee bee guns. On one Halloween we decided to concentrate on a single symbolic act of rebellion and see how many street lights we could gun down. At first we didn't have any luck because the bee bees merely glanced off the bulbs. I'm pretty sure Billy Taylor should get the credit for being the first to figure out how to get the job done. What you did was, you stood directly under the bulb and shot straight up at its flattened bottom. If the pellet hit the bulb at an acute angle, the bottom would break and fall out, and as you ducked out from under the falling glass the filament would burn very brightly for a few seconds and then fizz out in a puff of white smoke.

Then we ran like hell.

The thrill of running away made the sport irresistible and so for a week or more after Halloween the streets in Scarsdale became progressively dimmer with each setting of the sun.

This satisfied a secret craving deep in all three of us.

Our presence in the world was having a noticeable effect and we hadn't even been to college.

» » » » »

One evening while the Gunnison family was having supper the doorbell rang.

Since it was the butler's night off, my father answered it.

I heard muffled voices and then my father raised his voice and asked me to come out in the foyer.

The policeman's name was Jural. He was a motorcycle cop but his boots, leather gloves and jodhpurs didn't fool me for a minute: he was nothing more than just a grown-up other boy. We later were to play a two-year game of cops and robbers which is probably why I never learned his first name.

Jural explained to my father that there were reliable reports that I had been breaking street lights with my bee bee gun and that this had to stop and that if it didn't I would be sent to Children's Village, which was a terrible place where all bad boys ended up and never saw their parents or their sisters again.

I saw my father slip Jural a five dollar bill as he left.

That was an awful lot of money the year after the 1929 stock market crash.

Then my father gave me a brief lecture on acceptable and unacceptable behavior, character, and as I recall, the dreariness of jails.

Then he turned abruptly and ran upstairs.

I was bewildered.

I wasn't grounded. He didn't take my bee bee guns away, and his lecture, as Yeats once poetized "lacked all conviction" and was not "filled with passionate intensity."

Many years later my mother told me my father was delighted that night. She explained that because I had taken a strong interest in classical music about that time dad had been afraid I was going to be a sissy.

» » » » »

My father was different from other men.

Here are just two examples.

Late in 1928 he was president of a large nationwide advertising company and we were living in a rented house in Scarsdale while our house was being built.

One morning he was riding up in the elevator to his New York office on the nineteenth floor of the Donnelley Building when the elevator operator told him he had made $2,000 on the stock market the day before.

My father thought about that and suddenly realized that everybody was making money on the stock market and that this was too good to be true. I remember his exact words: "When people start making a lot of money on the stock market they think it is because they're smart, but this is not necessarily true."

He called his broker that morning and told him to sell all his stocks. For almost a year in 1929 he amused himself when commuting into New York by checking the stock quotations to find out how much money he had lost the day before by being out of the market. Several times he almost lost his nerve, but in the fall of 1929, when our house was finished and paid for, the crash came and my father was sitting pretty. He waited for the market to bottom out and then reinvested.

» » » » »

In the late thirties my father bought a 250-acre farm in Pawling, New York. Pawling was only seventy miles from New York City and many famous and affluent people who worked in Manhattan had permanent or summer homes there.

Because, and only because my father was friendly with all of them, I once played in a golf foursome at the Quaker Hill Country Club with Edward R. Murrow, Lowell Thomas and Thomas E. Dewey. Mr. Dewey's "caddy" was actually his bodyguard, because when Dewey cleaned up the rackets as New York's District Attorney, the mobsters had sworn openly that they would "get" him. That would have been hard to do since the "caddy" carried a machine gun in Dewey's golf bag. I thought that was cool, but don't get me wrong. The only reason I'm telling you this is because what I got out of this experience and other, similar ones, was a king-sized inferiority complex: I was moving about freely in an exciting and heady milieu with no credentials of my own other than my ability to break streetlights, and even that skill I had to learn from Billy Taylor.

And to add insult to injury, my golf score was the highest of the foursome.

When Dewey ran for president against Harry Truman my father decided that since Dewey lived in Pawling the town would be overrun by visitors and curiosity seekers when he was president, just as the case had been when President Roosevelt lived at Hyde Park.

Since from the very beginning all the polls showed that Dewey was a shoo-in for the highest office in the land, my father decided it would be a smart move to buy the Pawling Hotel, and quietly made arrangements to do so when the presidential campaign was in its infancy—long before the wisdom of such a move had become obvious.

I was working in Baltimore at the time and will never forget the shock I got the day after the election when I saw the photograph of a smiling Truman holding up a newspaper with the ironic headline "DEWEY WINS."

A few days later, during a phone conversation with my father, I started to commiserate with him over the Pawling Hotel fiasco.

"Oh!" he laughed, "Just before I signed the contract—actually when my pen was poised in the air—I had 'em insert a clause that if Dewey didn't win I didn't have to buy the fucking hotel."

It was uncharacteristic of my father to use a vulgar term, and to use one to describe a lovely old country hotel in which the new owner would be host to weary travelers seeking release from the woes of the world was foreign to my nature. Still I respected and was amused at his choice of words. Even the fact that my father was annoyed because circumstances had cheated him out of the chance to buy a profitable hotel on Boardwalk and use lonely travelers as pawns to win paper money was legitimate. That poker game was no place for pantywaists and I'd have had to be a pretty sorry son to criticize my father for coming out of that unfortunate turn of events smelling like a rose.

Everyone lives or dies by the system as he or she understands it.

However, our problem was simply that, for whatever reason, my father and I were on impossibly different wavelengths: he was always dialing into business reports while I was tuning into Mozart.

Motorcycles also spoke my language, and the pucka, pucka, pucka of an idling Vee Twin, as music for my soul, was every bit as potent, in its own field of delight, as Mozart.

I have just given you two quick examples of how my father's mind worked. There were many more just as sharp. It was clear to me at an early age that his was an impossible act to follow, and I didn't even try.

Instead, I became, along with many other unbusinesslike but immensely profitable things, a motorcyclist.

CHAPTER 6

1923 Was a Good Year for Indians

A persistent balance in motion memory I have about the years between nine and thirteen is that I often tried to make my bicycle sound like a motorcycle. I taped pieces of celluloid, isinglass and Bakelite to the forks (there was no plastic as we know it now) so that the spokes struck them noisily when the wheel revolved.

All these experiments were dismal failures, and what I learned from them, by simple trial and error reaction, was that in any field of human endeavor, by and large, there is no substitute for the real thing. No, not even philosophy.

This was of course long before television changed the course of the evolution of happiness and cultural history proved, to everyone's complete satisfaction, that I was dead wrong.

» » » » »

This brings us to 1932 and my odometer to 201,300 miles and your companion on these pages to age thirteen.

It has been said that in the United States in the early thirties, which were the darkest days of the Great Depression, it was possible to buy more transportation for less money than at any time in our history.

In those days gas stations often displayed signs (6 FOR 1) which meant you could get six gallons of gas for one dollar, but even at less than 17 cents per gallon people were selling their cars because they couldn't afford to buy gas. A new Willys cost $395.

You could buy a used model T Ford for $10 and drive it across the country.

Early in the spring of 1932 my streetlight busting buddy, Billy Taylor, showed me a classified ad he had noticed under "motorcycles" in the White Plains newspaper. It precipitated the following dialogue with my father the next morning at breakfast.

"Dad, do you remember when I was nine years old I asked you if I could have a motorcycle when I grew up?"

"Yes."

"And you said 'yes,' right?"

"Yes."

"Well, you see, I'll be fourteen next August and I think it's about time, don't you?"

"Well I don't know . . ."

"Oh I know I'm too young to ride a motorcycle but you see Billy Taylor and I have a chance to buy a 1923 Indian for $5.00 and it's in excellent shape except it doesn't run or anything and we got to thinking that if we owned it we could spend a few years fixing it up after we'd done our homework and learn something about mechanics because I want to become an engineer and it's never too soon to start and you see if we got it running in a year or two we could ride it around Billy Taylor's father's estate until we were old enough to get our junior licenses."

My father took a thoughtful sip of coffee as he looked long and hard at my mother.

My mother smiled at him and nodded her head almost imperceptibly.

"When do you need the money?" dad said.

There was a long pause.

"Well . . . now?"

Dad took out his wallet and handed me a five dollar bill.

I looked at the bill, I looked at my dad, and I looked at my conscience.

"I only need two-fifty," I said, "Billy and I are going halves on it."

My father immediately took back the $5.00 bill and counted out $2.50 in change.

"If you ever get it going I don't want you riding it on the street," he said.

"Thanks, dad," I replied.

As I was scooping up my pot of gold I decided to change my career from engineer to salesman, which is what I eventually did.

» » » » »

My father was a good man. He sent me to camp in the early summers, then to prep school and college. Shortly after I became interested in classical music and breaking street lights, he bought the finest RCA Victor radio and record player money could buy, although he had no taste for music. He fed me well, looked after my health and remembered me in his will. He loved to drink, but I never saw him drunk, and he taught me how to use alcohol with honor. But of all the things my father did for me the single act which gave me the greatest pleasure for the longest time was when he gave me $2.50 to buy half of a motorcycle.

» » » » »

I was well on my way as young lives go, and my way led to a farmer's barn where a neglected 1923 Indian was waiting to show two thirteen-year-old kids the fast lane to adult paradise.

The big red Indian Chief was leaning against a manger in a box stall. The set-up looked like a Nativity Scene when you still believed in Santa Claus.

Because it was about to be ours, it was the most exciting object I had ever seen. Billy and I stood there taking it all in for a few moments.

Then Billy turned and looked at me.

I turned and looked at Billy.

Neither of us said anything but we were thinking the same thing.

We had played our last game of mumblety peg.

» » » » »

Although Billy Taylor and I had several chances to buy Harleys, there was something in the name Indian that grabbed me. Back then kids played "cowboys and Indians" a lot. We got ideas from movies.

The cowboy parts were played by stars like Tom Mix, Hoot Gibson and Ken Maynard, who were all good actors, made big bucks and drove around in boat tailed Dusenbergs.

The Indian parts were played by extras who didn't have to know how to act. All they had to do was submit while make-up artists slopped brown paint on them and then go in front of the cameras and die gruesomely enough to delight every rapt kid who ever wanted to six-shoot evil off the face of the earth, but this bothered me: I had trouble with the thought that the closest the poor devils who were doing all the dying got to one of those boat tailed Dusenbergs was holding the gas cap while moonlighting as gas station attendants.

Another thing that troubled me was that the Indians weren't even real Indians, so when I had a chance to buy an honest-to-goodness Indian it seemed to me, in an allegorical sense, that this would be a logical step in my ongoing search for personal fulfillment and absolute morality.

Thinking back on those innocent days, I am astounded at how precocious I thought I was at the age of thirteen.

» » » » »

It doesn't seem as if there was ever a time when I didn't know what a carburetor, magneto or countershaft sprocket was.

It is a curious and little known fact that languages do not evolve slowly, over a period of many years, but spring up almost spontaneously in a very short time. This is true of all languages, including French, English, German and Swahili.

I reasoned with unprovable logic that as primitive people began to congregate in small areas their social interactions were chaotic until they created a language.

The need to express personal feelings was not only important for psychological health, but was also often a matter of life and death, so when someone made a noise which sounded like *prenez garde!*, or watch out!, or *aufpassen!* the phrase would catch on and become a permanent part of man's history in that localized area.

The 1923 Indian provided that same life-and-death urgency except that the language I learned was the language of happiness and the vocabulary of mechanics, while interesting, existed only to further that goal.

In retrospect, I think the part of my sales presentation that sold my father on letting his twelve-year-old son have a motorcycle was the bit about my being interested in mechanics and wanting to be an engineer. Perhaps, knowing how fired up I was about motorcycles, he may have decided that a broken down bike would provide an intense motivation for learning how it worked and how to fix it. He may have looked at it as a means of teaching me the pleasures of learning and, above all, that you can't give life your best shot unless you are turned on by whatever you're doing. (I suspect this is unfortunately something very few fathers understand.)

My dad may also have figured my survival instinct would protect me if Billy and I ever got it running. I can assure you with considerable authority that this turned out to be the case. After seventy uninterrupted years of putting my survival instincts through the ringer on motorcycles I only have three permanent marks on my body as a result, and two of them happened when the motorcycles were standing still and not even running.

My father was so smart the humiliation of merely being his normal son was probably unavoidable. This is an old story in many father-son relationships. But on one thing we understood each other perfectly. My father and mother both loved horses and rode together at every opportunity for over sixty years. I believe when I asked him if I could have a motorcycle, in his ever-young heart he felt that if our conversation had taken place fifty years earlier, I would have been pleading that I was old enough to have a horse.

And that pleading, in principle, bless him, he could not deny.

Based on the statistics in our family, horses are more dangerous than motorcycles, but that's not why they never turned me on.

It's just that I don't like to ride things that have their own ideas about where we're going and how fast we're going to get there.

What I like about mechanics is that although the principles are simple, their applications are profound.

The human body has a humbling similarity to a motorcycle engine. Both have esophaguses, stomachs, intestines and anuses. The only difference is that the bike doesn't have a clue what's going on. It doesn't know how much gas is in the tank, or if some klutz forgot to turn the petcock on, or when some son-of-a-bitch is going to cut the ignition and kill it.

Ah! But *human* life is different. We know things. Sure we do. We can deal in abstractions. We insist on knowing all about finite reality and unreality, even though this foolishness is a weird form of self-terrorization. The greater our imagination, the longer our concept of eternity becomes—particularly near the end. This leads to the conclusion that the main drawback to death is that we're dead for such a frigging long time.

It's enough to make anyone wish he or she was a machine.

This, I suspect, is one of the fascinating misconceptions that enables technology to take command of our lives, even though it is obviously out of synch with our heartbeats.

We can't be machines, but we can be part of a machine. We can interact with it, and we can use our imagination constructively to converse with it even if we can't have heart-to-heart talks.

"Excuse me, Harley old boy, but I'm going to push your gearshift lever down. Would you please be kind enough to engage your lowest gear?"

"Klunk."

See how easy it is? As long as we are absorbed in our machines, we haven't the leisure or the inclination to think of anything else— particularly dumb thoughts such as what we'll all be doing one hundred years from now. The machine has become our ultimate distraction, and it works. Our god is not carrying a cross, he's carrying a continuity tester.

This is great. I love it. It is legitimate. Continuity testers should all be gold-plated and kept in urns.

Having said the above, perhaps it is in our best interests to take this view a step further. As a motorcyclist there is no way you're going to catch me criticizing technology in principle, even though increasing numbers of the brethren are lamenting the fact that bikes are becoming so needlessly complicated few bikers know how they work anymore. This problem of deliberate alienation from human capabilities will get a full treatment later on but for now I can tell you with a conviction which has stood the test of time that even with my antique 1923 Indian and only a thirteen-year-old brain to work with, I could ride circles around today's vaunted virtual reality.

» » » » »

Truth! What a bummer. You have to begin a sentence with it to capitalize it without pretension.

But before Billy and I could find truth, capitalized or otherwise, we had to get the Indian running.

Fortunately Billy had an older brother named Ernie who was not only the handsomest and friendliest guy in the world, but who also knew all about everything that mattered. Early one cool spring afternoon he explained that there could only be two reasons why the Indian wouldn't start: either it wasn't getting gas or it wasn't getting spark.

"I checked out your bike and I know what the trouble is," he said, "but see if you can figure out what it is."

And with that he rode off on his three-year-old 1929 Harley JD.

Billy and I were pretty sure our motorcycle was getting gas, but the mysteries of electricity were beyond our reach. We examined the bike carefully, looking for an obtainable goal worthy of our expertise.

We noticed that the kickstarter return spring was broken, so fixing it became our first repair job. We untwisted the wire that permanently held the kickstarter upright and replaced it with a carefully crafted wire that was secured to the frame at one end and had a hook for the starter pedal at the other. This did the same job as the original wire, but was more efficient. We were proud of our fix. It had taxed our mechanical expertise to the limit and, including research and development, had taken all afternoon.

That evening it turned colder than a witch's tit. The wind rattled the windows in the flimsy garage, which wasn't really a garage, but rather a long, narrow and ancient chicken coop that Ernie had converted into a shop after building a new chicken coop out back. For a while it was even spitting snow, and we were worried about Ernie, who was still out in the dirty weather on his Harley, and I was getting an ominous feeling that these machines might be more dangerous than we realized.

About eight-thirty we heard Ernie's bike outside the garage door. Instead of blowing the horn he opened the muffler cut-out, which was standard equipment in those wonderfully innocent days. And—God!—when he rapped the throttle the unmuffled song of that big twin was my first audition of the "music" that begins where sissy music leaves off, and it hooked me on big twins forever.

Billy had to help me hold the door open against the wind as Ernie skillfully manhandled his bike into the glowing warmth and friendliness of the garage. He cut the ignition and laid it over on the sidestand and dismounted all in one graceful motion.

I watched everything he did as if doing it myself.

Ernie had just ridden in from the Armonk airport, where he had gone "to watch the night flying."

"God, it was cold riding home," he said, shivering. He took off his gauntlets, goggles, scarf and fur-lined aviator's helmet and rubbed and blew on his hands.

Then he unbuckled the straps on a black leather and chrome star-studded saddle bag flap and took out two spark plug wires. Holding one in each hand, he threw them, apart, to his brother who caught both in one hand with a deft sweeping motion, and such a winning brotherly smile thanks would have been an insult.

"Take the wire off only one spark plug and replace it with the new wire that's the same length: you can take it from there" Ernie said.

Then he took a quick pass around our Indian.

"Hey, I like the way you guys fixed the kick starter," he said over his shoulder as he started for the house and his hot bath.

I have long thought that the reason I have never been prone to envy is that I used up my lifetime supply of it watching Ernie that storm-tossed, ghoulish night as he strode out of the garage, missions accomplished, with the barest suggestion of a swagger, a senior license in his pocket, and the world and all the girls in it in the palm of his hand.

» » » » »

The next day after school we installed the new spark plug wires and pushed the Indian out of the garage and laid it over against a tree.

The kickstarter was on the left side, and after tickling the carburetor, I jumped on the starter pedal and made history: the engine backfired and my right foot went up in the air and came down on the bare starter sprocket, ripping a gash just above my sneaker. This gave me the distinction of probably being the first person in history, and certainly in Scarsdale, to injure himself on a motorcycle without ever riding one. I still have the scar.

One scar down, two to go.

Then Billy took over, and on his first kick the Indian burst to life in a cloud of exhaust smoke. We listened to the music for a while and then shut it off as the cylinders started smoking and we figured, probably correctly, that it was overheating. I often heard it said in those days that you shouldn't let a motorcycle engine run for more than five minutes when the bike is standing still.

The Chief was so big and so powerful and so mean looking we weren't exactly eaten up with impatience to ride it.

In 1923 motorcycles didn't have sidestands. Instead they had "U" shaped rear stands. Their sides pivoted at the axle and the bottom cross-piece snapped into a spring catch on the rear fender when not in use. They held the bike vertical with the rear wheel several inches off the ground.

Billy and I began to familiarize ourselves with the controls by starting the Indian while it was on the rear stand and then shifting gears with the rear wheel spinning like crazy well above the floor.

Late one hot sunny afternoon we were practicing our fake riding drill with the Indian facing the end wall of the long, ex-chicken coop garage. The doors were propped open, and Billy was at the controls. He was a showman, just like his brother. For example he always put his cap on backwards when he "rode" our Indian, and he always kept his elbows high and leaned forward into the "wind," even though there wasn't any.

While I was standing outside, away from the smoke and roar, Ernie drove up in his father's car. Putting his forefinger to his lips, he swore me to secrecy. I nodded deferentially to my idol, unaware of what he was going to do, or that I was about to betray my pal Billy.

As Ernie said after the catastrophe all he wanted to do was sneak up close behind Billy in the car and then honk his horn as if he wanted to pass him. It would have made a neat prank but unfortunately Ernie got too close and the car nudged the Indian off the rear stand just as Billy was opening the throttle, giving him a golden opportunity to make history in his own right.

First, there was the bump.

Then the fateful silence.

Then the SCREECH as the spinning rear tire hit the concrete.

This forced the Indian to attempt a backwards somersault, which gently eased Billy onto the garage floor too ignominiously unscathed to make even Scarsdale history.

Then the front wheel came down and the riderless bike accelerated straight as a die down that long flimsy garage, the rear stand bounce-bouncing behind.

I didn't see the crash because I closed my eyes but right after it I noticed that exhaust smoke was glowing brightly at the far end of the garage.

The splintering sound of a second crash out back was followed by a chorus of outraged cackling and clucking.

As the smoke gradually cleared the glow became focused into rays of sunlight which slanted radiantly through the end wall in an outline that approximated, to an uncanny degree, the frontal outlines of a 1923 Indian.

There was a prolonged silence.

Then a half-plucked chicken limped through the opening, cocked its idiot head at us in mild curiosity, and clucked.

» » » » »

Billy and I tossed a coin for the first ride on our Indian.

"Heads," I called.

Heads it was.

"Look, Billy," I said, "I'm a good sport. If you want to take the first ride that's o.k. with me."

"Oh no you don't," Billy said, "you lost the toss, you have to take the first ride."

Billy Taylor's back yard consisted of a field roughly two-hundred yards square. It was dead level for fifty feet behind the house, but then the whole yard suddenly sloped down to a little creek, where again there was a fifty-foot wide, two-hundred yard stretch of dead level grass.

As I rode along the level stretch at the top of the hill the motorcycle just felt like an enormous bicycle. I was apprehensive about turning left to go downhill, but there were no surprises.

The downhill leg was, again, like coasting on an enormous bicycle. I tested the brake: it worked reassuringly.

I turned left and rode along the creek, which was sparkling in the sun, all the more beautiful because I was moving too fast through time to take it all in.

I turned left again and started back up the hill. Everything was going great until I realized, with dread, that the motorcycle was slowing down, and that if I didn't do something quick it would probably buck to a stop and fall over on me.

I fed it a little gas.

The Indian picked up speed and chug chug chugged its way up that hill like it wasn't half trying and the sight of the grass blurring beneath my feet and the sound and sensation of those magnificent power impulses are as vivid and as visceral this moment as they were seventy years ago.

It was one of the great revelations of my life.

It was in the same class as the time I watched a load of #4 chilled shot spray the St. Lawrence River into the face of the daybreaking sun as the first wild duck I ever shot at unfortunately escaped with a life as precious as mine.

It was in the same class as the time my haphazard reading lucked out on Thoreau's 'Where I Lived and What I Lived For,' and I suddenly understood what a few trifling moments before had only been a quiet sense of desperation: that getting the most out of life was far more complicated than choosing the right woman from centerfolds or the right beer from enticing ads in men's magazines.

It was in the same class as the time I spent weeks and weeks building a Playboy Senior model airplane and installed a Brown Jr. gasoline engine in it and sent it aloft and never saw it again and was so astonished at what I had accomplished that I became a lifelong scale modeler.

It was in the same class as the first time I poised above class 4 rapids in a wood and canvas canoe with everything essential to my immediate existence lashed to the thwarts, and abandoned myself, scared shitless, to the suck of fate, and was so elated when I reached the pool below and threw my paddle high into the air that wilderness canoeing became part of what I have done at every opportunity, not for a living, but for life.

It was in the same class as the time I played the Liebestod from Wagner's *Tristan and Isolde* on a wind-up Victrola and first experienced the intense release that comes from the artistic principle that William Butler Yeats was to provide me with the words for many years later: "We begin to live when we conceive of life as a tragedy."

When Billy Taylor's turn came to straddle the Indian and take off on his own psychic adventure I wondered what his reaction would be to the experience that was so earth-shaking to me.

I never really knew the long range answer to that, and perhaps it doesn't matter.

For any real motorcyclist, it is enough to be grateful that he is among the chosen few who can, for endless, incredible moments, escape the sin of indifference.

CHAPTER 7

Like Father, Like Son

We rode the Indian around and around the same back yard. We never got anywhere we hadn't already been many, many times. Yet we loved it. The ride itself was the thrill. We weren't traveling. What we were doing was riding our motorcycle. That was all. That was enough.

For me, many decades later, that is still enough.

Traveling is only a bonus.

If I ever reach the stage where the government decides I am no longer fit to ride a motorcycle on the street, I'll build a circular "Wall of Life and Death" structure in my back yard and buy an original 1923 Indian and ride that scooter to my heart's content, and when I get tired of going around and around one way, I'll go 'round and 'round the other way until the engine seizes and I fall off the wall to the Answer, and after I hit the deck there will be dirt in my eyes because they will be wide open at the instant when the most exciting and mysterious example of a new experience changes their glistenings to a glaze.

» » » » »

Billy Taylor and Ray Devener, the guy who taught me how to fly his 1929 Fleet biplane, had one thing in common. They both had eyebrows that flared upwards into the hairline and made them look like devils.

They were neat guys to hang out with if you yearned to get out of the backyard and illegally ride your motorcycle on public highways and thus play cops and robbers with a self-satisfied society that had smugly and arbitrarily decided backyards were better for anybody under sixteen years old.

One hot summer day while we were all cooling off down by the creek—Billy, our Indian, and I—Billy brought up one of his flared eyebrow ideas that had frequently crossed my mind.

"You know," he began with diabolical casualness, "if we were riding our Indian on the highway, we wouldn't have to stop every few minutes like this and wait for it to cool off."

"Yeah," I replied, "and not only that, but then we'd get to find out what it feels like to ride it in high gear."

"Well, what are we waiting for?," he asked.

I knew the question was coming and I both welcomed and dreaded it.

"Billy," I said with resignation, "my father was good enough to let me have this motorcycle but he made me promise I wouldn't ride it on the street. I just can't do it, damn it."

"I envy you," Billy replied, "I never see my father because he's always in Europe on business and my mother's always upstairs drunk. I got my $2.50 from Ernie."

There was a long silence during which we noticed the cooling engine had stopped ticking.

Then we took turns making it overheat again.

For the next few days I was a one man think tank.

The first breakthrough came when I recalled that I hadn't actually promised my father I wouldn't ride it on the street. All he had said was that he didn't want me riding it on the street, but that didn't mean anything. He didn't want to sell all his stocks before the '29 crash either, but he went ahead and did it anyway. He defied the authority of his stockbrokers, who all told him to his face, "Mr. Gunnison, you're crazy."

The thought of myself thinking like my father, in my own way, of course, excited me.

Besides, every kid knows that if kids didn't defy their fathers, the world would become hopelessly old fashioned in a single generation.

I was lucky. My father and I saw eye to eye. I was sure the reason he didn't make me promise was because he didn't want me to feel guilty about taking the risk of being myself.

Despite this rationalization, I felt I still owed it to him to defy authority on reasonable grounds.

What if there hadn't been a stock market crash in 1929?

I analyzed my motorcycling portfolio as follows.

According to the New York State License Bureau, it was against the law for me and Billy to ride our motorcycle. When we rode it around his father's back yard we were breaking the law, and the only reason we weren't arrested was because Billy's backyard was outside the law's jurisdiction. According to the authorities this illegal act we were committing week after week was something we were too young to do.

The fact that we were not too young to ride, and in fact had already learned how to slide to a stop and spin donuts (by the way, what ever happened to that lost art?) proved to my satisfaction that the authorities were wrong, just like my dad's stockbrokers, and therefore they not only could, but should be ignored.

When I gave the street riding go ahead to Billy Taylor he smiled broader than I had ever seen him smile. That was when I first noticed that in addition to flared eyebrows his smile turned down more than up, and—oh yeah—his hair was red and his ears were pointed.

What a pal!

Considering what I was about to get into I needed to be in cahoots, and the devil incarnate filled the bill to perfection.

CHAPTER 8

Cops and Robbers

The man who takes only what's allowed accepts a miserable
life on earth.

—from Handel's opera "Ariodante"

The fifteenth century poet Francois Villon, who was a graduate
of the Sorbonne, a low life, and at least in my opinion the greatest
of the French lyric poets, once confessed that he became a robber
and highwayman in order to find out how much resolve it took to
place himself in utter opposition to society.

Based on a life of utter oppositions, and using the New York
State License Bureau as a symbol of society's opposition to my
God-given rights as a teenager, my feeling is that it doesn't take
any resolve at all to buck the system: you just do it. Despite this
feeling, why some people do it and others don't has always
fascinated me, and I suspect it has something to do with poetry.
Poetry is a means of intensifying language and, by extension, life.
In our hyperactive way, Billy Taylor and I were leading poetic lives.
For example, we considered shifting gears on our Indian a poetic
act. First gear moved us from a neutral, stasis-oriented life into an
existence with purpose, direction and goals. Shifting into second
gear hooked us into a still higher state of being in which the world
became a poem and began to rhyme. The heart of the poem was
the process itself which included that brief exquisite neutral between
1st and 2nd, that delicious reminder of what you're escaping from

and that momentary precursor of greater thrills to come. What motivated us to become rebels, therefore, was a poetic impulse in the form of a burning desire to get our Indian out of Billy's backyard and onto the world's great highways where we could experience the bliss of shifting into high in order to find out how much resolve it took to put life in utter opposition to fear.

Billy and I knew full well that what we were doing was wrong, or perhaps even wicked, but it was a joyful, irresistible wickedness and nobody got hurt. Now while it is true that someone could have been hurt, it was also true that all the people we kept passing in cars on our Indian were taking the same risk, and it quickly became apparent from the way they drove cars that many of them were taking greater risks than we were.

Not getting hurt was what the rear brake on our Indian was for. We used it at the slightest provocation and carefully adjusted the linkage as we wore it out. Later on, when we bought a '29 Harley with a newfangled front wheel brake, our fourteen-year-old rational minds had a problem with it. We reasoned that if the rear wheel brake was there to stop forward motion, the front wheel brake was there to stop rearward motion. The trouble with this was that we never went backwards, so for the first few weeks we only used the hand lever operated front brake when we stopped while going up a hill to keep the bike from rolling backwards.

But, ever curious, we began to play with the front brake when going forward, and discovered it was far more effective than the rear brake.

Then one day as I was turning into Billy's gravel driveway a neighboring Siamese cat ran out in front of me and when I squeezed the front brake lever with the passion of an animal lover the front wheel washed out and I took a nasty spill in the gravel. Bit by ignorant bit, we sorted out the plusses and minuses of the front wheel brake. Our adolescent episodes were microcosms of the history of technological innovations: thanks to the front wheel brake, the faster we could stop the faster we went.

The world probably doesn't know this, but metaphorically it is just one Siamese cat away from oblivion.

» » » » »

Computer games are kids' stuff compared to the game we played. Our game was for real, and if you're not playing a game that can kill you, you're messing around with non-life and the box the system packages you in as a child is likely to become the box you're buried in.

Francois Villon had it easy five hundred years ago. Society didn't have police cars then.

Billy and I also had it easy seventy years ago. We lived after the invention of the motorcycle and before police cars had two-way radios.

This is how we played the game. Our role was to keep out of the cop's jurisdiction by riding where they were unlikely to be, and their role was to catch us riding without licenses if they could, before we robbed society of its complacency. What we got out of the game was excitement and what the cops got was their weekly paychecks, so you can see it was a game we couldn't lose unless our motorcycle was confiscated. This was an ever present possibility and it really pissed Billy and me off because we considered excitement an absolutely legitimate and honorable goal. Why is it the guys who are only playing for money always play dirty?

You know, it would have been different if we had let the air out of their tires when the cops were in having coffee and donuts, but we never did that, and not just because that was intermission time when we could ride anywhere we wanted. We weren't mean, we just had better things to do, and it was a point of honor for us to play fair and square.

Billy even rode by the donut shop one time and waved to the cops.

I can't tell you how much I admired him for doing that.

We figured if we got caught we wouldn't be smart enough to talk our way out, but we also felt that if we were spotted on the machine it was quick and nimble enough to spirit us away. "Nimble" is the key word here. Our bike could go places police cars couldn't and a motorcycle cop, like our arch enemy, Jural, wouldn't go because we assumed (I think correctly) that it was beneath his dignity.

For example, we used to do something we called "hedge hopping." In those days Scarsdale had a lot of six-foot privacy hedges and we knew every gap in every hedge for miles around that was just gappy enough to enable our Indian to squeeze through and become invisible, and we became so adept at this that whenever we were spotted by the law, we knew within a tenth of a mile where the nearest hedge hop was.

One afternoon while I was enjoying an innocent ride on our Indian Chief I was spotted by Jural on his four cylinder Indian— bad news—and hopped the nearest hedge, only to discover myself in the midst of a lavish Scarsdale lawn party. It was embarrassing. There must have been thirty ladies there, sitting around two long tables about eight feet apart. Some of them had pink dresses and floppy pink hats and others had blue dresses and blue hair. Each table had a linen table cloth and iced tea in a couple of large pitchers, cut glass and probably Tiffany, that I knew were worth more than a couple of '29 Harleys.

I was distraught when I bulled my way through the hedge but quickly composed myself and rode as sedately as possible right up the alleyway between all that finery, nodding politely to left and right as my mother would have expected me to and hoping like hell mom hadn't been invited, but knowing somehow that if she had she wouldn't betray me.

I rode across the backyard and out the driveway and never looked back.

Jural wouldn't follow me. I knew that. He was too dignified. He had the prestige of society to uphold.

I wouldn't have followed me either. A guy would have had to be crazy to shove that gorgeous Indian four-banger through that tangled hedge-hop.

» » » » »

One of our big problems was that we never had enough money for gas.

One day Billy suggested in that disarming, casual way of his, that we get a hose and siphon gas out of cars at night.

I was against it. Sure, thumbing our noses at society was more fun than you could shake a stick at, but it was also more than that. It was a theoretical, symbolic act, with a distinct evolutionary flavor that I couldn't ignore.

(That wasn't what I would have called it at that time but that was the way I felt.)

But stealing gas was a raw physical act. It changed us from rebels to parasites. We were poets. We were latter day Villons, not common thieves. Even if we just called it swiping gas, I couldn't stomach the idea. It demeaned our noble calling.

Billy agreed with me, or so I thought.

But somehow there always seemed to be a little more gas in the tank than I remembered, and I figured that was because Billy's father was always in Europe and his mother was always drunk. If my parents had been hosing me like that I probably would have used a hose myself but what my pal was doing still bothered me.

I compromised my conscience by giving Billy more turns riding our motorcycle.

This wasn't an ideal solution, but then I was only thirteen, which was a few years before God in his Infinite Wisdom chose me to reform the world.

» » » » »

One hot summer afternoon I was riding our overheated Indian in Billy's backyard just for old times' sake and on impulse rode it alongside a lawn sprinkler to cool it off. It cooled off all right. There was a loud crack like the sound of an axe blade on my skull and a chunk the size of my hand without the fingers dropped out of the crankcase and about six chugs later the beast we had flogged with unmerciful zest for so long rolled over and died.

» » » » »

Many years later—many years ago—I had another run-in with a sprinkler. It happened on an unusually hot late spring afternoon while I was riding my 1971 Moto Guzzi Ambassador through a spectacular narrow valley in the Canadian Rockies.

At long last my odometer and I had agreed to call it quits for the day and I stopped for fuel because who wants to take time out from the next day's pre-dawn ritual to get gas? Under those conditions getting gas is like getting a condom from the medicine cabinet, and I want no part of that when I'm busting a gut anticipating that special first half-hour of the day's point-of-no-return orgasmic rush.

I had taken my leather jacket off because I had a long wait in oppressive still air for my turn at the pump, so I was riding in my tee shirt when it happened.

I had just made one of my all-too-rare genius decisions which was to treat myself to an air conditioned motel in a sleepy valley town a mile or so away where I planned to commit gluttony with a ganja appetizer and an 18" pizza and fall asleep watching TV as a special, well-earned treat: it had been a 700-mile day.

As I approached the town limits, I saw a humongous revolving sprinkler up ahead, which was spraying a solid geometric torrent of water about ten feet out onto the street at each revolution.

I slowed down and assessed the situation. In order to get the maximum joy from its refreshing coolness I had to synchronize my approach with the sprinkler's drenching path. With a little tweaking of the throttle I hit my approach dead center at about the speed of a fast walk and got the shock of my life.

The water was glacial runoff which may well have been ice as recently as when I pulled into the gas station.

I laughed out loud even as the icy water stung my cheeks like tears.

That evening, having thus lost all interest in the lukewarm blandishments of contemporary culture as exemplified by the motel, ambrosial pizza and sleep-inducing TV, I pitched my tent under the stars and tuned into the creation channel.

» » » » »

After our Indian's sprinkler debacle it was Harleys all the way. I don't recall how we did it, but somehow Billy got himself a '28 with one big headlight and I got a '29 with two bullet headlights. I kept mine in Billy's garage because I was only supposed to be riding it in his backyard. However, it was a rare occasion when both beat-up old motorcycles were running at the same time, so we had to ride two up on whichever one was usable.

I think these occasions gave me my first feeling for the wordless bond that unites all real motorcyclists.

In our pleasure-twisted minds Billy Taylor and I contended that the law against kids driving should be abolished because in addition to being alert for normal road hazards we also had to keep a sharp lookout for the police, which put us in double jeopardy. (We were heavy into legal terminology in those days.)

One day I rode, with Billy on back, the forty miles from Scarsdale to Lake Carmel to get a bottle of gasket cement which we could have bought in Scarsdale except then we wouldn't have had any reason to ride to Lake Carmel, which I knew would be shimmering because the sun was out and the wind was blowing.

As it turned out Lake Carmel was shimmering as predicted but since Billy wasn't into shimmerings he took my bike to get the gasket cement while I amused myself with a little think job on the lake.

Why, I wondered, was it so beautiful?

Clearly the beauty I saw was not in the lake itself, because if it was Billy could not have ridden my bike away from it with such obvious relish.

I decided the difference in our outlooks had nothing to do with the lake and everything to do with where it was. For Billy

Lake Carmel was in Carmel, New York, which was also where, more importantly, the gasket cement he wanted was.

From my point of view, however, the Lake Carmel I was feasting my eyes on was not in Dutchess County, New York: that was an illusion. The proof of this was the fact that I could still see it in my mind's eye even if, at that moment, I had been in Carmel, California. From this borderline whimsical beginning I suddenly suspected, with a stiff jolt of Enlightenment, that Lake Carmel for all practical purposes was not in front of me at all, but existed inside my brain, and the beauty of it therefore had to have something to do with how the hell it got there.

I had no way of knowing at that stage of my development exactly how much water my skull could hold even assuming my brain wasn't straining at the seams to take up all the available space, but I knew it was considerably less than the amount of water in Lake Carmel. Yet there it was: the whole frigging lake was inside my head along with the surrounding trees, rocks and meadows—to say nothing of sky. I thought of my marble-sized eyes and my thread-like optic nerves and realized with a tingling thrill that I was on to something our family doctor and even Einstein could not explain, though that quirky bastard Zeno might have taken a pretty good shot at it!

When my pal Billy returned with his gasket cement I started to tell him about the close call I had just had concerning the nature of beauty but decided I was not up to the challenge. Seventy years later, when I wrote the above paragraph, I realized I was still unnerved by the implications of this traumatic mystery.

I suppose computer freaks know what keys to punch to solve this mystery, but I am too proud of my computer illiteracy to beg for what would probably turn out to be nothing more than rational data.

» » » » »

On the way home we decided to go by way of Somers on the odd chance that some motorcyclists were hanging out there, as they often did.

We were riding with three potential strikes against us: no licenses, no plates, and no pillion seat.

In those days there were three ways to carry a passenger. Two were illegal and the third was expensive, dangerous, dumb and legal.

In the first way the driver sat on the gas tank with the passenger on the seat. This was very awkward and uncomfortable especially for male drivers, and was only used for short distances. The second way was for the passenger to sit on a cushion placed on the rear fender, holding on to the driver and hooking his shoes on the axles or if they were too short, the frame. The third way was to buy a pillion seat, which was a complete bolt-on unit consisting of a seat with a handle to hold on to and pegs for your feet. Pillion seats cost almost as much as we paid for our old motorcycles, and were beyond our reach.

In addition, the pillion seat was an ugly, ungainly, and heavy apparatus and its weight, plus that of the passenger, was too far back, so that riding double with a pillion seat definitely made the bike handle as if it were suffering from vertigo. When the passenger sat on a cushion, he could move forward on the fender and hunker up to the driver and the bike was solid as a rock.

Well what happened was that we were high-tailing it into Somers with Billy cushioned on the rear fender hugging me from behind. I thought I could feel his head against my back, turned to the right since this was his favorite position when we were really hauling ass and only touching down where the road had high spots.

What I didn't know was that Billy wasn't looking to the right, he was looking straight ahead over my shoulder.

I knew a road was about to become visible on the right where the cops liked to hang out and I kept looking to my right because if you watched closely from the hill we were on you could see the cops before they saw you and turn around and slip away.

Just as we approached the cops' hideout Billy shouted "WATCH OUT!!"

I thought he had spotted a cop and kept looking to my right just long enough to hit some heavy gravel in a roadwork zone, just ahead. I thought sure we were going down but somehow we didn't and thirty yards later I was back on solid pavement cruising along for a while as if nothing had happened.

But something had happened.

The bike felt different.

I felt sick.

Billy was gone!

I turned around and rode slowly back to Somers, scared to death and promising to obey the law starting the next day and go to church every Sunday all winter for the rest of my life.

Billy was sitting on the stone wall by the Somers cemetery laughing like an immortal idiot.

He didn't have a mark on him.

But on the crown of the fender where Billy's cushion had been there was now stuck a broken bottle of gasket cement, smeared label, wooden stopper, wire, dauber, and all.

» » » » »

Not long after that Harley Davidson introduced their Buddy Seat, and since it was illegal in New York to ride "double up" on a motorcycle without a pillion seat, a test case was held at the White Plains courthouse. Billy and I attended as self appointed expert witnesses. Some men wheeled a brand new Harley equipped with a Buddy Seat, which tickled the hell out of us, into the courtroom and demonstrated to the courts' satisfaction that the Buddy Seat was a big improvement and that the pillion seat should be illegal.

What was hard for Billy and me to take was that society considered us too immature to ride, and yet we had been riding for two years without incident and even knew more about riding two up than those who made the laws did.

» » » » »

In the early thirties there was a motorcycle shop in Somers owned by a black man named Johnson. He sold Harleys and Royal Enfields.

Billy Taylor and I used to ride over to see him on our Harleys just for somewhere to ride and he always kidded us about riding without licenses. I could tell he probably did the same thing when he was our age, which couldn't have been long ago because he didn't look much older than we were, although, of course he was.

In retrospect I think he may have enjoyed watching two kids having a whale of a good time while living in a state with a highway department that was dead set against any such goings on before the age of sixteen, when they let you drive with a junior license for two trial years before getting a senior license.

Some time later, when we had gotten our junior licenses, we rode over to Somers and fast talked our way into free demo rides on a new Royal Enfield by telling Mr. Johnson we were thinking of selling both our junkers and sharing one brand new bike. This of course was a lie. Harley riders in those days thought Royal Enfields and other diminutive British bikes were only fit for children.

Mr. Johnson agreed right away to let us try the bike. He did, however, beg us not to go fast because the engine was not broken in but we ran the guts out of it anyway.

I can't speak for Billy Taylor, but I have always obsessively regretted what we did that day. Mr. Johnson was a wonderful guy. He deserved better.

For some reason, as the years went by and especially when I moved to the Midwest and knew nothing about his fate, I thought of him. Before I moved I used to see him at the Somers hillclimbs once a year or so for maybe ten years and he never seemed to age.

It was uncanny.

I remember he used to say, "Motorcycles keep you young," and the older I got the more convinced I became that in some black magic way they do indeed keep you young.

Sure, I know black magic has evil connotations, but the way I figure it, when the magic is clearly doing you such unbelievable good, its color is irrelevant.

Just recently I learned that Mr. Johnson had been elected to the Motorcycle Hall of Fame, which warmed the cockles of my heart.

» » » » »

Let me backtrack here because the above reminiscence lured me ahead of our cops and robbers story, with two episodes left to relate.

The first one involves a close call Billy and I had on my '29 Harley while we were waiting for a traffic light to change. The Harley's rear fender was missing and Billy was sitting behind me on Indian's version of the Buddy Seat, which we had adapted to our Harley, and which, so help me, they called the Chum-Me seat. I think that name is why Indian went out of business.

As it happened, a police car slipped through the intersection just as the light changed and sure enough I saw its brake lights go on and knew we'd been spotted.

Although Billy was holding on to me, he wasn't paying attention when I jazzed the throttle and dumped the clutch, so he slid off the back of the Chum-Me seat, and his most public and most private parts landed solidly on the wildly spinning rear tire, which threw him forward and high up on my shoulders. This knocked me down on the gas tank and I broke a tooth off on the handlebars as we zapped the intersection and vanished through the nearest hedge hop, bloody but still very much in the game of cops and robbers.

Billy couldn't even sit on a motorcycle for a few days after that, but that didn't do me any good. I couldn't ride it either because I was being driven back and forth to the dentist, who cautioned me in a fatherly way to stop climbing and falling out of trees or I would break more than a tooth.

Why is it that the bigger the fun you have, the bigger the lies you have to tell?

The system's whopper lies are all based on this kind of misinformation.

» » » » »

I just sat there and waited for him.

It took Jural what seemed like ten minutes to swagger from his blood-red Indian four-banger to my olive drab Harley. I despised him for that. I could understand how he would want to savor what was probably the greatest moment of his life, but he wasn't being paid to savor. He was playing dirty. He should have done his savoring on his own time and not over-savored at my expense.

And another thing. I hate it when a motorcyclist arrests a motorcyclist. There is something horribly wrong about that. Any motorcyclist low enough to do that is riding a bike for the wrong reason. He is in the same class as a vice squad cop who doesn't understand the first principle of compassion and who therefore poses as a hooker to cash in on the primordial urge that made her own life possible.

"Let me see your license and registration." Jural's words were right out of the rule book.

It was all I could do in my highly nervous state to keep from laughing in his face.

"License and registration," I said innocently. "What are they?"

Jural's face turned Indian motorcycle red.

It was the wrong thing to say but I don't regret saying it because that's how I learned once and for all that modern society is all statistics and paperwork, and lacks the fire in the eye that has kept the human race and prostitution going for thousands of years.

If this was it, if I had to go out, I resolved to go out in style. This was the beginning of my lifelong obsession to do something worthy of my father. Although I had chosen to be, among other things, a motorcyclist rather than a businessman, that didn't mean

I planned to be a bum. It just meant that the enjoyment of life was more important to me than the enjoyment of money, and if I had a chance to have some fun, as in the situation at hand, I worked as hard at it as an ambitious junior exec brown-nosing for a promotion.

It just so happened that my Harley's generator had packed it in, and I had removed the battery box cover in order to strap four series wired dry cells half in and half out of the box with a belt. The bike would not run without these dry cells. It was no longer self-sufficient and was running on total loss ignition.

It also just so happened that Jural had nailed me on the Boston Post Road at rush hour: it was a mad house.

"Ride directly to the Scarsdale Police Station," Jural said, as he started back to his Indian. This meant the bike was about to be confiscated.

"And no funny business," he called back, "I'll be right behind you."

"No, sir," I called back humbly.

While Jural was taking his sweet time swaggering back to his motorcycle I quickly kick-started my Harley, then reached down and unhooked the belt that held the four indispensable dry cells against the battery box, while I kept them from falling out with my right leg.

My last ride on that wonderful old hedge-hopped, battle scarred Harley was sweet beyond belief, just as my life has always been sweet beyond belief because I know it too will one day be confiscated.

I held back, savoring, savoring, until the rush hour traffic was heaviest and worked my way into the thick of it. Then, dog that I am, I lifted my right leg on every motorcyclist who ever arrested another motorcyclist, every vice woman who ever spoiled a horny man's evening, and the whole total-loss adult shebang.

PART II

*Education is not What
it is Cracked up to be:
it is just Cracked up*

CHAPTER 9

Stand up and Take a Bow, Henry!

My respect for the range and integrity of Henry Adams's sublimely analytical mind is so great that my only honorable choice is to begin this chapter with a quote from his autobiography which, with uncanny force, annihilates all the reassuring pap the popular culture has been feeding a timorous populace ever since I can remember:

> Every fabulist has told how the human mind has always struggled like a frightened bird to escape the chaos which caged it; how—appearing suddenly and inexplicably out of some unknown and unimaginable void; passing half its known life in the mental chaos of sleep; victim, when awake, to its own ill-adjustment, to disease, to age, to external suggestion, to nature's compulsion; doubting its sensations, and, in the last resort, trusting only to instruments and averages; after sixty or seventy years of growing astonishment, the mind wakes to find itself looking blankly into the void of death. That it should profess itself pleased by this performance was all that the highest rules of good breeding could ask; but that it should actually be satisfied would prove that it existed only as idiocy.

—from *The Education of Henry Adams*

» » » » »

Henry Adams was the scion of one of the most illustrious families in American history. Both his grandfather and great-grandfather were presidents of the United States. His maternal grandfather was the richest man in Boston and his uncle was president of Harvard College. With a lineage like this one would think he would have become either President of the United States or a wastrel, but he was neither.

In my opinion his potential contribution to man's fate was infinitely greater than that of his illustrious ancestors. The fact that his century-old insights will continue to be ignored until it is too late—as he predicted—constitutes the most brilliant, yet tragic miscalculation in the history of human life on earth.

Through accidents of birth and intelligence he was privileged to move freely throughout his life in the company of world leaders. At the age of only twenty-two he became secretary to his father, who was ambassador to Britain during the Civil War. This was a highly sensitive diplomatic job for the father/son team because British leaders had the same pigheaded hostility for the Union cause that they lavished on their colonists prior to the American Revolution.

Henry's contribution to the United States' cause also included the position of London correspondent for the New York Times.

Henry Adams soon found most of the world leaders to be scoundrels. Again and again in his twelve history books, he exposed in great documented detail the deliberate dishonesty of famous world leaders.

He was also quick to give credit to intelligence and altruism if and when he occasionally ran across these traits in famous people.

But it is the *range* of Henry Adams's mind that expresses the full measure of the man. For example, he had a deep romantic appreciation of the earth, as in his refreshing comment on "the endless delight of sense impressions given by nature for nothing." Note the exquisite sledgehammerish twist in the last two casual words. Adams's prose is full of such stuff.

When a principle, insight or even a hunch is based on sound evidence, it is amazing how the pieces of the identified problem fit together even a century after the fact: reconsider recent American political and corporate scandals, for example, in Henry Adams's century-old context.

Such ancient lacunae spring forward to life in page after page of Adams, whether he is writing about radium, education, the environment, guns, or science's "so-called accidents." The range of his interests enabled him to reinforce his insights with stunning parallels with the ancient world, literature, and above all his stilled-voice anticipations of our anxieties a century after his death. In the tradition of such giants as Tolstoy, Montaigne, Goethe, Melville and Wagner he expressed his vision of life in universal terms simply because it was his nature to probe as deeply as possible into the covert recesses of our common human heart.

Faced with such a daunting array of complex, unresolved subjects, a lesser mind probably would have tried to find solutions through the mechanisms of education—the system—but here again Henry Adams exhibited the extraordinary depth of his perceptions. After receiving excellent grades throughout his classical education, and even after teaching history at Harvard for seven years—beginning at the age of thirty-two—he was not only able to summarily reject the total edifice of education, but concluded that what it neglected to teach him was what would ultimately destroy civilization.

Today short quotes from his various commentaries on education read like epitaphs in a Cemetery of Lost Opportunities:

The more I was educated the less I understood.

I am weighed down by the rubbish of sixty-six years of education and still desperately hope to understand.

I was aching to absorb (such) knowledge and helpless to find it.

Nothing in education is so astonishing as the amount of
ignorance it accumulates in the form of inert facts.

The practical difficulty in education is not in theory, or
knowledge, or even want of experience, but in the sheer
chaos of human nature.

» » » » »

The reason for this chapter—the reason for this book, actually—
is that in the century following Henry Adams's death I discovered
through my own experiences in classrooms and elsewhere how
staggering his analysis of the conflict between human nature and
the machine age was. I consider these matters to be of paramount
importance at the beginning of the present millennium. Also,
because Henry Adams has been unjustly ignored for too long, I
am writing this update of his views as they appear to me after
eighty years of living in a now—suddenly—exponentially shrinking
scientific straight jacket. This book is my way of expressing my
homage and gratitude to the world that has given me such intense
pleasure, and if it sometimes lapses into my notions of carefree
entertainment it is only because of my persistent but totally
unrealistic desire to get Henry Adams's vital insights into the hands
of as many voters as possible.

» » » » »

Although Henry Adams's Pulitzer Prize winning autobiography
is an absolutely legitimate American classic, I completed all the
course work for a Ph.D. in American Literature without ever hearing
it mentioned. It is either being systematically ignored as antithetical
scientific data sweeps all before it or because academics will forever
resent its swipes at their barren lives.

In this regard we might say that Henry Adams also wrote his

own obituary when he commented on the history of several ground-breaking books which were *treated with a conspiracy of silence such as inevitably meets every evolutionary work that upsets the stock and machinery of profitable culture, or which demands new thought machinery.* I don't see how any intelligent reader can read *The Education of Henry Adams*, then look objectively around him and proclaim the above quote to be sour grapes.

The fact is that Henry Adams was in fact singularly aloof from the current enthusiasms of conventional lives. From my perspective, as an octogenarian burning midnight oil to get this book published before I die so I can enjoy the result of all this toil, one of the most impressive decisions Henry Adams ever made was to insist that his monumental classic be published posthumously: for the greatest writers the greatest joy is in the work itself.

However, this delay in publication was only partly out of concern for the families of people he raked over the coals. He was better at this than perhaps he should have been but could not resist the impulse to think of all popular phenomena in terms of human evolution. For example, this is what he had to say about President Grant who "fretted and irritated him," and who (like most Washington correspondents) he considered "vicious, narrow, dull and vindictive." But the important thing here is what he makes of this low-grade topical material:

> He had no right to exist. He should have been extinct for ages. The idea that, as a society grew older, it grew one-sided, upset evolution and made of education a fraud. That, two thousand years after Alexander the Great and Julius Caesar, a man like Grant should be called—and should actually and truly be—the highest product of the most advanced evolution, made evolution ludicrous. One must be as commonplace as Grant's own commonplaces to maintain such an absurdity. The progress of evolution from President Washington to President Grant was alone evidence enough to upset Darwin.

I never drive by the famous tourist attraction of Grant's Tomb in
New York City without wondering what Henry Adams would have
to say about "one-sided evolution" if he were to compare Archimedes
with the latest fabulously rich Silicon Valley wonderchild.

Henry Adams consistently maintained that his insights would
be ignored, and this has not only been the case, but poignant proof of
this is implicit in the copy of his autobiography which I am currently
using. In the 1995 Penguin edition of The Education of Henry Adams,
Jean Gooder, a distinguished member of the English faculty at
Cambridge University, wrote a brilliant scholarly introduction in which
her erudition and especially her comprehensive grasp of world literature
clearly reveal the working of a superior mind. Based on my experiences
in graduate school my admiration for her as exemplifying all that is
productive and valuable in higher education remained boundless right
up to the moment when she almost incidentally—as if it was of little
import—dropped the offhand remark that "many of (Adams's)
ideas . . . (on) science, for instance, have not stood the test of time, if
they were ever plausible."

In her unelucidated remark, which was sanctioned by one of the
oldest and most universally revered institutions of higher learning, it
is not at all difficult for me to envision the onset of the Age of Default,
which will be followed almost immediately by the Age of Chaos and
Misery, unless we are lucky and the end comes quickly.

But now for the hard part. Despite the above conclusion I find
myself honestly wishing I could justify Jean Gooder's overall views.
Although a detailed discussion of her consistently fine commentary
would take us too far afield I am torn between respect for her scholarship
and horror at her inability to understand the essence of Henry Adams's
complaint: "the more I was educated the less I understood".

Come on, now, Ms. Gooder, what is so hard to understand about
the fact that a knock-down-drag-out fight was going on a century ago
between science and humanism, when the evidence was first becoming
obvious, or that today humanism is hanging on the ropes, bloodied
and incoherent? How could a supposedly impartial appreciator of a

classic humanistic document blandly champion the reverse of what Henry Adams stood for? Were you bought off, Ms. Gooder? Do you drive a nifty little sports car with four-on-the-floor?

If Jean Gooder's remark was dead wrong, as I believe it to be, she nevertheless unwittingly expressed our almost universal psychologically oriented functional indifference to science's immense destructive power. However, this lack of concern can in no way be equated with the intellectual inability to understand absurd complexities. Humanists are losing ground to scientific dogma at a sharply accelerated pace and the losses are almost all by default. The world is a long way from grasping the significance of science's effortless invalidation of humanistic education which is taking place for very simple reasons: technology is convenient, distracts us from grim realities, and is good for the economy.

We are now faced with the hopeless task of using a system of higher education which is utterly controlled by science to delethalize science after the fact.

» » » » »

In what Edmund Wilson called "the ecstasy of imaginative vision" Adams clearly saw, at the end of the nineteenth century, what would happen if we continued to welcome scientific advances indiscriminately without giving the slightest thought to their consequences. This was not entirely theoretical or philosophical speculation: oddly enough he was able to document his findings by analyzing coal production figures in the years following the invention of the steam engine.

Here are his conclusions based on his coal "statistics":

> From Hammerfest to Cherbourg on one shore of the ocean—
> from Halifax to Norfolk on the other—one great empire
> was ruled by one great emperor—coal.

> The (power) of sex could not be overcome without

> extinguishing the race, yet an immense coal-black force,
> doubling every few years, was working irresistibly to
> overcome it. One gazed mute before this ocean of darkest
> ignorance that had already engulfed society.

I leave Henry Adams's actual statistical analysis of coal production to the care of the accountants, and the rule of the greatest tyrant of all—oil—in the inept hands of the academic historians.

In the famous chapter in his autobiography titled "The Dynamo and the Virgin," Adams describes his visits, at the age of fifty-two, to the 1900 Paris Science Exposition. The primary enthusiasm in scientific circles at that time was the dynamo. They were represented in all shapes and sizes: some were forty feet in diameter.

The conclusion he reached on the basis of the primitive evidence available in 1900 was that scientific progress had been so rapid since he attended the Chicago Science Exposition of 1893, that "in just seven years man had translated himself into a new universe which had no common scale of measurement with the old." He had "entered a supersensual world, in which he could measure nothing except by instruments," and he concluded that "the neck of history had been broken by the sudden eruption of forces totally new."

These forces were so complex, varied and plentiful that Adams wondered if the most comprehensive mind in the world could grasp anything beyond a small percentage of the knowledge necessary to use them wisely, if for no other reason than the limitation of the human life span.

As we might express the same idea today, both individually and collectively, homo sapiens is getting in way over his head, like the scores of dinosaurs which died in an outwardly inviting but treacherous water hole 20,000 years ago south of Sturgis, South Dakota. Those poor beasts were pikers: each year we kill 40,000 of ourselves on our highways—over 2,000 of them on motorcycles—

yet do you hear me complaining? The fact that I deplore the slaughter yet am a hyperactive contributor to the chaos says it all, the brave words in this chapter and elsewhere notwithstanding.

I now ask you to consider Adams's century-old views in the context of my life: this book was written with fifty-seven ballpoint pens by a man who, computer-wise, became a "functional illiterate" within the short space of ten years. What is most significant about this is that a hundred years ago, when "in just seven years man had translated himself into a new universe which had no common scale of measurement with the old" there were still two thriving, healthy cultures. One was spiritual, the other material. Although increasingly they were unable to communicate with one another, each was still an awesome entity. Together they represented the complex potential of the human race. Together they were major parts of the variety in all living and natural things which act as checks and balances and which, *as ecologists have demonstrated a thousand times over, are necessary for our survival.*

Today, a measly hundred years later (as the Raven flies), it is no longer a matter of "no common measurement with the old," because for all practical purposes the old humanistic (or spiritual) culture is getting uncomfortably close to extinction and is hardly more than an annoying barrier to scientific progress. Early in life I used to see evidences of this trend yearly. Later it became monthly, then weekly. Then daily. Lately it has become hourly. What a mere century ago was a healthy conflict between science and man's spirit has been reduced to a single boilerplate culture in which reasonably high tech gizmos compete only with ultra high tech gizmos and that's it. Take it or leave it and become a laughing stock.

» » » » »

Henry Adams used the dynamo as a symbol for the power of the emerging Technological Age, and the Virgin as a symbol of the power which for many centuries before 1900 resided in man's spirituality.

On the one hand you had a thing, a dynamo, that could be manufactured and transported to provide electrical energy anywhere in the world and thus create material progress.

On the other hand you had the concept of an innocent Virgin, as symbolized by the great High Gothic thirteenth century cathedral at Chartres, that represented five centuries of humanistic thought and provided man with spiritual energy.

Henry Adams remarked that man considered the dynamo as a "moral force" at the beginning of the twentieth century, and that we viewed it "as the early Christians viewed the cross." Note his withering irony. He saw the dynamo as a symbol of diversion from nature and reality. By contrast "the planet itself seemed less impressive, in its old fashioned, deliberate annual or daily revolution." Note how his words interlock with today's problems: it is far easier to pollute an "unimpressive" planet. Above all, he saw the dynamo as "*a symbol of latent destructiveness and irreversible technology.*" (Emphasis mine)

The Virgin, on the other hand, represented "spiritual forces, such as the great religions of the world, which were the highest energy ever known to man, [which included] the creation of 4/5ths of his noblest art, exercising more attraction over the human mind than all the steam engines and dynamos ever dreamed of."

Please bear in mind that the above words were written a century ago, when they were true. The fact that they are no longer true, and haven't been since approximately August 6, 1945, does not invalidate his fundamental point, which is that exponentially dynamic forces have been unleashed on the world which are lethal, unstoppable and are clobbering all spiritual forces.

Adams looked for a synthesis of these opposing forces. All they had in common was their power to attract, but the problem was that there was no agreement among individuals as to what was attractive: the sheer chaos of human nature was relentlessly doing us in. Consequently he was never able to reach a satisfactory rapprochement of what Leo Marx later referred to as "the machine's incursion into the garden" and I concur with Adam's conclusion that he ended his life basically uneducated, as I am about to do. He did, however, leave a clue that enables me, if not to find a synthesis, at least to work out a solution I can live happily with— primarily because I am over eighty years old. He said the Virgin had no interest in perfection other than her own. I take that to mean that we should seek to perfect the self, rather than waiting, as science keeps suggesting, for someone to perfect rocket ships on the outside chance that absolute happiness will be found in the ether rather than the ethos.

Don't get me wrong: I'd be all for a trip to outer space if tickets become available during my lifetime, but of course only on the condition that they let me take my canoe.

When I was young scientific progress was made with pen and ink and mathematics was a function of the brain. Remember the brain? It's the thing we used to use to turn the lights on on our cars before rational minds decided we were too stupid to notice the difference between daylight and darkness.

Anyway, I was married and had two kids before cheap manual adding machines became available and I began to do my budget on one. That was the point where I first began to suspect that mechanical was not automatically better. This was a difficult concept for me to accept because I loved mechanics and machinery and often thanked my lucky stars that I had been born into the modern era: I'm sure I don't have to sell you on *that* feeling.

However, I had to admit that the adding machine didn't do anything for me that I couldn't do with more pleasure myself. I have always enjoyed arithmetic. It is a game I play with my brain. Games are an important part of its capability, its self-awareness and its health, just like the art of writing, which is also, at heart, nothing but a game. All my life I have tried to increase the speed and accuracy of my calculations, and today, at 83, I get a special bonus each month when my brain and I do my budget and find that my quaint, almost turn-of-two-centuries mind can add faster today than it could ten years ago. Doing my budget with my brain alone is akin to the pleasure of checking the compression on my vintage motorcycle and finding both cylinders right on the money. This monthly mental health proving exercise, sustained by a lifetime of enjoyable effort, was made possible because my frame of reference has always been the life forces at my disposal, rather than the number of machines I bought with money earned slaving in somebody else's system.

» » » » »

Based on this updating of Henry Adams's views I am convinced that technology has peaked and that the pendulum is about to start moving in the opposite direction if it has not in fact broken lose from its pivot.

The computer triggered the burnout. Without the computer, science could never have reduced itself to the brink of absurdity in such a short time. What is so frightening about this development is not the speed with which the sudden frantic increase in tiny, insignificant and predictable advances have taken place, but rather the slowness of our realization that we are satiated by too much of too many slightly better things. The ubiquitous and dirt-cheap timer is running most of the show: it rings the bells and blows the whistles while it turns life off. Newness is losing its allure. Perhaps the real culprits are not the gadget scientists but rather the behavioral scientists who know exactly where all this is leading but are apparently too busy awaiting their turn on the Internet to alert the world to what they have known for years—that given the built-in limitation of humankind's sweet tooth, life in a candy factory is only paradise for a couple of centuries or so.

To my knowledge what follows is the most lucid and concise description of our current plight in existence, which is remarkable when you consider that Henry Adams wrote it over a century ago.

> In the earlier stages of progress, the forces to be assimilated
> were simple and easy to absorb, but, as the mind of man
> enlarged its range, it enlarged the field of complexity, and

must continue to do so, even into chaos, until the reservoirs
of sensuous or supersensuous energies are exhausted, or cease
to affect him, or until he succumbs to their excess.

The gist of the above 100-year-old quotation is implicit in the
prideful, oft-repeated phrase, "it boggles the mind."

As that phrase indicates, we don't even know what we are really
saying anymore, and if we don't even know what we're talking
about, is it any wonder that we reserve our highest praise for objects
which increasingly distract us from the systematic obsoleting of
our already outmoded brains?

» » » » »

Like Henry Adams I realized in mid-life that "the times had
long passed when a student could stop before chaos or order," and
that we "had no choice but to march with the world."

Still, as a practical matter, he relied on two atypical forms of
knowledge. The first he called self-education, which is somewhat
self-explanatory and egotistical and sounds ominous only until
one considers the legendary limited imaginations of run-of-the-
mill pedagogues.

The second he called "accidental education." His most notable
illustration of this type was the dated circumstantial fact that Edison
invented the gramophone. Through the repetition which records
suddenly provided, he was able to "learn" and thus to appreciate
classical music, which enriched his life enormously.

I consider the fact that I spent the better part of my life in the
hi-fi era to be the single most important aspect of the chronological
lottery of my birth date.

Now that we have Adams's two fundamental concepts of
education under our belts, let's see how they can be applied to my
education in the 20th century.

That will be the subject of the next chapter.

CHAPTER 10

Homemade Education

Beginning in the fall of 1932 my father sent me to the Berkshire School in Massachusetts for three years and then to the Taft School in Connecticut for two. I regret that for literary reasons I must limit commentary on this phase of my life to Berkshire, as I have fond memories of each and feel a deep obligation to both.

Contrary to how most prep school boys used to put it, my father did not "ship me off" to school. Every fall he drove me up to New England and helped me in with my bags. I like the look of what I have just written: I want everyone who reads this book to know that for all our often bitter differences, Raymond M. Gunnison was the best man he knew how to be, which is saying a great deal and needed to said here.

» » » » »

I loved Berkshire. The air was crisp and clean, the fall foliage transcendent, my friends the greatest, our green and grey uniforms dotting the athletic fields the vividest, and the shouts and laughter echoing—*echoing*—in the Berkshire Mountains were the most exciting sounds known to adolescents. The years I spent there were tremendous. They had everything I needed for happiness except girls, but they were waiting in the wings for my vacations. Berkshire gave me a rich academic sense of the sweep of cultural history, a timeless rush of anticipation and a wonderful feeling of security. In retrospect, knowing what I learned largely on my own since then, I rarely went outside for athletic practice without expecting to see banners waving in the wind while proud fifteenth century Nürenberg Meistersingers cheered us on with a song contest of their own, or perhaps catching a glimpse of a damsel in distress and a knight on a shining motorcycle racing to her rescue. The fact that these fantasies never materialized was more than offset by the sight of punted footballs spiraling squinting high before tumbling out of the naked cold-blue sky to be clutched to a uniformed breast like an absolute truth, only to be ground underfoot by a phalanx of wrong-colored uniforms.

My real-life roles as a right end, right wing and catcher were played with the utmost seriousness, and I defended the values Berkshire instilled in me against the evil values that football, hockey and baseball players from Taft, Hotchkiss and Choate tried to ram down our throats.

Most of all I loved the ski-trailed mountain behind the school buildings to the West which cast its ever-lengthening shadow across the playing fields in mid-afternoon, adding a chilled sense of urgency to our festivities, degree by delicious degree. It set up razor-sharp contrasts: what could be cozier, after a cold late fall afternoon on a football field, than the sensation of steam heat, the other-warmth of ancient wooden floors and oak wainscoting and a delicious hot supper enhanced by a wolfish appetite? Finally there was recreation—homework, the evening's bull session, and black night's foretaste of oblivion.

Berkshire was a "prep school" or preparatory school. Like all the others, it was designed to prepare students for college, particularly "ivy league" colleges, such as Yale, Harvard and Princeton.

As I understood this setup the purpose was to simplify everything.

What I considered to be the "ugh" subject—Latin—was a good example.

Amo amas amat. I love, you love, he loves—get it kids?

Yes sir.

Ha! Now go out in the world and try to fight for your place in the sun armed with an obsolete language and an impossibly simplified concept of love.

Unimpressed by such "knowledge," I had my own idea about what a prep school was. I wasn't interested in being educated for higher education because that struck me as a self-enclosed process in which education was the goal. Education was not my goal: in my book it was a given. My goal was a happy life, and for that, since *my* happiness was at stake, I had to do a lot of figuring out on my own and not accept all information on trust just because it proved to be valuable in someone else's pursuit of happiness. The prospect of a happy adult life *for me* was the "prep school" I was going to while I was enjoying life at places called Berkshire and Taft.

» » » » »

Let me give you an example to illustrate this principle. I was taught at Berkshire that Copernicus was a greater person than Ptolemy because he proved Ptolemy was wrong about the earth being the center of the universe, and that the earth revolved around the sun and not the other way around.

All my life I have contemplated sunrises and sunsets with assists from clouds, mountains, prairies and oceans, to say nothing of the life and death perspective of duck blinds and goose pits. I have always been awed by each coming and going of the sun without ever thinking about Copernicus because his genius and his life were irrelevant to the infinitely more-than-satisfied situations I found myself in. His dry mathematical concepts were eclipsed by the exciting immediacy of my individual life's daily beginnings and endings.

Although I never mentioned thoughts like the following one on my prep school exams for fear of being flunked out of my paradise, my private feeling was that Ptolemy, right or wrong, had it right in the first place, because if mankind believed, as Ptolemy did, that the earth was the center of the universe, then the rest of the so-called "universe" would be irrelevant, or at least of no practical value, and we could devote our time to appreciating sunrises and stars purely as aesthetic experiences, which I have always assumed was how the heavens were intended to be used in the first place.

Not the least of the great values of this (which, along with aesthetics, is of course not taught in schools), is that people could enjoy these experiences every day instead of standing around humming to themselves while futurists prepare rosy never-never days for them.

Copernicus, perhaps more than anyone else except the three contenders for the honor of inventing the telescope, instigated mankind's preoccupation with its self-made abyss. He was like a mendicant priest who grabbed the universe by a drumstick and realigned it on the platter so he could carve it up more expeditiously for the hungry friars.

Copernicus was the progenitor of all the talk we hear about conquering space and frankly I don't understand why we're trying to conquer it. What did space do wrong? Has it been raiding our villages or perhaps stealing our cattle at night? Does it look funny? Talk funny? Has it taken your job away?

» » » » »

I knew I was privileged, not just because my father could afford to send me to private schools, but because I was having such a wonderful time while still only on the threshold of life. (What an ache it gave me to write that line sixty-five years after the fact: this is one of the joys of writing, believe it or not, because even an ache is more alive than numbed avoidance.)

Like all teenagers I was insatiable when it came to having fun, so I decided to put a plan into effect which would enable me to systematically milk life's pleasures for all they were worth. I really don't think I was motivated by greed, self indulgence or Blake's "I want! I want!" It was just that I didn't want to overlook anything important through lack of caring.

Each night's foretaste of oblivion made this obligatory.

The first project in my master plan was to learn how to walk. When I was in my first year at Berkshire, at about thirteen, it occurred to me one morning while taking the three hundred yard walk from the dormitory to the classroom building that I'd be doing a great deal of walking in my lifetime and therefore should think seriously about the best way to go about it. After all, people have to learn how to play tennis and golf, so why shouldn't I teach myself how to walk, especially since walking was not on the school academic or sports agenda.

With this in mind, every morning when I walked over to the classrooms I enrolled in a course of my own and experimented with walking options. As I traipsed along with my school chums I made minute adjustments in the length of my stride. I tried to break the monotony of precision with freelance hops and skips and sometimes walked backwards or sideways to see what effect non-standard walking had on my outlook. I conducted graduate courses for myself on ambling, strolling and sauntering, and even took a brief fling at moseying. For variety I sometimes left for class early and checked out the pleasures of lolling along; other days I started late and lolloped to class. I experimented with arm-swinging options and couldn't wait for the first heavy snowfall so I could practice my trudging.

As you can imagine, most of these experiments were failures, but they were an important part of my self-education, which was based on the principle of not taking anything for granted. I did not want to live the rest of my life wondering if I was missing out on a better way to walk.

Along about this time I got into a discussion with one of the masters (teachers) about Latin. My position was that it was a waste of time to study the grammar, vocabulary and pronunciation of a dead language for four years when the time could be better spent reading people like Caesar, Cicero and Virgil in translation and thus get an understanding of Latin not as an exercise in discipline, or as a means of learning how to memorize, but rather as a fascinating literature which proved that the little blue flame of our common humanity was burning brightly well over two thousand years ago.

To illustrate my position I tossed off a few gems from Latin literature which were suffocated in Latin grammar classrooms.

"A sound mind in a sound body." (Juvenal)

"Seek not immortality, oh my soul, but explore the limits of the possible." (Pindar)

"It is impossible to argue about taste." (Granted, even a person with a sweet tooth could have written that.)

The master wasn't having any. He ignored my quotations. Instead, he lit into me for transgressions I didn't even know about. He recited a litany of all the things that were wrong with me and used the word authority so often I thought I was losing my mind.

And when he had finished unraveling the rope that held me together and reached what he thought was the end of it, he looked at me kind of funny as if everything about my presence was so far out of whack that his right eye could not believe the evidence of his left eye. Then he said, "You've got to try harder to respect authority. We can help you—I've been observing you walking to class and, heck, you're thirteen years old and you haven't even learned how to walk yet!"

» » » » »

As part of my master plan to explore the stratospheres of life's pleasures I had made a list of projects, and painting was next on my list after "walking." I pored for hours over books of great paintings, looking for the elusive ethos that no one I had ever known had been able to appreciate, and when I finally realized that I too was defeated, the defeat was also a triumph of self-knowledge. This meant that I would never have to pretend that I loved something that was clearly beyond my capacity.

Still, every once in a while I go to an art museum to see if anything has changed, or perhaps I go the way you go to visit a sister who lives far away and with whom you have little in common, but you go anyway just because she is your sister, and you love the feeling that you shared a common womb.

About twenty years ago I discovered Goya, who wrote a moving description of man's fate in paint: had my self-quest in art at Berkshire finally paid off?

Classical Music was next on the list. Like everyone else I liked popular music so much I was sure my tastes would never change, even though I had an apparently premature interest in serious music the last fall I spent in Scarsdale. I reasoned that classical music was probably the equivalent of painting with sound, and since I preferred photos to paintings and loved pop music and was impatient with minuets, I almost skipped over my resolution to *make sure* I wasn't overlooking a good bet, but fortunately I have never been able to check off an item with real potential unless the check mark carries all the weight of a thesis.

In all of Berkshire there were only two people who knew anything about classical music. One was a math teacher named Somerville who used to drive us all nuts in the springtime playing classical records with his windows open, and the other was Bill Jones, a student in our dorm who liked classical music but was less self-assertive about it.

Fresh from my humbling debacles with walking and great painting, but still loyal to the principles of self-education for the greatest thrills, I asked Bill how a guy might get interested in classical music. He explained that it was easy and that I had come to the right place. All I had to do was give him five dollars. He would then order me three Victor Red Seal classical records. I was then supposed to play them over and over on the wind-up Victrola my grandfather had given me, and in about a week I would be hooked forever on classical music.

In a few days the records arrived. They were all overtures and closing scenes from Wagner operas. I played them for a week and Bill Jones was right; I lost all interest in popular music and was forever hooked on classical.

One day a month or so later Harry Ely asked me how a guy might get interested in classical music. I told him it was easy and that he had come to the right place. All he had to do was borrow my three records and play them over and over for a week and he'd be hooked forever.

A week later Harry returned my records.

"Well?"

"Naw," Harry said, "any good Dixieland band can buy and sell all that symphonic junk."

Almost everyone I know claims to enjoy classical music but I have never had a single friend who loved it enough to know who wrote the dance symphony or acquire an extensive classical record library and a first class hi-fi, though many could easily afford them.

Something unnecessary is wrong. I'm not sure I know what it is but as the result of my adolescent experiences as both a student and a self-teacher I think it has something to do with the obsolescence of those damned amos, amases and amants.

CHAPTER 11

The Dismal Science of Economics

Perhaps you are wondering how Scarsdale, whose very name conjures up dreams of wealth, advantage, high culture and the super-refinement of the good life, ever got so screwed up that a fifteen-year-old kid could scoff at its community values which, to be fair, were earned by hard work, self-denial, brain power and persistence.

Was this because that spoiled brat was, as he once admitted, a dog?

I don't think so, but even granting with a smile that this might be a blanket rationalization, several traumatic episodes early in life turned my mind inward, and before I knew what had happened I was living in an intense perverted world in which white was often black and black was often white. I considered grey illogical and redundant and instinctively avoided it many years before I began to study the craft of writing. I associated a certain white with the white of a loved one's eye, a certain black with a black eye, another black with the abyss and the most passionate white of all with the adored fact that I was not on the edge or the bottom of it. That was my world, and I left grey at the disposal of the system for painting its battleships.

I began to reject all the obviously silly adult options almost in the order they first presented themselves. They started on that fateful morning in 1927 after the granddaddy of all snowstorms had filled my curious heart with a new experience almost beyond its capacity for joy while the authorities were doing their damnedest to keep my grammar school open and thus minimize that haunting aesthetic bonanza.

Another adult option was the opportunity to live according to the precepts of economics.

I accessed this option and arrived at my conclusion one morning when I was about twelve years old while walking with my father from Grand Central Station to his office at 305 East 45th Street, as I had done several times before.

It was one of those solid spring days that affirms everything that ever was or is about to be and I was enjoying the imperishable energy in each of my young steps. My mind was playfully speculating on the mystery of why my father had just walked us four blocks out of the way to the Donnelley Building.

Not wanting to break the spell, I didn't say anything, nor did my father, for reasons of his own.

Then he did something I would never have expected him to do in a million years: he stopped at a candy store.

"I buy all my gum here," he said with the emphasis and the air of a school authority imparting a profound truth, "because they sell three packs for ten cents."

Ah ha! So that was the mystery!

Economics.

For the last sixty-eight years I have defined economics—in purely personal terms, you understand—as the science of buying three packs of gum for ten cents.

How did I arrive at this perhaps oversimplified conclusion?

Well, for starters, I picked up on the fact that dad didn't mention what kind of gum he bought. See, I liked Wrigley's Juicy Fruit which had just come on the market and wasn't always available. Were the authorities telling me I should walk four blocks out of my way and perhaps be forced to buy three packs of Spearmint just to save a nickel? Jesus: I hated Spearmint.

Clearly, if I wanted to add a human factor to the economic process—in this case the enjoyment of my taste buds—I would have had to call the candy store from Grand Central Station to make sure they had Juicy Fruit in stock.

But the phone call would cost a nickel.

The plot thickens.

If an economist is willing to walk four blocks to save five cents how much will the shoe leather he wears out cost? That depends on where the candy store is: if it is in a rundown area of the city, with rough sidewalks, the leather will wear out quicker. Granted, the chances are that even after deducting the cost of shoe leather you will still save money on the three packs for ten cents deal, but it stands to reason that even if the shoe leather only costs a small fraction of a cent, you're no longer saving a nickel, but only pennies.

Now for the biggie.

Suppose you're a modern, world class economist, and you underwrite a scientific analysis of shoe sole materials. You study coefficient of friction statistics and pore over digitally generated graphics comparing the abraidability of leather, rubber and the latest high-tech materials in order to determine the greatest economic return on your four block, three for ten cents gum enterprise.

The way I sized up all this busy work was to conclude that the trouble with the science of economics is that it forces you to take a vital interest in subjects which are not in themselves interesting.

For my money the abraidability of shoe sole materials is one of those subjects.

I imagined myself as a grownup and someone asking me what I did for a living, and I heard myself replying, "Oh, I study shoe sole materials."

So why do economists concern themselves with such lifeless junk?

Because they are even more fascinated by little discs of metal and larger rectangles of paper which, in an unimaginably perverse way, are in themselves not only uninteresting, but in terms of taste buds, virtually worthless.

These were my thoughts as I accompanied the system in the

form of my father from the candy store to 305 East 45th Street, but I didn't have the guts to lay my childlike four block Adam Smith odyssey on the president of the Ruben H. Donnelley Corporation.

Besides, I couldn't chew gum anyway because it would get all tangled up in the braces my father bought me with the pennies he saved buying three packs of gum for ten cents.

» » » » »

When I was in my late teens I was convinced I had once lived an exemplary life in a greatly inferior world. How else could I explain being born again into this paradise, this technological nirvana?

This nirvana went far beyond the Victrolas, the cameras, the model airplane engines, the repeating shotguns or the 1935 Ford convertibles with white sidewall tires. No. Above all, it was the ever present, ever tantalizing, ever-just-beyond-reach promise of fresh ingenuities, of bigger, better unheard-ofs.

As you can see, I was still a few years away from seriously considering the possibility that there might be more to human progress than reducing friction and increasing velocity and prices.

However, I had occasional moments of ruffled bliss. One occurred when I was reading, ironically enough, Life magazine.

When I was sixteen I practically lived for the latest models of cars—particularly Fords. I realized that a new 1935 Ford was impossibly beyond my resources and suspected with an ache and a dread that unless I radically changed my absurd notions about how to buy Juicy Fruit I would never have enough money to buy one. My problem was that I was also convinced if I could own a 1935 Ford convertible I would never know greater happiness.

While enjoying the second-rate experience of challenging Life, with every flipped page, to have something, somewhere, to hold my interest, I lucked on to a full-page photograph of a brand new 1935 Ford. It wasn't a convertible, but it did the trick.

It was lying on its side, as graceless as a bull with a matador's sword through its heart. Flames and smoke were shooting out of the windows, which had been shattered by angry blue collar workers wielding baseball bats. The green sheen of new motor oil lent a sickening texture to the glass-littered street and I was shocked that a system which had everything for everybody could have gone so terribly wrong.

Jesus, did those guys hate that car!

Hmm—I wondered, why did they hate the object I loved? Was it because they lived in Detroit and I lived in Scarsdale? Or did it go deeper than that? Was the idea that machinery is creating the best of all possible worlds a myth?

I studied that photograph for what seemed like ages trying to answer my own questions and finally went back to flipping pages looking vainly for something pertinent, somewhere—*anywhere*.

I was years away from owning a new Ford, but in the meantime I decided to keep closer tabs on the world and the machinery around me. Don't get me wrong—everything was great, absolutely great—it's just that something seemed not quite right even when I was sixteen. I had to wait until I was forty before Lewis Mumford explained all this to me in lucid detail in his monumental, beyond-praise book *The Pentagon of Power: The Myth of the Machine*.

Meanwhile, despite my early vague doubts the years of my life flowed sweetly on like Niagara Falls at the height of the honeymoon season.

CHAPTER 12

Back-to-Back Accidents

One chilly winter morning a few years later (probably as the result of the previous evening's loosely—orchestrated debauchery) I was late for my freshman English class at the University of Louisville.

Because snowflakes were in the air, here and there, I let my BMW sleep over on its centerstand and kicked my Triumph dirt bike out of bed. The Triumph and I were old friends. We had endured many hard enduro miles together, and I always maintained it race-ready, which included full knobby tires front and rear. The knobbies weren't worth the powder to blow 'em to hell on pavement, but they would at least keep me from getting stranded if the snow accumulated while I was in class.

Against my better judgment—because of the tires—and in a vain attempt to outrun my conscience, I was hotdogging to the campus on Eastern Parkway when my frankfurter fell off the front forks into the fire.

The light was green and the driver was parked beneath it waiting to make a left turn. His left turn signal was blinking. He obviously was waiting for me to clear the intersection.

The imminent dysfunctions were not technological in origin. They were, as Nietzsche would have said, "*human, all too human.*"

The driver's timing error was perfect: he delayed his turn until I was in the dead center of the danger zone.

What saved my butt was that in my two wheeled commutings to college I had memorized all the intersectional escape routes.

The crisis at hand involved carefully threading my way between a telephone pole and a large free standing mailbox shortly after jumping an oddly radiused six inch curb. The curb was the easy part and I stood on the pegs and lofted the front wheel, but the oddball radius threw me off my line and my left peg—with my boot heavy on it—hit the mailbox and snapped off like a piece of peanut brittle. Now off my line and out of shape as well, I was luckily able to find the rear brake pedal and laid my bike gently down on the uninhabited sidewalk, as unscathed as a butterfly alighting on a lily pad.

As I picked up my Triumph I glanced over at the intersection—there wasn't a vehicle in sight.

This didn't bother me because to be perfectly honest I don't know which is worse, speeding or leaving the scene of an accident.

As I resumed my ride to the university, now of course going faster than ever to make up for the lost time, and with my boot resting awkwardly on the left engine case, I suddenly realized I had not escaped unscathed. My left foot felt repulsively hot and sticky, as it would if my boot was filling up with blood.

But I had a class to go to so I gave my system a dreg shot of adrenaline and tried not to think left foot.

I was a serious and conscientious student. I had done my homework for the English class with great care and, yes, perhaps even devotion.

Although the bell had rung ten minutes before, all the students were still there. I put my helmet on the desk and went quickly to the blackboard. My class had been reading George Orwell's *Such, Such Were the Joys*, which is his personal testament to the rewards of the literary and creative life.

I began to put an Orwell quote on the blackboard.

"*Nationalism is no longer warranted*" I wrote, "*because to be French or Russian or German or American . . . .*"

I stopped writing, disconcerted by the feeling that my left boot might by now be filled with blood and that it would shortly overflow or perhaps start leaking between the sole and the vamp.

Glancing nervously down, I was relieved to see I was not leaving bloody tracks.

I was writing the quote in a continuous line on the board and at the word "American" the blackboard ended where it intersected with the side wall. Partly because I didn't want to walk back to the other end of the blackboard on the theory that it would pump more blood into my boot, and partly for the delight I have often experienced from obeying ninety degree impulses, I continued chalking out George Orwell's words, finishing up on the side wall where there was no blackboard.

The quote ended with the phrase " . . . *is to be less than we actually are.*"

Frankly I was tickled by what I'd done, because in my extensive experience college classrooms tend to be places where life is taken far too seriously.

Since one thing usually leads to another, to cap off my impromptu performance as a stand-up comedian, as I turned around to face my class I tossed the chalk into the air and was going to catch it with a flourish.

But I never did.

While the chalk was in the air there had been another potentially fatal accident involving thirty people at the intersection of Blackboard and Side Wall.

In the shocked, horrified, mouth-open-astonishment registered on almost every student's face I could see what was wrong with higher education.

If college students are horrified by chalk marks on the wrong wall, what are they going to do when they get out in the real world and their shoes start filling up with blood for no reason at all except that they had just seized an opportunity to have a little unsanctioned fun?

» » » » »

Frankly I enjoyed the contrast of discussing the vicissitudes of George Orwell's intellectual life while blood resulting from a recreation my colleagues disapproved of was leaking into my boot. It gave me a delicious sense of having just escaped from the moribund system while standing in front of thirty students and conscientiously promoting the concepts of George Orwell, who had done his level best to bring that system back to life. I also loved the sweet beyond belief contrast between the physical and the intellectual side of man's nature, which adds up to the concept of wanting it all in the context, of course, of our abilities and limitations. It was a memorable day, for sure.

Perhaps, dear reader, you're having trouble with all this. That's understandable. After all, blood in your boot is not everyone's cup of tea. Besides, if you accept everything I'm saying at face value you're doing something I would never do. To paraphrase Thoreau, how do you know that when you have decided to live as I live, I will have decided to live differently?

Ah! But that's another day, another school and besides, the bell just rang: this class, this concept—such as it is—is over.

CHAPTER 13

Truth or Consequences

I read the George Orwell quote aloud.

"Nationalism is no longer warranted because to be French or Russian or German or American is to be less than we actually are."

"What do you suppose this means?" I asked, with the feeling that since my wonky chalkwork had put me off my line, I was about to hit thirty inflexible objects and be out of shape as well.

The students were mute and sullen. Helen glared at me. Helen of the C—minus written on scented paper in her exquisite calligraphy: lordy, if writing were only that easy!

"Helen?"

"Who is going to clean the chalk off the wall?" she wanted to know. She was really pissed.

"Gee, I don't know, Helen," I said, "That's not a faculty concern. It's a staff job. If you really want to know you might check with the janitor," I said, "or the janitress," I added hastily, determined to avoid subsidiary trouble. There was no way I could deal with the absurdity of the situation without humbling Helen's intelligence, just as mine had been humbled hundreds of times in the course of my education.

The class giggled, but I couldn't tell if it was at Helen's grasp of fundamental concepts or my unprofessional elitism.

I opened the throttle a tad.

"Tell you what, Helen—since you're so anxious to get your higher education in rooms with chalkless walls, why don't you check with the janitorial department and write a paper on what kind of rags they use?"

This time the students not only giggled, they also tittered and snickered.

But this time I was the target for sure.

Great! If feigned elitism doesn't do the trick, deliberate sarcasm never fails: *the class was beginning to react.*

Truth is always subversive.

Still, I wasn't kidding myself. Pretending to have two nasty personality defects was probably an unnecessary sacrifice. While it was one I would redeem before the class was over with an objective discussion of the nature, use and dangers of elitism and sarcasm, the fact was that what became known as "the chalk episode" in future classes was more entertaining than George Orwell. I somehow managed to make my day by getting Helen cleansed and laughing with me. Everyone had an opinion about chalk on the wall and as long as we were discussing that nobody had to figure out what the stupid quote was supposed to mean.

My boot had apparently stopped filling with blood, probably because my heart had started to bleed for the students.

» » » » »

My conditioning as a student within the system began at the age of nine at the Fox Meadow Elementary School in Scarsdale.

One day Miss Witherspoon noticed that I was chewing bubble gum in her class, but I didn't see anything wrong with that. Heck, I was even blowing bubbles. I was good at that and proud of my skill. An ordinary bubble burst with a sound like a cap pistol, but I had mastered the knack of opening my mouth wide at the explosion so that the sound reverberated like a shotgun blast.

"Herbert, please come up to my desk," Miss Witherspoon said.

I did so, triggering a shotgun blast on the way up.

Miss Witherspoon patiently and politely explained why I shouldn't chew gum in class.

"A class," she said, "is a community of people just as Scarsdale is made up of people who live together in the same area. It is important to be a part of that community. You should never do things that other members of the community cannot do. What is wrong with chewing gum in class is that you are doing something that no one else can do. Have I made myself clear?"

"Yes," I said.

"This is very important. Do you *understand?*"

"Yes," I said, "I understand."

"You may be seated."

I licked my fingers, took the gum out and dropped it in her wastebasket.

Then I sat down, elated.

I was in love with Miss Witherspoon.

The zoology of my situation was akin to the mating ritual of the ruffed grouse, in which the cock struts and puffs himself up to excite the hen. And since I was in love with Miss Witherspoon, I spent the rest of the day trying to think of a way to make her realize that I wasn't just another cock.

The next morning I seasoned and prepped three balls of bubble gum before class, and shortly after the bell rang I blew the biggest, the most spectacular bubble I had ever blown in my entire nine years of existence. It blocked out my whole head and through its rubbery sweetness the blurred image of the woman I loved appeared like an angel in paradise.

"HERBERT!!"

Startled, I lost control. Before I could suck back a little air the bubble burst and flattened against my face, covering it like a blister pack.

"Come to my desk," Miss Witherspoon continued, ominously ignoring my plight.

I managed to pull the gum away from my nose so I could breathe, then I reached in my desk and got the bag and bowl before walking up to her desk. My face looked like a corpse that had revived while the death mask technician was plying his trade.

"Didn't I tell you yesterday not to chew gum in class?"

"Yes, you did," I blubbered, "but I've solved your problem."

Whereupon, strutting and puffing like a grouse, I produced the bowl and twenty-one balls of bubble gum.

"There is one for each member of the class, including you," I said proudly, "now we can all chew gum together."

In the next few seconds I got enough education to last a lifetime.

When I got home with Miss Witherspoon's note explaining that I had been sent home for "insubordination" my mother asked me what happened.

I told her, scared to death, about the awful thing I had done. She laughed.

Then she stroked my hair, looked deep and lovingly into my eyes, and explained in great and lucid detail what had just happened to me and why, and what I had to expect for the rest of my life unless I changed my ways, which she advised me not to do.

That night, lying in bed reviewing the day's events, I decided to dump Miss Witherspoon.

» » » » »

There was a lot more going on in my classroom than the students realized. When you are hired to teach on the university level you are sometimes required, as I was, to sign a statement to the effect that you will not use your authority, or prestige, or whatever, to sell your own ideas.

On the surface there appear to be good reasons for this: for example, if you are teaching a course in government, and you happen to be a staunch democrat or socialist or anarchist, it would be easy to present your academic material from the point of view of a politician, stressing or minimizing facts so that they conform to the way you think people should be governed.

In the situation I was in with the chalk episode I was technically not performing my job. I had not been hired to teach the principles of creativity. In fact, there was no such course. Although I felt this was a major void in higher education, and much as I regretted having to dig this information out entirely on my own, I could not in good conscience let the present discussion be protracted, because what the university wanted me to do was help the students reach an educated understanding of George Orwell's view of society and the joys of his work, and not my own views on how the creative process works.

This would have been well and good except that the paper I had signed ironically prevented me from teaching what I believed in because of my sense of obligation to my employer.

For this reason I decided to get the discussion back within the syllabus for Freshman English—that is, back to Orwell. Specifically, back to the quote on, for the most part, the blackboard.

The chance to do this came in the form of Peter, who was famous in my class rollbook for not doing his homework. His face registered more than anger or outrage. It was full of hate.

"Peter," I said pleasantly, "you look as if you'd like to say something."

"Yes, I would," he said.

Silence.

"Yes, Peter, go ahead."

Peter spoke with obvious emotion: his words came slowly. They were evenly spaced and had an identically heavy emphasis.

"Neither-you-or-anyone-else-can-make-me-unpatriotic," he said.

"Who is trying to make you unpatriotic?," I asked.

"You-are."

"How is that?"

"With-your-damned-writing-on-the-blackboard."

"Peter," I said, glad he had given me the opportunity to say it, "there is something you have to understand here. No one is trying to make you unpatriotic. You're no longer in high school. This is a university, and a university is nothing more than an organized opportunity for self-education. You always have the option of calling your own shots."

"Okay, then," he said, "I'll-call-my-own-shot. I-think-you-should-be-fired-for-writing-that."

"But Peter, I didn't write it. George Orwell did."

"Well-then-he-should-be-fired."

"But he doesn't work here."

"Well-then," Peter fumed, "our-government-should-send-him-to-Russia."

"I'm afraid we can't do that, Peter, because he's British."

"Well-then-he-should-be-deported-from-Britain."

"That would be very hard to do and there really wouldn't be much point because he is dead."

Peter looked furtively around the classroom like a trapped animal—his eyes beseeching—seeking help and reinforcement from his fellow Americans.

He didn't get any, but I had a sickening feeling that this wasn't because the rest of the class did not agree with him.

Unlike most other disciplines, education in the humanities usually begins when you hear something you don't want to hear.

There is a saying among salesman that "the selling begins when the prospect says no." In other words, if the prospect buys the product as soon as he is told about it the salesman hasn't sold him, he has merely taken an order. Selling is the art of changing a no to a yes. This is rarely easy, and for those who are good at it, it pays handsomely.

Peter had said no.

My job was to change that to a yes. I was not selling a product, or even an idea. At this point I was selling knowledge, and knowledge begins with words. Poignancy lies at the heart of all the most exciting words.

Mommy. Daddy.

Peter's problem was that in previous years it had never occurred to anyone to teach him the difference between the words patriotism and nationalism. His problem was exacerbated because, aside from not doing his homework, his intentions were above reproach. He was really trying to understand. When a teacher told him that patriotism was love for, or devotion to one's country, he was moved—perhaps even thrilled by the concept. Thus the feeling of love and security he got from his parents—who were probably also patriotic—was augmented by the feeling that his country would take care of him, no matter what. The irony implicit in this self-seeking psychic reassurance went right over his head, just as it had once gone over my head when I felt the way he did and didn't know what the word "irony" meant either.

» » » » »

One of the great self-educations of my life—greater, perhaps than building my Playboy Senior model airplane and watching it spiral up, and forever out of sight—was reading a newspaper account of a soldier home on leave who died of a heart attack in Brooklyn.

I was about nine years old: it hit me like a ton of bricks: I thought khaki: how could this be? I visualized him lying in a coffin, about to be abandoned under tons of dirt while all dressed up in the khaki uniform of the United States Army, which up to that point I honestly believed protected everybody from everything forever.

» » » » »

It was a welcome relief from the growing tension to explain to Peter with as much sympathy and reassurance as I could muster—as to a brother—that, unlike patriotism, which is simply a natural love of one's country, nationalism is the belief that the welfare of one's country is more important than the welfare of the world. It assumes that national boundaries—lines drawn on maps by cartographers—somehow negate the fact that all human beings are brothers and sisters, who should enjoy each other's company and perhaps especially their differences instead of killing each other.

Having thus elevated the discussion to a scholarly level in which

words are used with precise meanings, I then explained that George
Orwell's quote says, in effect, that when they are allowed total
freedom to do as they choose, human beings are, for the most part,
noble, and to the extent that they fall under the influence of ignoble
people who are governing them, they become less than they are—
far less than the highest form of life.

Many a bombardier who wouldn't kill a fly in his role as a
human being has killed thousands of fellow human beings in his
role as a nationalist. And one in particular has killed scores of
thousands and probably got a medal for this, though not much is
said about that.

Oh, but I could tell Peter wasn't buying.

And he was not alone.

I was sick at heart. What the hell was I doing standing in
front of a group of tomorrow's leaders trying to influence the
course of human evolution? What good did it do to quote from
one of the most objective and prophetic minds the human race
has produced? What good did it do to defend Orwell, who in
recent years has actually become the target of scornful ignorance
by people who think artists should always be held scientifically
accountable for the validity of their fantasies and who have no
concept of the supra-validity of timeless first principles? Then,
recalling H.G. Wells' comment that the survival of mankind
depended on the outcome of the race between humanistic
education and technology, it suddenly dawned on me that the
first vital force was largely unappreciated and the second was
too powerful for its own good.

What a laugh—you might as well race a poet on a magnificent
stallion against me on my ninety horsepower sport bike, and since
I've had two bikes stolen God help anyone who tries to take my
present technology away from me. Let me temper any full-of-myself
tendencies you detect in this memoir with the admission that as
far as contributing to the irreversible downside of technology is
concerned, I readily admit to being as guilty as everybody else.

I was relieved when the bell rang. The students filed out of the classroom exchanging local gossip, unaware that quite possibly they had just taken part in a preview of the end of civilization as they were enjoying it.

It had been a hard day. I'd already had two school-related accidents, one physical and the other psychological. I didn't want any more. All I wanted to do was go home to my model shop and leave the fate of the world to the politicians.

As it happened I was working on a museum scale model of Baron Von Richtofen's World War I Fokker DrI triplane, which I had been building for over a year. My airplane was rich in historical associations: the Red Baron faced terrible dangers and gave his life for his country, which just happened to be Germany, which just happened to have a nationalistic government at the time.

In a few weeks I'd take my airplane out to the model airport and fly it with radio control equipment. This skill is hard to learn and requires great persistence, because model airplanes are always at risk in the pins and needles sky, and a new, untried, and untrimmed model is always at heavy risk on the first flight. However I am a philosopher and I figured that if I totaled it I'd have the pleasure of building another model—who knows, perhaps a British Sopwith camel, a French Spad, or an American Curtis Jenny.

My model shop has always been a haven. It provides me with a non-lethal, non-polluting and absorbing outlet for the technological side of my nature. A day in my shop working with internal combustion engines or electronics gives me a deep sense of accomplishment, and when I put a favorite plane through its paces the amount of coordination and concentration required, plus the romance of miniaturization, brings an earned sense of a high state of being easily within reach.

But the thing I like most about the whole process is that the only conceivable purpose for all this delightful activity is play— honest, unashamed adult play.

Modeling is my way of escaping from a short memory world culture in which a titan like Baron Von Richtofen, who acted on the noblest of impulses, had been reduced, a few short years after

his supreme sacrifice, to a subsidiary role in the comic strip
"Snoopy."

The only reason Snoopy's cartoonist gets away with his
desecration is because he studiously avoids mentioning Arlington
National Cemetery or its equivalents throughout the world.

CHAPTER 14

The Plusses and Minuses of TV

The difference between TV and life is the difference between watching it and being on it. I don't know what the odds against life are in this respect except that they are dreadfully stacked against it, so when I was invited to be on a talk show at Louisville's WHAS-TV I jumped at the chance to put a few licks in for life.

This opportunity came about because a local high school teacher had been fired for teaching <u>The Catcher in the Rye</u> and I had written a letter to the Courier Journal in defense of literature in general and the unfortunate teacher and Salinger's masterpiece in particular. The moderator of a regional program called "Casing the Classics" read my letter, called me from his home in Cincinnati, and after a brief discussion invited me to be on a program in which the pros and cons of The Catcher in the Rye imbroglio would be discussed.

The first thing that impressed me about being on TV was that you could not do it in the comfort of your home lying back on your tufted coffin decor couch upholstery.

No: for this experience I had to travel from my ancient log house in Prospect all the way downtown to the studio. It was raining but I rode my bike anyway because from River Road the Ohio is breathtaking in the rain, especially when you too are being rained on. It was a mystical real-life experience with overtones of Siegfried's Rhine Journey echoing pantheistically in my soul.

I noticed two things about being on TV: first although the studio furniture was threadbare, this defect did not show up on home TV screens, and, when I looked up at the huge hearse-like video cameras I got the feeling gods were eyeing me for possible candidacy for heaven, but because my heart was triphammering with New Experience excitement I dismissed that prospect as overkill.

In addition to the moderator the panel included a sixteen-year-old high school girl, a well-known minister, and me. The host introduced the girl as representing the high school student body, the minister as a moralist, and me as a literature "professor" at the University of Louisville who had written an "inspiring" letter on the subject. He then read my letter to start the discussion.

Everything went along reasonably well. In a short while I warmed to the situation and my heart, suddenly realizing it was not threatened in my present situation, decided not to blow a gasket.

In the course of critiquing Salinger's contentious book I unintentionally aroused the ire of the minister by quoting in quick succession from two literary classics which, considering the name of the program, I considered entirely appropriate. But with that, the minister suddenly slapped his hand on the arm of his chair and declared with visible emotion, "You can quote Tolstoy and . . . that other man all you want, but let me tell my friends in TV land this—I have a cousin who had a real mixed-up kid, a troublemaker just like Holden Caulfield, but he shipped him off to a military academy and those men straightened him right out!"

» » » » »

On my ride home along the Ohio I recalled the joke about the pollution consulting firm which had been commissioned to determine the ratio of water to raw sewage in the Ohio River, and their conclusion was that there was no ratio because there was no water in the river.

I rocked my bike from side to side in my favorite mechanized version of side-splitting laughter.

But inside I was gloomy as gloomy can be.

What we had done to the Ohio River we were also doing to the life-sustaining resources of our literature.

I thought long and hard about Salinger's exquisite fable of absolute morality, about his becoming a recluse, and if that would perhaps be my solution to the identical problem.

I began to think seriously about what I did for a living and the role literature plays in cultural evolution. I decided that if anything it only reinforced the status quo, which entrenches itself all the more the more literature takes swipes at its values. The evidence was everywhere and it was staggering.

In my immediate experience, one of the most easily documented proofs of this was the case of the TV production of Anna Karenina, where Tolstoy's profoundly human insights, which have been revered for a century and a half among people who care deeply about the quality of their lives, were reduced to a small-screened spectacle, a pagented toilet-watered cake of soap. The show's producer, who was not fit to shine Tolstoy's shoes—shoes Tolstoy made and repaired himself, by the way—declared in print that he decided to "help Tolstoy out" and make Anna more appealing by giving her a sense of humor. However, in Tolstoy's monumental and skillfully interwoven dramatizations of the attributes which create sublime marriages, so-so marriages and out-and-out disasters, one of the reasons for Anna's tragic end was that she lacked a sense of humor.

Tolstoy created her that way for a humanitarian reason. He hoped to vivify women whose marriages were failing because, among other things, they were taking themselves too seriously. His game plan was to show them the light through the seemingly innocent pastime of reading a novel.

The TV producer, whose name neither of us know, in effect hired out one of the great tragic heroines of literature as a common whore and sold it to the highest bidding advertiser.

And if you, dear reader, have a sense of humor and want a bellylaugh, conjure up the scenario of Mr. and Mrs. Couch Potato telling all their neighbors that they saw *Anna Karenina* on TV, and that they just love Tolstoy, with the funny part being the look on their faces when their neighbors tell them the exact same thing, which amounts to the larger unfunny truth that the Einsteins of imaginative literature are no match for couch potatoes.

Anna Karenina was one of the books I taught at U. of L. Although it has many great themes, some of them of enormous social significance, I limited my overviews pretty much to husband/wife relationships because I felt those insights would be of greater value to college students, as they have been to me throughout my life. Early on in our discussions students began requesting that their spouses or girl or boyfriends be allowed to audit the course. I was gratified and gave my permission without asking the authorities if it was all right, because I suspected, knowing what I already knew about higher education, that it probably wasn't all right.

Experiences such as this and the one I had just had at WHAS-TV convinced me that if I ever wrote a book it would be, like this one, wholly without moral purpose. I therefore can tell you unequivocally that I harbor no secret desire to make the world better. All I am working at is to depict modern life realistically and responsibly and with as much good humor as my frustrations will allow. If a reader gets an idea here and there that he can fit with advantage into the bag of tricks he uses to heighten the thrills he gets out of life I will be excellently compensated for the enormous amount of work it takes to write a book of this nature. And out of gratitude and respect for those teachers whose intentions were finer than their perceptions, and who tried their best to give me a "proper" education, I promise to spend the money I make wisely, which means giving chunks of it away to my various alma maters.

CHAPTER 15

Creativity, Anyone?

Tell me what I must do
to speak that sweet language.

Goethe
"Faust," part II

In the no-man's land which separates a writer from his or her audience, which has always fascinated me, you have the supreme example of a one-sided conversation. I can say anything I please: you can't even say "but." It is not fair: it's not even polite, but it is all we've got.

It's the system.

Neither of us can change the system, but you can at least circumvent it in your own secret life and in this very moment, which is all that matters.

How do you do that?

It's easy.

Agree with me.

» » » » »

Creativity is simply the process of doing or saying something that isn't being done or said trillions of times a day: cleverness is the same process except that the arithmetic is more like 100,000 times a day and is therefore hardly worth mentioning even though journalists swear by it and often get a surprising amount of mileage out of it.

Almost from my first day at school I concluded that education is not only useless but actually a drag in the creativity department whenever the math reaches unimaginable proportions.

Since there are no courses in creativity per se, students who think it might be nice to be creative and would like to take the fling are in a catch-22 situation. How can they be what everyone secretly wants to be if none of the authorities who are telling them how to be know diddly-squat about how to be what everyone secretly wants to be?

The best ways I know to run this roadblock are to do as much of what you do all by yourself and to pay close attention to what you observe and especially what you read. Once you're over these hurdles creative writing is a snap: you just say what everyone is afraid to say, such as that you cannot run with the herd and be creative at the same time.

The primary concern of anyone who aspires to creativity is to resist the deadly influence of mass attitudes which are revered for the cowardly reason that they constitute a reassuring majority.

However, it is not enough to be a rebel as a matter of principle: if you don't have a gripe of reasonable, perhaps even provable stature, you are nothing but a troublemaker.

For this discussion therefore we need examples, and they are now forthcoming. The first one appropriately enough is from the world's canon of imperishable literature.

» » » » »

Whew! At last this chapter is off and running. (Let me tell you, that was one pesky first olive!)

» » » » »

Well over a hundred years ago Thoreau had a shrewd insight and drew a vital conclusion from it.

In essence, he said in reference to our insatiable appetite for news and data, that if you read about one cow that wanders on the railroad tracks and gets killed by a steam locomotive, or one jetliner that gets highjacked, or one runaway horse that injures an old woman, or one tank truck that explodes, or one politician caught with his hand in the till in any century, then what you have just read or seen on TV constitutes a principle, which is that cows will walk on tracks, jets will be highjacked, et cetera, et cetera, *ad nauseum.*

Thoreau's conclusion was that once we understand the principle, we no longer need myriads of examples of the same principle, which only amounts to treading water.

Many a man who has read Walden and professes to love Thoreau's concept of simplicity also watches the news on TV every night and claims to love it for the same paradoxical reason, which is not that he finds equal value in his warring loves, but rather that his overriding concern is to promote his image as a with-it personality.

All things to all people can't be all that bad.

Unless, of course, you are hung up on the notion that the creative process exists independently of mass-produced self-helps and is, in terms of strictly human satisfactions, the invention to end all inventions.

One of the latest irrational examples of mass-produced hog wild "creativity" is the vaunted E-mail, which was designed for technophiles who either think Alexander Graham Bell has been hopelessly out-teched or who just don't like the sound of a loved one's voice.

E-mail is also an example of the recent onset of flakiness in scientific progress, which is becoming increasingly retrogressive and appeals to those who prefer inferior things like e-mail and the sonics of Internet music, primarily because they're free. Are we getting so selfish and miserly that we're not willing to pay ten cents a minute to hear a friendly or loving voice? The telephone is a far more humanizing device than e-mail and provides unexpected creative opportunities for joy. A girlfriend I had a stormy affair with once phoned me while she was taking a bath. Midway through our conversation I heard water sloshing and was electrified when I realized that she was pleasuring herself with a highly creative erotic deception. In fantasy I suddenly saw the world through her eyes and infinite opportunities for breaking the bonds of ordinary conversation opened up to both of us. The sexually modulated voice-to-voice exchange which followed was as profoundly human as it gets in a world where the criteria for judging excellence are inexorably trending towards the cheapness and the newness of the technology.

What has happened to spelling is another illustration of my thesis.

Originally, spelling was a function of the brain. There were national contests where spelling was treated as a game and the winners were probably rewarded with medals or scholarships or other symbols of unnecessary excellence. I use "unnecessary" somewhat loosely because spelling does not fall into the category of vital knowledge stored in the brain.

Instead, it is a form of data which can quickly and often profitably be looked up in a dictionary, since flipping pages for spelling data often exposes the conscientious and word-curious writer to a wealth of word meanings he or she had never dreamed of. Even a spelling dictionary robs the writer of these frequent contacts with the source of his creativity—word meanings—and to what end? Speed and convenience. But have you ever heard anyone say, "Oh, Harriet is a fine writer, she writes very fast and conveniently."

I understand there is some kind of a gadget you can attach to a word processor that corrects your spelling. Chances are, being young and computer literate, you know what I am referring to. But even though I am old and illiterate, I am against word processors and spelling gadgets on principle. Why should I turn my delight in processing words over to a machine that knows nothing of delight except how to spell it? For that matter, why should I use a word processor? I prefer to do all my word processing in my mind before routinely transferring the results to paper, and besides I greatly enjoy the soundless sensuality of flowing ink and the endless signature implicit in my calligraphy.

While we are on the subject of software perhaps you should know that the boilerplate gadget that corrects your grammar is flattening creative language to the level of Hallmark cards without the sentimentality. These machines won't even let a novelist use the passive voice to subtly reveal a wimp's ineptitudes. However, they are the perfect present for anyone who believes the gift of writing talent can be bought the way you might buy a rattlesnake in an exotic pet store.

The Discovery Channel is another example of the electronic short-circuiting of creative human impulses. You pay through the nose for this channel because it isn't a discovery channel at all: it merely informs the viewer what has already been discovered, and limits his or her curiosity to what's up for grabs on the evening's programming. Each member of the vast audience gets identical information gleaned from the commercial potential of various phenomena. Thus the programs create the illusion in each viewer that he has discovered something valuable which in fact is nothing more than what every other viewer has "discovered" on a given night. For this reason each honest attempt the viewer undertakes to make himself more interesting only amounts to treading water. Discovering is an individual learning, rather than a group-watching process. To really and truly discover something you have to go where no one ever goes, such as the North Pole or the library.

» » » » »

There are two kinds of knowledge. One is the information we have stored in our brains and the other is the data we know where to find. The former vital type comes from experience supplemented by reading and contemplation and the latter, ho hum type, lies waiting to be of service in the reference section of all libraries or by doing whatever one does on the Internet.

Since nourishing a successful life is largely a matter of making yourself more interesting to others as well as yourself, we can all profit by differentiating between provocative memories and information known only to ourselves and data available to anyone on the Internet.

The importance of this difference is illustrated by the following experience I had at age eighteen.

» » » » »

When I was at Taft the school arranged for the editor of a publishing company to talk to students interested in writing careers.

There was a large turnout of privileged adolescents.

During the question period a student asked how important spelling and grammar were. It was a question we were all interested in because we were getting heavy doses of both in English classes.

The answer straight from the horse's mouth was that they were not at all important. The spokesman explained that publishers were looking for people who could communicate original ideas, who had fire in their eyes and fueled their imaginations with gasoline.

As for spelling and grammar, he added indifferently, anyone who puts his or her mind to it can master these skills and for that reason publishers could, in his words, "hire hacks for peanuts to do the window-dressing."

He then noted that Hemingway, Thomas Wolfe and F. Scott Fitzgerald were all notoriously poor spellers and concluded with a Mark Twain quote: "The ability to spell correctly is a God-given talent and is a sign of intellectual inferiority."

At this point in that long ago but unforgotten afternoon all student eyes aligned themselves like feathered darts on the English teachers who up to that point had been sitting smugly on the rostrum. Watching them squirm in humorous discomfiture was a joy for all the students to behold.

Meanwhile my friends and I treated the titanic subject of

creativity with comic unconcern, and let it slip quietly out the back door of the auditorium without so much as a glance over our collective shoulders.

» » » » »

When I was very young and had my whole life and a mountain of homework to look forward to, I used to think my brain was my Achilles heel. I was convinced that my poor memory would sooner or later do me in.

School authorities up through college and even including graduate school tended to confirm this. I operated as best I could with this handicap until I embarked on my self-education career and discovered that while memory is crucial if one is determined to lead a creative life, it is of little importance in the sense with which memory is traditionally taught. The greatest blunder educators can make, by far, is to equate memorizing with understanding, yet this continues to be the rule. Knowing what happened in 1066 means absolutely nothing if you don't understand the difference between nationalism and patriotism.

In the larger scheme of things it turns out that I have a wonderful memory: I forget 98 percent of what I learn.

To the creative aspirant the primary function of memory should be to filter out all information that is not memorable. Success or failure will be determined by what you consider memorable, and you should forget the sales literature because no machine can determine that for you.

That is why the Internet is the most unimaginative device imaginable. By throwing unlimited data at you it stultifies the creative process while creating graphic illusions that it is opening up new worlds. Thanks but no thanks: the Internet is to the creative impulse what a mud slide is to a house designed to profit most from a view of a lovely valley. If you want to be a creative writer you will sink or swim according to the sprightliness of the intellect with which your line-by-line decisions are made.

And you no sooner squeak through one blank page crisis than you are confronted with another. It's an exciting life for sure.

How many times have you heard someone say that so-and-so is brilliant, that he or she has a "photographic mind"? Who in his right mind would want such a dreadful thing? A mind like that has no mind of its own, yet it is as revered and envied as if it had invented the camera.

Do you know there are people who can stand on a busy street corner all day and "photograph" the license plate number of every car that passes by? Such a brain is sick: it is pathologically unable to discriminate between what is important and what is of no consequence. In advanced stages of this disease, which is terminal in our culture, the patient buys a machine which metaphorically enables him to access the license plate data of every car currently licensed, and he can do this without any effort other than reading an owner's manual, pressing a few arthritic keys, and looking at an uninspiring, puke-green screen.

Is that what we want?

I guess so!

Let's drop the subject and turn the evening news on good old T and V. If we're lucky perhaps a tank truck has exploded.

It has been fun spinning my wheels for you: it momentarily diverted me from the worldwide, well organized and systematic dismembering of my sources of happiness.

CHAPTER 16

Death in the Classroom

Of all the insufficient authorities as to the total nature of
reality, give me the 'scientists' . . . their interests are the most
incomplete and their professional conceit and bigotry
immense. I know of no narrower sect or club, in spite of
their excellent authority in the line of fact they have explored,
and their splendid achievements there.

—William James

One morning I looked around the classroom at the innocent
faces of kids who, if they wanted to live out natural life spans,
would have to solve gigantic problems related to minuscule things,
such as planktonic organisms and substances infinitely smaller than
the point of a pin.

All these problems were caused by people who, for the most
part, were professors in institutions of higher learning, such as
Harvard College, St. Lawrence University and West Point Academy.

I remember in 1938 when a professor stood in front of our
inorganic chemistry class and told us with a perfectly straight face
that the physical world was composed of 92 absolutely basic and
irreducible elements. This was just three years before Pearl Harbor.
Surely that bastard knew that his colleagues were on the verge of
breaking those 92 elements up into something of more use to
mankind than rocks, rills, woods and templed hills. He also knew
that this work was theoretical, which meant that although the

conclusions made sense on paper they would ultimately have to be proven experimentally.

Sure enough, they were.

At Los Alamos.

I never knew until several decades after the fact, even though I had a college education and read newspapers and listened to the radio regularly, that when the first atom bomb was detonated the purpose was to determine experimentally if the chain reaction it initiated could, as they hoped on the basis of their calculations, be stopped. They also wanted to find out if the atmosphere would catch fire.

On the day that test was made, the life of every man, woman, child and animal on earth was placed in jeopardy with consummate irony to win a war.

How did I find out about this criminal, world-wide experiment physics professors committed secretly, without referendum?

From a *literary* professor named Hannah Arendt, who also made what I consider to be the most devastating comment on mankind's ultimate fate in print. Quoting from seared-in-the-brain memory, she wrote that "the most frightening aspect of the nuclear bomb is not its awesome power, horrible as that is, but rather *the speed of man's acceptance.*"

Since mankind has parlayed itself into the absurd position of being deathly afraid to die on an individual basis and blithely unconcerned about the extinction of homo sapiens, let's reinterpret Hannah Arendt's remark with all the objectivity we can muster to see what we can salvage from our knowledge of secrets the man in the street knows nothing about.

If we try to fault the nuclear scientists responsible for the Los Alamos experiment—which put 2 1/2 billion of our human lives at risk—we are attempting to solve a problem using only half the available evidence.

Consider the following incontrovertible fact as the other half of the evidence: *when scientists put everyone else's life in jeopardy at Los Alamos, they put their own lives on the line as well.*

This changes everything. It cancels all written philosophy from Plato to Pirsig and replaces it with the handwriting on the wall. It proves that nobody, including what today are generally considered to be the brightest minds, can resist the fascination of science. Technology is a more potent force than the fear of death, which we were obviously burdened with for—God help us—survival purposes. This fact alone should tell us all we need to know about our future as a race. What more evidence do we need that technology is dehumanizing, or that the dehumanization process is, in the most literal sense, a form of terminal mental illness?

It should be obvious from the drift of this discussion that I am expressing the artist's view of the Age of Science and Technology. This means that, like all artistic personalities, I am concerned only with strictly human values. Thus on the basis of our common predicament as outlined above, I have no choice but to call into play the concepts of remorse and compassion.

To this end I now ask you to re-read the William James quote at the beginning of this chapter, not with bristling animosity, if you happen to be a scientist, or with smug self-righteousness, if you are a humanist, but rather with compassion for the chaotic human conflict that lies buried beneath the two ways of looking at our most pressing problem.

Remember, as you re-read the quote, that the key to understanding what even a genius like William James did not fully understand can be expressed in a single word: compassion.

My favorite compassionate passage from literature, and the one most appropriate to the subject of education, is in George Eliot's *Middlemarch*. In the following quotation her remarks refer to the sterile academic character Casaubon, who every passionate and imaginative reader has grown to loathe. In an electrifying three-word reminder that she has just assumed the role of author omnipotent ("for my part") she suddenly describes Casaubon, not as a famous novelist doing her tricks, but as a human being forced by a male-dominated culture to use the pen name George Eliot:

> For my part I am very sorry for him. It is an uneasy lot at
> best, to be what we call highly taught and yet not to enjoy:
> to be present at this great spectacle of life and never to be
> liberated from a small hungry shivering self—never to be
> fully possessed by the glory we behold, never to have our
> consciousness rapturously transformed into the vividness of
> a thought, the ardor of a passion, the energy of an action,
> but always to be scholarly and uninspired, ambitious and
> timid, scrupulous and dim-sighted.

Since this is a memoir, and because as a writer I cannot afford
to have inhibitions, I will now reproduce, verbatim, the notes I
discovered in my handwriting in the margins adjacent to the above
quote in my well-worn copy of George Eliot's masterpiece.

> (These notes were made the following day.) This is the
> incredibly coincidental point where Joan suddenly appeared
> out of the tent on the banks of the Peace River with lipstick
> on and a beautiful pale blue slip. That ended the reading
> abruptly. Afterwards I finished the chapter with a slightly
> guilty feeling. Later, when I mentioned this feeling, and the
> circumstances of this chapter at her appearance, she was not
> at all perturbed but said, 'what a wonderful mixture of art
> and life!' It rained on (our) tent last night—how cozy it was!
> We still have three days of canoeing to look forward to.
> What joy! What sustained happiness!

» » » » »

I now ask you to consider the George Eliot quote in the context
of this chapter. Couldn't her compassion for the sterile scholar
apply with equal emotional impact to Henry James's sterile
scientists? After all, aren't the scientists eternally frustrated because
of their fundamental dissatisfaction with the earth? I feel sorry for

them. It must be awful to be constantly trying to make tomatoes grow bigger and brighter red, and forcing every living thing to follow that example. Wouldn't it be easier and more fun to augment life as exemplified by the pleasure of eating tomatoes, by exercising to work up an appetite and adding garlic?

The science-oriented mind reveals its bias in many ways, but most notably, I think, when it borrows icons from art, usually without sensitivity, to demonstrate the author's versatility. Take Pirsig's reference to ". . . a sterling performance of Beethoven's 'Ninth Symphony'" for example. What is "sterling" about the Ninth? Sterling has connotations which fit a military band playing a note-perfect march more than the experience of being passionately possessed by the transfiguration of Schuller's "Ode to Joy" through music. "Sterling" suggests at best nothing but cold and a generalized ideal. It is perfunctory. As music criticism it never gets off the ground and the reason he devoted mere lip service to Beethoven is because Pirsig had more important things to explain to us, such as his ideas about the true nature of quality.

Well, suppose we grow to enjoy the catharsis that results when the George Eliots of this world elevate us to higher states of existence. Would this help us to deal with the nagging problem of runaway dehumanization?

In short, does this discussion have any practical value?

I think not.

Alas, any benefit I can dream up has to be purely romantic. What I am saying, in effect, is that since both intuitive and concrete evidence suggests that we are probably either going to become extinct in the next century or so (the good news) or else be permanently and unimaginably miserable, we should at least be preparing ourselves for our upcoming bizarre awakenings to the true nature of joyless, scientific reality.

Let's accomplish this goal with the nobility, resolve and purpose of ancient Greek tragedies during the Golden Age. Let's admit that we are all guilty, all programmed to short sightedness. Let's exchange smiling regrets while helplessly committing major and irreversible ecological transgressions: after all, someone has to do this. Let's let a rueful smile be the height of good breeding. Let's rehearse our farewells. To go down bickering among ourselves would be the ultimate dehumanization. Can't we do better than that? Who knows, maybe a vastly superior strain of the blue-green algae will start a recycled evolution leading to a super responsible race capable of tracking us down, even in our collective nothingnesses, in order to purify the earth once and for all. No, don't laugh: religions have survived for centuries on less likely apocryphal fantasies. Isn't it time we made an unabashedly off-the-wall religion out of our irrationality?

Above all, let's be optimistic about the end of the world we have learned to love. Let's explore the fun options for suicide. Let's congratulate ourselves for eliminating all diseases in one fell swoop. And as the end draws near let's salvage something from the error of our ways, even if it is only a party to end all parties in which the cost of our mechanized sybaritic pleasure, at long last, is irrelevant.

» » » » »

The experience in chemistry class with which I opened this chapter took place when I was a student at St. Lawrence University in Canton, New York. Those four years transformed my life by giving it focus, substance and ammunition. Oh, not from the chemistry prof, but from Dr. Rutherford E. Delmage, who turned me on, in his delightful way, to the joys and obligations of literature.

At this writing "Doc" is still alive, still has all his diamonds, and I visit him as often as I can, not only for the pleasure of breaking up over his wit, but also to transport him from his nursing home to where I can share his delight in eating ice cream cones and riding on merry-go-rounds.

But above all I make these 300-mile roundtrip pilgrimages to remind him of the specific value of his life, as many of his former students are doing.

But here I was, thirty-three years after Doc's revelations,

standing in his shoes and trying to set the world back on its pintles at the University of Louisville.

Even though I could never hope to equal Doc Delmage's impact I like to think that in my last years one or two former students might drop by to remind me of the specific value of my life as an educator. However I do not think this is likely. Let me explain.

I once spent an entire class period in freshman composition explaining how decisive the opening lines of a written work of art are. I cited experiments which proved that most people do not enjoy the physical process of reading, and therefore the only way you can entice them to read is to grab their interest right off the bat.

To illustrate this I quoted several of my favorite first lines: They included the beginning of *Anna Karenina*: "Happy families are all alike; every unhappy family is unhappy in its own way."

Next I quoted the off-the-wall opening of *Kafka's The Metamorphosis*: "As Gregor Samsa awoke one morning from uneasy dreams he found himself transformed in his bed into a gigantic insect."

And my all-time favorite opener from Ambrose Bierce's short story "An Imperfect Conflagration": "Early one June morning in 1872 I murdered my father—an act that made a deep impression on me at the time."

Finally, just to let the class know they were not being taught by a robot, I quoted the first line from one of my own short stories: "Joe had been dead a long time, if such a thing is possible."

A few days later while editing and grading the papers resulting from my discussions of opening lines, I came across this gem: "The car was upside down. The wheels were still spinning. The street was littered with glass, and lying on the street there was a severed human arm. Now that I have your attention, I would like to tell you about our Sunday school picnic."

The first page of this student composition is framed and hangs in my study as a memento of my career as an educator.

My father's house in Scarsdale

My grandfather's summerhouse in the Catskill Mountains.

My humble abode in Flatbush.
Entertaining my sisters.

Daytona Bike Week, the beach, the ocean, the love of my life, and
the Alligator enduro coming up tomorrow. Mere happiness couldn't
handle such a formidable array of blisses.

I thought this 1931 Harley was a great bike and put over 100,000 miles on it.

The bike I used for my cross-country record attempt. Eight-gallon fuel tank has yet to be mounted on port (rear) side. Photo by Earle Flanders who had his service men give this bike a thorough going-over for free, which I greatly appreciated.

Over the top of the infamous "block and tackle hill" on the Jack
Pine where 25% of the contestants were disqualified for being over
an hour late. The hill was steep, long, sandy and full of ruts and
switchbacks ~ generally a hellacious obstacle. Note that my tongue
is sticking out, which it always is in tight situations and which
means it could be bitten off if I landed on my lower jaw in a spill.
I figure this tongue-out business is my body's way of putting one
of its key parts at special risk so I will stop doing what I am doing
and go home before being rendered speechless for the rest of my
life—but I could never control the habit.

Finishing a grueling 500-mile Jack Pine on time is something to smile about even with a tooth knocked out in a spill. 1960.

Why the large funnel? Because everybody is nervous and since every minute counts on an enduro. Also, spills are dangerous on hot engines.

Me at 82 getting ready to ride 100 miles home from Linder's Cycle Shop in New Canaan, Ct. Linder's is my favorite cycle shop.

When I am paddling down a seemingly endless river, I am immortal for as long as you can be immortal if Class 7 rapids are ruled out.

A little boy—now full grown—with the metaphorical cowboy hat takes his last fill of mountains before starting out on an unforgettable 200-mile canoe trip to a lonely outpost in northern British Columbia. The Tuchodi River had 50 miles of Class 4 rapids.

It took me a week above timberline to find a mature ram with horns large enough to be taken legally. After a day of stalking I shot him on my 55th birthday. Having a birthday supper of Stone sheep ribs roasted over a willow fire was a once-in-a-lifetime gustatory birthday thrill. Any way you cut it, death in the mountains is a profoundly bittersweet experience. It took me two days to pack the meat down the mountain because I wanted to come home with every bit of it—knowing that I would never kill another ram.

Class 5 rapids on the Tuchodi River after our sheep hunt. They had to be negotiated and were hairy in a heavily loaded freight canoe with two men, two stone sheep and a caribou.

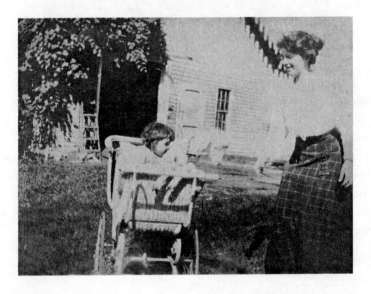

A phantom photo of me. In this snapshot my mom was three months pregnant with me. She was trying to extricate a goat from my sister's baby carriage. Isn't she beautiful?

Me with father and grandfather. Two impossible acts to follow.

This would be more thrilling if this beast had two wheels instead of four legs.

If you were a pretty receptionist for a bank president's office and this man waltzed in and asked for an audience with the president, would you forget protocol and usher him right in? Photo of Foster Gunnison judging <u>Beaux Arts</u> festival in New York.

Author in Berkshire School's baseball catcher's outfit. On the bus ride over to our game with Taft, a motorcyclist followed us for about 20 miles. He was having a great time.

Kyle. My fine stepdaughter deserves her place in this book for two reasons: first, I want to be a kind and considerate stepfather and second, I love her and enjoy pleasing her.

An unusual photo of Gunnisons: everyone is smiling broadly. Author and granddaughters. Do the smiles mean we are successful?

Joan is a crack shot. Here she has garnered enough geese for Thanksgiving, Christmas and New Year's feasts. Birds in background are decoys.

Joan on what was once the site of my grandfather's house in the Catskill Mountains.

David Ziegler was my father's black butler and chauffeur, and we were great pals. He was never critical of me and had a ready smile. He was a happy man and I loved him. He taught me how to fish and play baseball.

Running water line from hand-dug well at bottom of glacial creek to cistern for house 300 feet higher.

Me cutting stair access to basement of my own log house.

Photo of our house taken in late August. Note snow on Selkirk Mountains behind house.

This house, built by a little boy with a cowboy hat on a site picked out when he was full-grown. View is breathtaking in all directions.

PART III

*7,500 Miles
of Looking Back—Through
Rear View Mirrors*

CHAPTER 17

Maps and Road Signs Versus the Joys

of Dead Reckoning

I can see by my odometer that if I know what's good for my book I'd better resume the narrative of my trip.

When I got to the outskirts of Louisville I stopped at a gas station and washed all the dirty words out of my mouth before visiting my two daughters and three granddaughters.

One would think that with my addiction to earthy language I would have engendered something with the word "son" in it, but I have long suspected that females are earthy in a way that puts the foulest mouthed, beer-belly Harley rider to shame. It may have something to do with the bloody mess of having babies and cleaning up after them. It may also be that their clean spiritual language is a come-on, which, may be why when a pretty girl uses the F-word outside a workable context, she doesn't seem as pretty anymore. All I know for sure is that women are infinitely superior to men, though I would never want to be one. I'm not man enough to put up with what they have to contend with.

But I'm woolgathering . . . .

» » » » »

When I left Louisville my plans were to wind up in Sturgis, South Dakota, where every year in early August there is a world-class motorcycle rally. As far as getting there was concerned, however, it wasn't a trip. I wasn't traveling in the ordinary sense of that word. What I was doing was riding my motorcycle. I could ride by the *Taj Mahal* without giving it a second glance if there was the slightest question about the road surface up ahead. My motorcycle is my world and the only reason I need the earth is because my bike takes up an ungodly amount of space when it's turning four grand in high.

I don't ever want to know where I'm going and sure as hell don't want to know where I've been. I'm always afraid if I get too preoccupied with the future or the past I'll forget to give the present my best shot and do something really dumb, like forgetting to breathe.

I wouldn't drive my car across town without sending away to the AAA for the best route and making sure the umbrella was still in the trunk, but a motorcycle is different. A bike puts you one on one with the universe, which is that exciting little mass between the lining and the tightened chin strap of every sane cyclist's ever-present helmet. For navigating in that world you don't need a road map, you only need East and West, a clear day, and an elementary knowledge of astronomy. If the skies cloud over, keep 'er steady as she goes, avoid an odd number of 180° turns, and remember that every cloud has a silver lining. If that cliché doesn't get you exactly where you're going exactly on time, and with no surprises, then we're all in deep shit.

I attribute my admittedly curious lapse in touring savvy to a brief conversation I had, when young and impressionable, with a cartographer I met at a party.

It went like this:

"Oh! So you're a cartographer, eh? Then you make maps, right?"

"That is correct," he replied.

His formal reply and the plastic sleeve for pens and pencils in his breast pocket plus the fact that parties are supposed to be fun all reminded me how much I hate to tread water.

I stretched my toes, reaching for the bottom of something—something worth remembering.

"Well if you make maps you must love wars, right?" I asked as if this was the next logical question.

"No, as a matter of fact I do not," he replied, "What makes you say that?"

"Because wars change boundaries and therefore ought to be good for the cartography business."

He had no concept of irony and therefore no idea of what I was talking about—even though he had recently been working in Central America—and was obviously relieved when I found an excuse to wander off by myself and reflect on what there is about formal, scientifically created lines on paper that make people lose touch with their humanity.

Now that I am old and relatively set in my ways, I can't figure out why motorcyclists like to stop every five minutes to study maps drawn up by minds with no imagination, no sense of humor, no business sense, and above all no nagging secret desire to own a Harley.

I know, dear reader. I know. You're right. I'm all wet. Even arrogant. I made an unwarranted generalization from a single chance conversation. That poor mapmaker might have been so unnerved by the shoot-to-kill world we live in that he actually thought there was a difference between lines drawn on paper, lines drawn in the sand, and lines chiseled in granite war memorials.

Perhaps if I hadn't come on so strong with my smart-ass view of the world I might have learned a thing or two worth remembering from that cartographer. You know, something important to me as an individual, something unavailable in home entertainment centers—*something that gives me an edge.*

He might have told me, for example, that many maps have an intentional error on them to prevent unethical people from copying them and selling them as originals, and that these "errors" will stand up in court.

Be all this as it may, the fact remains that I can't talk about cartography for five minutes without getting into long-winded discussions of the personality of your typical mapmaker, ethics,

business practices, wars, and copyright lawsuits: in short, all the
pissant stuff I'm trying to avoid by riding my bike as far away from
reason as it will take me with the leisure and money at my disposal.

» » » » »

As I headed West out of Kansas City I saw two signs, one on
top of the other, on the thruway.

They read U.S. 70 West and U.S. 35 West.

Even though I was in a highly euphoric state, I had a problem
with those signs.

I "euphorized" that if the word "West" meant what I had been
taught it meant, then in order for two highways to go west from a
single point up ahead, one would have to be on top of the other. I
knew this was unlikely, but on the other hand why was one sign
on top of the other?

The fact that one highway might be on top of the other was
no reason to get upset; that kind of public money boondoggling
takes place in highway departments everywhere: always has, always
will.

It was their goddamn one-on-top-of-the-other *signs* that freaked
me out: had the corruption become blatant—were the bastards
starting to advertise?

On an impulse, I took the next exit and began the following
detour through the labyrinth of my mind. Come on along—and
oh! bring a ball of twine if you don't have a satellite activated place
locator.

» » » » »

If you happen to be in the market for a metaphor which will
give you a feeling for the comic disparity between the promised
land theoretical scientists are leading us towards and their specific
directions for getting there, it would be hard to beat the lowly
highway sign.

Let me begin at the top, with a classic illustration of the nature of the engineering mind.

Many years ago, an airport in Louisville was named Standiford Field in honor of a local pilot. As the city progressed so progressed the flying field. Eventually the runway was lengthened and paved for jet traffic.

Meanwhile progress was taking place in surface transportation. Civil engineers masterminded the inner belt and outer belt thruways, and in order to keep the airport from being lost in the shuffle highway engineers requisitioned large, expensive signs which all said "STANDIFORD FIELD."

If you think this was a natural mistake you don't understand how an engineer's mind works. Even when the complaints started coming in, it took *years* for highway engineers to realize a human equation should have been part of their supra-human calculations.

By the time the engineers got around to changing their signs to STANDIFORD AIRPORT all the out-of-town businessmen in their rented cars had learned the hard way that Standiford Field was not the local ballpark and began showing up for their flights home.

There must be something about supervising the pouring of thousands of cubic yards of concrete that makes it difficult for a civil engineer to grasp abstract concepts, such as the notion that not everyone who uses his roadways has lived in Louisville since the days when Mr. Standiford was making a name for himself in local flying circles, and when airports were referred to quaintly as "fields."

For those among my readers who have bought the system, may actually have friends who are engineers, and feel I have just tried to deprive them of the pleasure of living in their engineered paradise, I offer the following conciliatory personal experience that also took place at Standiford Airport. It is the other side of the coin. Let's call it an example of do-it-yourself human engineering.

The difference between human engineering and scientific engineering is that the former makes your day while the latter is always promising to make your tomorrows. In the following anecdote making my tomorrow would not have done me any good.

I once had the pedal to the metal in my car, was nailed in a radar trap, and pulled over by a county patrolman right under the landing approach to the main runway at Standiford Airport.

He began with the classic "What's your hurry?" but before I could answer an incoming jet thundered overhead, making conversation impossible, and giving me just enough time to think.

As the aircraft began to settle and the roar of its engines subsided I pointed at it through the open window and said, "Officer, I'm on my way to Chicago and if I'm not on that jet when it takes off I will lose my job and this company car."

The officer took a step backward, told me to cool it, and motioned me to go ahead.

I drove ahead a hundred yards and took the off-ramp to the airport.

After about an hour at the airport I decided it was safe to go back out on public highways.

What I had done was ethical to the highest degree. You cannot treat an anvil ethically: ethical conduct is always a direct or indirect interaction between two or more *human beings*, but I wasn't interacting with the cop: he was an innocent bystander just earning his living. I had been legally forced by technophiles to do my interacting with a machine, a radar gun, which was just the tip of one iceberg in an ocean which now has more icebergs than water in it.

It was an interaction I could not hope to win without using a radar detector, which I refuse to use on moral grounds: two wrongs don't make a right.

You know, being moral and ethical like me isn't all that bad. What's bad is that you can no longer tell the good guys from the bad guys because the bad guys are all respectable presidents of electronics or insurance companies. Give me the good old days when the bad guys hid honestly behind bushes and chased you fair and square. Give me back the time, as the saying goes, when tits and wheels were the only sources of trouble for a fair-minded guy. But today it's not love or the internal combustion engine that are doing us in.

It's electronics: it is electrons in the wrong hands.

We can't feel 'em, taste 'em, see 'em, or smell 'em, yet they have mankind by the short hair.

» » » » »

U.S. 70 West

U.S. 35 West

I can see from the signs we're back on the way to Sturgis: for a moment there I thought we were lost.

Any fully functioning motorcyclist homogenized in 75 mph rush hour traffic who suddenly picks up on two self-canceling signs like the above would have stopped and studied his map.

Not me. I had daydreams on my mind and they were all too pleasant to interrupt. Besides, in order to study a map you have to stop, and long experience has proven to my satisfaction that I always know more about where I'm going on a moving motorcycle than I could ever find out on a parked one.

I think this has something to do with instinct. You can quote me if you like.

Anyway, one of my pleasant daydreaming reminiscences had to do with the time many years before when Bill Chescheir and I were riding back to Louisville from Topeka and stopped for lunch at the Stockyards Inn in Kansas City. We wolfed down a couple of fantastic steaks while a thunderstorm took it out on our bikes, which were parked just outside our cozy window.

Why is it that there is nothing more forlorn looking than a bike parked in the pouring down rain, and nothing less forlorn feeling than riding one in the rain?

I think this has something to do with poetry, but please don't quote me.

On that trip Bill was riding a 250 cc Honda and I was on a

new 1963 BMW R69S. Bill had been hinting for days that he
wanted to ride my Beemer for a while, but I wasn't having any. I
was riding what I had chosen to ride, and Bill was riding what he
had chosen to ride. If he found his choice uncomfortable on long
trips, then I figured if he was forced to live with his mistake for
another 700 miles or so it would prevent him from making that
mistake again. That's why I stood my ground: after all, what are
friends for?

About 200 miles east of Kansas City and twenty miles west of
St. Louis, Bill pulled his Honda over on the berm up ahead and
stopped.

I pulled up beside him.

Bill was just sitting there staring with his eyes closed at his
Honda's silver gas tank.

His bike wasn't running.

"What's wrong?" I said.

Bill slowly turned and looked me straight in the eyes. His
expression was heartrending. He was in deep trouble.

I waited apprehensively.

"Herb," he whined, "for God's sake, let me ride your
motorcycle—please just as far as St. Louis?"

» » » » »

Anyway, there I was, careening around in 75 mph traffic,
wondering if Bill Chescheir had ever forgiven me, while I tried to
choose between two signs which said essentially the same thing.

The choice looked innocent enough. I knew that Sturgis was
West, and so, on the assumption that highway engineers were as
meticulous as cartographers, I took U.S. 35 because it obviously
didn't make any difference. West is West: everybody knows that.

I rode out the balance of my day, pleased with my choice
because I was seeing pretty country I'd never seen before and
because the setting sun was not in my eyes. I vaguely remember
buying gas a few times in Oklahoma, but it wasn't until I came to

the outskirts of Albuquerque the following evening that I began to suspect I had made a slight miscalculation.

I stopped for the night at one of my favorite campgrounds, which was on top of the hill west of Albuquerque, and paid extra for a site which gave me a breathtaking view of the city lights.

While supper was cooking on the picnic table I got out my map and flashlight to see what was what.

From Kansas City to Sturgis was 766 miles. From Kansas City to Albuquerque was 842 miles. From Albuquerque to Sturgis was 890 miles. When I got to Sturgis I would have ridden 1,731 miles from Kansas City to go 766 miles to Sturgis.

Map or no map, I couldn't see how a motorcyclist could have any more fun than that without going too far out of his way.

CHAPTER 18

The Morning After

Teach me to live that I may dread the grave as little as my
bed. Teach me to die.

—Children's Bedtime Prayer

When I woke up the next morning the panoramic view of
Albuquerque had lost all its glamour: I was feeling out of sorts.
There wasn't much to go on—just a slightly upset stomach and an
occasional fleeting pain in my chest. I figured both symptoms
would go away when I got out on the road.

But there was more—why was I hiding it? I had that ancient,
vague, spacy feeling I thought I had licked forever: I was disoriented.
This episode, however, was more complicated. Although I had
some entertaining experiences with psychosomatic problems during
my dirt bike competition days, what I was now experiencing had
nothing to do with somatics—it was pure psycho, as in the
Hitchcock movie.

I knew and dreaded the symptoms. I'd had three episodes of
mental illness severe enough to land me in the hospital. On one
occasion I was behind locked doors for three months right in the
middle of the bike riding season—now that's *crazy!*

What made my concern so complicated was that I had long
ago discovered that motorcycling was the anxiety preventative
par excellence. So why was I uptight after having just ridden
2,100 glorious miles, with 5,400 sure-fire glorious miles to

go, including a full week of immersion in the motorcycling hot tub of Sturgis?

The minute I asked myself the question, I knew the answer, but like I said, it's complicated. For the answer we have to go back to Brooklyn, New York, as it was in 1927, when I was eight years old.

Seventy years ago there were no refrigerators in Flatbush and ice was delivered every few days by horse-drawn wagons. One afternoon just as I walked up to Tony's ice wagon, which was parked in front of our house, a double chain drive Mack truck backed up into the wagon shafts, snapping one with a sound like a rifle shot and driving a splintered end deep into the horse's chest. The animal staggered back, its eyes ablaze with horror, made an ugly gurgling sound, and as it fell down in the traces, twisting the shaft, a heavy stream of blood spurted out and struck me in the side. For a moment I didn't react. All I knew was that something repulsively wet, sticky and hot had happened to me.

» » » » »

That night, for some reason, I had trouble getting to sleep.

"Mom!"

My mother was a very beautiful woman in every respect. She also knew everything there was to know about everything that had ever happened or ever would happen. She would help me. I just knew it.

I was startled at how quickly she came into my room after I called.

For the first time in my life I experienced the ecstasy of having a beautiful woman sitting on the edge of my bed preparing with the mystery of her sex to whisk the rubbish out of my life.

My mother looked deep into my eyes and stroked my hair back again and again and again while giving me her heart-stopping smile.

"What's the matter—can't sleep?" she asked sympathetically.

"No—I mean yes, I can't sleep."

"Do you know *why*?" she continued in that probing way I knew so well.

"No."

Mom just sat there stroking my hair for a few minutes, but just as I thought I might be drifting off to sleep I noticed a scary change in the smile I knew so well. I couldn't have described it then but I can now. Perhaps this is because I always do my writing in the morning, when the spooks are asleep: her smile was as warm as it ever was, but now it looked like a picture of a lovely woman smiling—a tiny heart-stopping picture in an enormous flat black frame.

My mother had just decided I was old enough to have the rest of my life rendered glorious.

"Do you think what happened to Tony's horse has anything to do with your not being able to sleep?"

The minute she mentioned Tony's horse I knew what was bothering me. What had happened to the horse was going to happen to me, sooner or later and one way or another. My shock, though severe, was temporary. Now mom would explain what I was too young to understand. It had something to do with why I was so fortunate to be a person and not a dumb animal pulling a stupid ice wagon.

"You shouldn't let those things bother you," she said. "Why—you're only a child. You have your whole life ahead of you."

That's all she had to say. I took it from there. What mom had told me was that I had been wrong from the beginning: my fears were well founded.

I started to say something but mom was light years ahead of me: she was committed. There was no turning back. She lowered the boom and explained the principle of wishful thinking and the limits of knowledge.

For weeks after that mom used to read Billy Whiskers stories to me until I drifted off to sleep, dreaming about that adorable old billy goat. I've often wondered if along about that time my sister Alice had stepped on her pet hamster and squashed it, and then called, "Mom!!" at bedtime, if mom would perhaps have told her about heaven and the angels just so she could spend more time with her husband.

Mom loved the truth as much as I loved her. However, she was not a kook about it. She still encouraged me to believe in anthropomorphic billy goats and Santa Clauses. She knew the value of the diversion we call fantasy. I think she figured fantasies were okay as long as you didn't build your life on the idea that they were true, but used them constructively to stimulate your imagination.

Who would have thought a horse that was hauled away to a Brooklyn glue factory would clear the mind of a touring biker in Albuquerque almost seventy years later?

Once I knew what was bothering me I could handle it. I knew a pain in my chest could be the ultimate pain in my ass. My problem, if such was the case, was not "why me?" because at 75 all that question does is announce to everybody with problems of their own that you're an ungrateful wretch who wants more than his fair share.

I remember when mom had her heart attack at 82 and courageously fired up her heart-stopping smile on the way to the hospital and said it had been beautiful and that it was time for her "to make room for someone else." Poor mom! The shoe was on the other foot, but I couldn't give back to her what she had given me in 1927. But even if I could, I wouldn't have had the heart to tell her the world had changed, that it was no longer a romantic place to live, that it now lacked her generosity of spirit and that nobody gave a shit what she said about making room for someone else because everybody was into overpopulation because it was good for business.

She spoke her last words to the cardiologist. By chance, they were uttered at the stroke of midnight: "I don't want you to hook me up to your goddamned machinery."

If I had been there, if I had actually experienced what I have just recreated out of fantasy and from what I knew about my mother and what I learned later, if I hadn't been 3,000 miles away, if I hadn't been, by chance, making love when she was bringing her last words to life, I think her final act on earth would have been to bring the world full circle for me.

In my imagination I often have a freak-out in which she rolls

her head away from the cardiologist and winks at me as she smiles
her last heart-stopping smile.

» » » » »

I had to get my juices flowing again, and fast. Everything had
to be tightened up. If "why me?" was selfish at my age, then "why
before, instead of after Sturgis?" struck me as a reasonable gripe
any motorcyclist could identify with. But I didn't even ask that
question. I had my mental health back in spades. Those 2,100
miles had paid off after all.

At my age you either learn to live with the inevitable aches
and pains or fritter away what's left of your miserable existence in
self-indulgent misery. Piss on that. I decided long ago to ride flat
out until I either run out of blood or the sheriff catches up with
me, and figure if I don't tailgate and keep checking my rear view
mirror I stand a good chance of realizing my life's ambition, which
is to outlive my life insurance agent.

I have never been able to figure out why people who would be
mortified to the bone if they fell asleep during their marriage
ceremony actually hope to be asleep for their death ceremony.
You're either into rituals or you're not.

I dearly love rituals and want to go out in style.

At the very least I want a splintered wagon shaft in my chest.

I want to make some lucky kid's day.

» » » » »

I struck my tent and hung it up to dry, unaware that I was
about to live through the most harrowing day of my life.

CHAPTER 19

What Would Life be Without a Little Thunder

and Lightning?

While I was busying myself striking camp between mouthfuls of Grape Nuts and powdered milk I kept looking down at the view of Albuquerque, which was nestled in the bottom of a bowl the size of a moderate sized lake.

Thirty years ago, almost to the day, I had ridden a BMW dealer's bike up into the same area while mine was being repaired and watched a late afternoon thunderstorm give the city a real going over. The thundercloud wasn't very big; in fact it wasn't even as big as Albuquerque and environs, but what this baby lacked in spaciousness it made up for in venom and purpose. It grew darker and darker and meaner and meaner. It wasn't kidding: this cloud had a uranium lining.

As a lover of contrasts and as one committed to reality, I sat bathed in sunlight way up on the hillside and prepared to savor that storm until it had shot its last bolt and all the debris had been washed away.

The sun was shining brightly, cheerfully, and perhaps even bravely everywhere except where that vast dark bag of water was getting ready to jettison jillions of tons of wetness on the city. When the bottom of the bag ruptured I followed the first sheet of raindrops all the way to the ground. After that it looked like a gigantic shower except for one surrealistic detail: the shower head was not connected to any plumbing. But even with this surreal assist my imagination wasn't up to it. For the life of me I couldn't imagine where all the water was coming from or why the cloud didn't shrink as it emptied.

Meanwhile an occasional streak of lightning zapped earthward, each one more impressive in its lean, concentrated and elemental way than an explosion in a fireworks factory. Each flash was followed seconds later by the thunder, but I wasn't counting the seconds to ascertain how far away the lightning was: who in his right mind would be making calculations at a time like that? Hell, a single thunderclap could reduce Beethoven to an indolent wannabe flunking out of his first semester at Juilliard. For that matter, who would want to run and get his camera? What could a photosensitive layer of silver halide suspended in gelatin add to the experience? One recollection is worth a thousand 8 x 10's.

I was having the time of my life imagining all the fellow people stranded in doorways, making a run for it with the day's newspaper over their heads, sitting impatiently in fog-windowed cars while waiting for the nuisance to go away, as I might have done had I been trapped in their perspective, so they could take their clothes to the cleaners or perhaps meet a fresh illicit love for cocktails at a funky hideaway.

After awhile I got a downer sense that the storm was running out of fury, as if the Artist was losing his inspiration.

But no, the lightning suddenly snapped flashier and sassier, the thunder drummed more thunderously, and the awe soared to inspiring crescendos as the music-drama seethed to climax in the finest operatic tradition. It looked for a few minutes as if Albuquerque were on the verge of floating away. What is it about this milestone in the life of a thunderstorm that makes us so aware of the disaster of time? Is it a coincidence that, as I write this storm up, the ink in my ballpoint pen has started to run dry and I have to keep pressing harder and harder, until the white heat of what I want to say is reduced to a slight indentation without substance?

As I watched the storm's impassioned final climax build I was already one regretted step ahead of it. What was going to take the place of that serendipitous, sufficient-unto-itself storm? What would replace my all-too-rare mountaintop perspective?

The pathetic remains of the rain cloud drifted aimlessly off to the East, as if looking for a way out of the Albuquerque basin but didn't have enough substance left to do much of anything.

A few whisps of diehard rain followed it like a silent benediction, and before I knew it the sun was everywhere.

I had just watched a local thunderstorm, which wouldn't even be mentioned on the evening's TV, blow away centuries of scientific progress.

Without mirrors.

And much as I hate to admit it, it also did a number on humanistic progress—at least the musical and literary branches of it.

Without metaphor.

I turned away and walked over to my borrowed bike. Compared to my high tech R69-S, which was the most powerful motorcycle BMW made thirty years ago, the dealer's R-50 looked almost ladylike, as if the fenders should have been trimmed with something pink and lacy and hemmed so they could be let out if the bike ever grew up.

It was a sorry specimen with which to defend technology from the onslaught of that unforgettable storm, but it was all I had.

I held the bikelet out at arm's length and booted its oddly designed kickstarter straight out, straight down.

Then I mock-thundered my little putt-putt down into the now steaming city, kicking up my own storm while glorying in the rain-washed sky. I was back on the prowl, full of venom, full of purpose, lusting for whatever came next as long as the perspective was from my two-wheeled mountain top.

I was smug, unrepentant, even insolent in my defeat, but I wasn't proud: I'll be human any way I can.

CHAPTER 20

My Two-Wheeled Ambulance

Even though I wasn't feeling up to snuff, I couldn't resist using the picnic table to write the thunderstorm episode you recently read because it took place almost exactly thirty years after that eidetic storm became part of what I am. Those three decades made it an occasion for a celebration, for a formal creative ritual rather than exhumed passive nostalgia.

This is one of the ways I trick time into doing things my way.

Celebrating as intensely as I could, after all, was a major part of what my 7,500 mile trip was all about. How often does a guy get to celebrate his diamond birthday with a month-long party in which he does practically nothing, day after day, but the one thing he can do, day after day, without ever having his joy bog down into mere pleasure?

Given the above parameters, it may be easier to understand why I have trouble with official maps and government signs. This should explain why I rode a thousand miles out of my way to express my gratitude the best way I knew, as a fanatical lover of storms and stress, at the site where one of my greatest affirmations of the beauty and terror of the earth had taken place.

I hit the road about one o'clock, had a nostalgic lunch at an oft-visited quick-and-dirty diner, and headed East on U.S. 40 about two p.m. The first sixty miles took well over an hour because I kept having to stop and wait for the scenery to cross the road.

About sixty miles from Tucumcari my chest pains got noticeably worse, and I stopped on a desolate stretch of road and got out my map to try to figure out what to do. The only piece of medical information I had was that there was a hospital in Tucumcari where I had stitches removed from my hand a few years before. I really didn't have any choice, so I continued traveling east on U.S. 40.

As soon as I started up again, however, the chest pains became acute. I was now in a crisis situation and had to get to the hospital as quickly as possible.

For the past quarter of an hour or so I had been picking up on the fact that there was no oncoming traffic: I learned later that an accident East of Tucumcari had blocked all westbound traffic. All I knew was that if I wanted to get to the hospital in a big hurry, there was nothing to stop me short of the law.

This was an old story that went back to Billy Taylor and our 1923 Indian. We didn't allow the law to stop us from our pursuit of happiness then, so why should I allow the law to keep me from rushing myself to the hospital well over the legal speed limit while experiencing the agony of what I was now convinced was a major heart attack?

I decided to go for it.

What did I have to lose?

» » » » »

Once I decided to go for broke, I reacted with a sudden eagerness that made me smile, and in a matter of seconds the speedo was indicating ninety. How many times had I done this on the wackiest of excuses? Once, as an adolescent with a limited understanding of how an internal combustion engine works, I ran flat out for fear of running out of gas. Then of course there were the mature times when the road was long and straight and empty and just asking for it.

In psychological terms 90 is a far less significant speed than the magic "ton" or 100 mph. At 90, which on most speedometers is only about 85, you are merely ticking off the fuzz, but at 100 and above you are giving the finger to the mindset of Western civilization.

I increased my speed to 100, then to 110 to allow for any speedometer error: it was a philosophical adjustment.

One would think that in a world with massive documentary evidence that human overpopulation is the most deadly form of pollution, motorcyclists would be given tickets for running under the ton, especially where conditions were unsafe. One would think that in a country in which 85 percent of its top scientists are working full time supplying the Department of Defense with devices which zero in with laser accuracy on the destruction of human life, a biker pulled over for endangering life at one-hundred-per would be given a medal instead of a lot of bullshit. One would think that in a democracy in which the common consensus is that technology can do no real wrong, a motorcyclist would be encouraged to use his high tech machinery to the fastest limit of its no-real-wrongness—to enjoy, nay, to rejoice in its power to outrun hypocrisy itself.

An odd thing had just happened.

Really odd.

Even weird, perhaps.

When I accelerated from 90 to 110 my chest pains went away.

Could it be that something mysterious and soothing happens to the human nervous system between 90 and 110? Was the "ton" more than just a figure of speech? Was it possible that technology was leaking into my consciousness, giving my aliveness both substance and peace, like a cutting-edge generator, or perhaps zapping my chest nerves into nullity like a spark plug? Had I in some predestined evolutionary way become a Ninja Mutant motorcyclist?

I got very excited, as I always do when I suspect I'm flirting with a new concept.

The reason I have trouble planning my life around the opinions of most philosophers is that they do all their thinking in easy chairs. And not only that, but they think their stuff up when in the prime of life, when death is not a daily concern, but rather something to toy with, like making plans for a long vacation in a far away land sometime in the distant future when you are rich enough to afford it.

The only philosophy that invariably makes sense to me is the one that hits the sweet spot when you're riding a motorcycle over the ton. If a line of thought makes your problems disappear under those conditions then you've got something to work with, some ideas to build what's left of your life around.

For the moment, even though I was racing to a hospital emergency ward, I didn't have a care in the world.

Nothing in my previous enjoyment of technology had prepared me for what I was about to learn about it. However, I had inklings of my present situation whenever I visited an art museum and borrowed a battery operated wheelchair, reserved for disabled people like me, for my "walk" through the genres of world class art.

I say "inklings" because clearly if a battery and electric motor could make my artificial hip not only "well" but also painless, then what use was the art? If science could nullify the supreme drag in my life by making me comfortable and mobile, what need did I have for the storm, the stress and pain which make artist-types so happy? The self-propelled chair turned the real picture of art to the wall, leaving only pretty paintings enjoyed from the comfort of a mechanical chair that transported my body wherever my mind wanted it to go by the slightest movement of thumb and forefinger. It was doing more for my existential moments than the world's most enduring art. Unfortunately, however, the wheeled techno-crutch prevented the art from teaching me what I needed to know when I had returned the state-of-the-art wheelchair and was back to normal with my cane and my pain.

If the silly-wheeled dynamo was not life, what was its non-lifer occupant doing in an art museum? In such situations I always felt like a bank robber cashing a personal check at his own branch bank. I became an impostor: without a gun in my hand or a gun at my head I was just a Sunday school teacher out for an uplifting afternoon.

You understand, of course, that this art museum analogy was not part of my race to the hospital, but was "recollected in tranquillity" (Wordsworth). At the speed I was traveling there was no mind space for it: there is an ironic lesson for modern man in Tazio Nuvelari's remark that "death is not hard to face behind the wheel of a race car" because in order to play God like this you've got to be speeding like the Devil.

I held the needle on 110 for a few minutes, milking my brief vacation from life for all it was worth.

I even became cocky. I ran the clock up to 120 and then, just for the fun of it, deliberately tried to think about death. It was no contest. Death had no clout at all. How could it, when I not only had my hands full staying alive, but was astride a Gothic cathedral?

I could see it all now: technology has us eating out of its articulated claw because it is the supreme diversion from life. But unfortunately— and this is crucial—it has the major limitation of having a short shelf life. Because 120 mph for five seconds is a lot faster than 120 mph for five minutes, after a couple of minutes I became jaded with speed. This automatically placed me deep into the mystique of our runaway civilization, in which boredom and boredom-canceling new technology were racing neck and neck to the abyss.

I slowed down to thirty-five because I saw a large dog way up ahead, and as I did so the stabbing pains in my chest returned. When I had passed the dog, and before I accelerated, I stood up on the one peg available while standing (on my much altered bike) to see if a good stretch would ease the pain. From my upright perspective I looked down at the gorgeous horizontally opposed BMW engine, with the highway streaking beneath it, which is something I dearly love to do. But this time the experience was different. Perhaps my traumatic state and my recollections of Henry Adams's views earlier in this book had fused in my subconscious, but I suddenly looked at the BMW engine as if it were a late, twentieth century dynamo.

Nothing had changed since the Paris Science Exposition of 1900. The basic promise remained unfulfilled. The machine can never engender authentic human emotion. The beemer engine wasn't gorgeous the way a startled wild stallion is gorgeous. Sure, it was interesting, fascinating, even exciting, but it was not gorgeous. What it lacked was a legitimate aesthetic value. It lacked the same quality scientists lacked when they went on record as saying a nuclear explosion is "beautiful."

Beautiful my ass.

That's my philosophy.

Since no philosophy is worth a rat's patooty until it undergoes a trial by fire, as a service to my fellow philosophers I cranked my beemer on all the way. The older I get the faster I go because the less I have to lose, and in this circumstance if I'd been riding one of the new sport bikes that goes like stink I'd have run its clock to infinity for sure. However, as it was I was on a slight downgrade, and I have a lightened flywheel and a few other mods on the bike, so the 135 mph indicated probably wasn't all that far off. I had the ride of my life, and the pains in my chest evaporated.

There was no doubt in my mind that this was the best of all possible worlds, my bike the best of all possible bikes, and my philosophy the best excuse for a philosophy one could possibly imagine under my life and death circumstances.

It had taken me 75 years to achieve this ultimate state of earned exaltation and I will be forever grateful to technology for every second of its ten minute diversion from my impending doom.

With no regrets, but suddenly feeling like an old man, I slowed for Tucumcari and followed the signs to the hospital.

I parked my bike on a patch of dirt by the rear entrance to the emergency room.

As I shoved my way through the heavy glass door I glanced back at my motorcycle and noticed that the kickstand was in a slight depression, so that if the ground was softened by a heavy rain the bike might fall over.

I went back through the heavy glass door, scrounged around for a flat rock, lifted my bike vertical with my bad hip, and nudged the rock under the kickstand with my boot.

As I shouldered my way back through the glass door for the last time, I looked back to make sure my bike wasn't too vertical and in danger of keeling over the other way.

I felt like a man holding the door open to the next world, while taking a fond look back at this one.

I approached the nurses' station, relieved to be able to put my fate in the hands of professionals, and told them I had severe chest pains and was having difficulty breathing. Then I made a sepulchral stab at merriment by asking the nurses with exaggerated innocence if they had any idea what it might be.

"Do you smoke?" the prettiest one said.

Oh Jesus no, I thought. Pretty woman, don't make me tread water at a time like this. But having just failed to check out in a 135 m.p.h. blaze of high performance profundity, I was willing to settle accounts, if it came to that, with a quip.

"Why do you ask me if I want a cigarette at a time like this?" I asked the pretty woman.

Perhaps it wasn't all that funny, at least to someone who wasn't living through a flat-out human hell, desperate for distractions.

But like I said, I'm not proud. I'll be human any way I can.

CHAPTER 21

Sturgis or Bust

When I left the hospital the morning after my Tucumcari escapade I felt like a thirteen-year-old. I was fit as a fiddle, the weather was perfect, and except for one minor detail I was all set to spend still another childlike day scootering through the paradise gardens.

The one minor detail was that I had to find a welding shop before I left town: this disabled man had been riding a disabled bike too long.

I guess it's time to tell you about the special controls on my bike and my artificial hip that makes them necessary. I once did a high speed "endo" on the Jack Pine Enduro, which is a wicked wreck in which the bike flips end over end. It gave me a black-and-blue spot the size of a pie plate on my right hip, and made it too sore to sleep on for a couple of weeks, but aside from that it was okay.

Or so I thought.

Eight years later, when I was 60 years old, I won the East Kootenay Regional tennis tournament at the Radium Hot Springs County Club in British Columbia, Canada, defeating a 23-year-old kid who I heard remarking in the locker room, when he didn't know I was within earshot, "Who is that old guy?" Our final match was long and hard, the 23-year-old was a better player than I was, and the reason I won was partly because I was more experienced but mainly because I was in better shape and outlasted him. After his last shot went wild I threw my racket in the air and jumped over the net, but my right heel touched the net like a let ball, and I almost would have been forced to end this paragraph with a self-induced mishap of embarrassingly comic proportions.

That was my first intimation that the bottom was about to fall out of my life.

I filed the incident away under "Things to worry about when you have nothing better to do."

A couple of months later I was trying a new dirt bike on for size and as I swung my leg over the seat my knee hit the seat and I didn't make it.

I didn't buy the bike and instead filed the incident away under "things to worry about when you have better things to do."

That fall, on a bighorn sheep hunting trip in the mountains, my hip became a serious problem and I saw my doctor as soon as I got home.

Apparently what had happened was that when I did the endo I didn't break any bones but I got a hairline crack in my femur. Then, because I later developed arthritis, it got into the crack and destroyed my hip joint over a period of many months. I had a hip replacement, but complications developed due to the inability of medical science to keep my femur from growing into the prosthesis, which it does in one percent of hip operations. What a lottery to win! I've had three hip replacements, and each time it gets worse. I finally realized that since I could still paddle my canoe in a kneeling position, which is the best way, and ride my motorcycle, which I dearly love to do, I would let well enough alone.

» » » » »

What I have just written bothers me more than I like to admit. Why?

Because I am in the throes of writing my memoirs and have just boasted about a minor tennis victory and bored you with my medical history. Since page one I have been uncomfortable with the need for this sort of thing, but it is an unavoidable hazard built into the memoir genre, so I ask you to bear with me while I defuse it with a few comments on the pitfalls of memoir writing so we can resume our narrative with a modicum of ego-related stress.

I keep telling myself you do not have to be famous to write your autobiography: you just have to be entertaining, or lacking that, interesting, or as a last resort, in jail for a heinous crime. Being dead would get me off the hook in the ego department but that is more trouble than I am willing to take right now and besides that bonus will accrue to me soon enough without any effort at all.

It is the effort that kills me. It is downright scary to roll out of bed every morning facing a six hour obligation to entertain, interest or shock people you don't know, will never meet, and whose religious, sexual and vocabulary preferences are unavailable as commercial guidelines.

I sometimes wish I was a novelist, so that all I would have to do is be novel because the pesky rules and niceties of correct behavior would apply to imaginary characters instead of the author's flesh and blood.

I am glad to get all this off my chest and hope you appreciate the sacrifices I make on your behalf. After all, if it weren't for my determination to be honest with you I could have won Wimbledon.

» » » » »

You and I are each taking two journeys. One is metaphysical and the other is just a plain old motorsickle ride. Since for obvious reasons I'm doing both the talking and driving I'm well aware, as a friend should be, that from time to time you must be having anxious moments in your role as pillion passenger, particularly if you believe in observing speed limits. If it makes you feel any safer remember that as far as the physical journey goes, you're not going to buy the farm no matter how fast I go because if that was going to happen you wouldn't be reading this.

The metaphysical trip, however, is a whole other ball game. When a biker is riding faster than his ability, it's called "riding over your head," and anyone who does a lot of this is bound to get hurt. However, that is kid stuff compared to riding over your mind in the world of ideas: this is because a mind trip is infinitely heavier than a body trip.

I remember once reading that at the moment of death the human body gets lighter. This data was science's way of playing God and "proving" that we have substantial souls. It struck me as significant at the time that they didn't provide the corollary data on elephants, jackasses, or even pet cats, if you know what I mean, but let's let that ride. I don't know and couldn't care less how wonderful a scale has to be to come up with this information, but for my money nothing illustrates the difference between the scientific and artistic outlook more than the technician's assumption that this weight difference is significant, because if it was, how come we need so many pallbearers?

» » » » »

The account of a seventy-five-year-old man who is disabled and rides his sixteen-year-old motorcycle 7,500 miles, alone, and is still going strong five years later would seem to have all the ingredients for an inspirational book: however this scenario is inconsistent with my life and, to a certain extent, with the facts. While a very small percentage of bikers my age and older are still active in the sport, when you consider the total number of bikers that small percentage represents a surprising number of guys who are doing what I do each summer, and who, like me, hardly give the idea that it might be unusual, or dangerous, or the culmination of an idiosyncratic philosophy of life a second thought.

What I am able to do today, at eighty-three, is the result of the way I have exercised my brain and my body throughout my life. I sure wouldn't want a bunch of old guys like me rushing out and buying motorcycles and taking off alone for the hinterlands, because life just doesn't work that way.

Way back in the glorious period in human evolution when the

Age of Romanticism was flourishing in Europe, Goethe, who played a major role in its inception, wrote a book called *The Sorrows of Young Werther* about a passionate and intense poet who had an unhappy love affair and was so devastated by the loss of his beloved that he killed himself. It was, and is, a wonderful commentary on the rewards and liabilities of the artistic life, but it was so moving that it inspired an epidemic of suicides among poet wannabes.

These tragedies bothered Goethe very much, but the damage had been done. The unenlightened young men lost their lives either because they had not read enough of Goethe to comprehend the absurdity of their acts or because they did not understand the irony in his story, or perhaps the greatest tragedy of all was that they were lousy poets.

As a man who has built his life around a passionate addiction to the principles and beliefs of Romanticism, it would bother me terribly if even one old man with little or no previous experience was inspired to buy a motorcycle and strike out on an adventure of his own and ended up on a slab in the basement of a small town hospital.

Please don't do it, brother.

» » » » »

All my life I have gotten off on contrasts. The sharper the contrast the more joyful, poignant or fascinating a subject or event becomes. I am sure the following scenario has actually happened many times in various ways.

A guy robs a bank. It's the result of months and months of planning a big heist, and it's successful. He is celebrating in a motel room with his gorgeous girlfriend. They have two tickets to Acapulco. A suitcase of unmarked bills is open on the luggage rack and money money money is scattered around the room, joyously thrown in the air by happy hands. The guy is stoned, his gorgeous girlfriend is acting kittenish, he has a blue thumper of a hard on and is in absolute heaven when there is a knock on the door.

"This is the police: open up."

That is roughly what it feels like to live the kind of life I lived for over sixty years and then hear the long-dreaded knock on the door when, after years and years of taking excellent care of your body, you are jumping a net in sweet affirmation of your way of life, and your right foot almost doesn't make it . . . .

Ironically that's when my love of contrasts paid off. My tennis days are over. My dirt bike competition days are over. My exercise program has been severely curtailed. These and several other out-and-out disasters occurred about the time my writing life began because up until then I was too busy living to sit home and write. That was when I cashed in on my lifelong love of classical music and opera, and substantially upgraded my hi-fi and record collection. That was when my scale modeling hobby paid off in spades. That was when I began extensive flat-water canoeing, which is a perfect aerobic exercise. And perhaps most important, that is when my motorcycle touring life began with a vengeance, because I knew it would probably be the next passion I'd have to learn to live without.

» » » » »

If this book may be said to have a single nitty-gritty, it is this: *don't let the bastards get you down. Never quit. Keep doing what you love to do despite all surmountable obstacles.* If you are a biker do it on a motorcycle until they take it away from you. Then get a sidecar. Even if you go blind, don't quit riding: get in your side hack and let a friend drive you around the world. You will still hear the great power impulses of a big twin, feel the wind in your hair, and perhaps in your mind's eye see the Taj Mahal on a moonlit summer night before you die.

Every other idea you run across in this book is just an attempt to stir up some shit so I don't have to tread water. All ideas are nothing but games where those who win are rewarded with more vibrant lives.

» » » » »

I have always considered myself lucky that I didn't have to change myself to accommodate my disability since that would have been physically impossible: I only had to change my bike.

I did this by adapting its ergonomics to the fact that I cannot sit upright or hold the bike up with my right leg while I shift into first with my left foot. To meet all these requirements I have to sit rather far back and a little sideways on the seat, so I have a double set-back for the handlebars. The right rear peg is located at the rear axle, and the rear wheel brake is just below it. Because of this arrangement the right muffler had to be replaced with crossover pipes, a collector box, and a Super-Trap muffler on the left side. This also meant that Joan, who was the best damned passenger I ever had, could no longer ride with me because I sit too far back and she would have no place to put her right leg. The upshot of this is that, Joan being Joan, we still ride together, but now on two bikes: she learned to ride when she was 65.

The problem of not being able to hold my bike up while shifting into first gear was handled by a rod attached to the right side of the gas tank. By pushing it down with my hand, a series of linkages pushes the gearshift lever down on the left side of the bike. Once underway I can shift with no problems, and in every other respect I can ride my bike as if I had no disability at all, even though I cannot walk without heavy dependence on a cane.

The victory inherent in the razor-sharp contrast between the act of snapping my leaden cane out of sight in its clip inside the fairing and then zapping away from the curb with the élan of a 23-year-old is not a triumph over old age and disability and in fact is hardly worth mentioning because that concept of what I am only exists in other people's consciousness. On the contrary, it is the infinitely sharper contrast between what our culture considers me to be and the glorious affirmation of the fact that as long as I am in my element I do not envy my young traveling companions because the rights and privileges of my youth are still not only intact, but vibrant: this joy exists within my mind.

At first I used to drop my bike a lot. Then I went for several years without dropping it. In the past four years I've dropped it twice, both on the side of my good leg. This doesn't bother me a bit. Every cyclist drops his bike occasionally and dropping mine on my good side gives me a delicious sense of being normal: the trick is to always be on the lookout for joy, and if this takes a little harmless lying, what the hell—go for it!

What caused my "heart attack" was that the linkage had broken in my hand shifter, so in order to shift into first gear I had to lean way down and do it manually. Riding out from Albuquerque, every time I stopped to enjoy a view, which happened frequently in that beautiful country, I stressed my back because I had to lean down close to the ground in order to shift into first with my left hand. Since I have arthritis in my back, all that stress began to pinch a nerve, which caused severe spasms in my chest. Muscle relaxer pills solved my problem and a visit to a welding shop removed the cause.

It is a well-established fact that people who in their fifties and sixties have severe heart attacks and almost die often suddenly take a new and even extreme interest and joy in life. I got a similar lift from my ersatz heart attack, but it was really more like simple relief, rather than a change in my point of view towards existence, because my lifelong sense of the wonder and beauty of this moment was fire-formed that fateful night, eons ago, when, as a mere child, my mother lovingly lowered the boom on me.

» » » » »

The welding shop was next to a restaurant. I had a troubled breakfast while my shifting linkage was being repaired because I had noticed the remains of a 500 cc Triumph that had been cobbled together from mismatched parts and crude welding which made it look as if it had been infested with bloated caterpillars. Luckily, when I picked up my bike it was easy to assume the guy who mutilated the Triumph didn't work there anymore.

As I was about to pull out on the highway a disheveled and forlorn-looking young man, obviously down on his luck, asked me if I could spare a dollar but I was hot to trot and shook my head as I rode away. A couple of miles down the road I remembered I'd left my dark glasses in the restaurant and rode back for them. The guy was still standing there, if anything more forlorn than before, and again I ignored him. As I left the restaurant and approached him for the third time I spared him the pain of making another useless plea and rode right up to him and stopped. I handed him a five dollar bill, which I already had in my hand, and as I gave it to him I told him I was sorry about before and that I had been in his spot myself, which I had on more than one occasion. Then I rode off feeling as if I were almost too good to be true and thinking of the temporary respite I had given a man to whom life, I'm afraid, was just a series of temporary respites.

Conscience is a wonderfully funny thing.

One time John Duthie and I were driving back to British Columbia from a hunting trip in Saskatchewan when we passed a line of twenty or thirty hitchhikers at the Trans Canada exit to Banff, Alberta. I asked John what he would do if he was thumbing and had to get at the end of that line. True to form, John came up with an idea that in a way explains why he was driving a fancy camper back from a successful wild goose shoot rather than hitchhiking to nowhere. He said he would walk a half mile beyond the last hitchhiker and then start thumbing. His theory was that while a motorist is passing up twenty or thirty poor devils his conscience bothers him on an ascending scale. When he passes the last one his conscience-torment peaks. Then suddenly, a half-mile ahead, he discovers, almost with joy, that he has a chance to redeem his conscience. Along with the hitchhiker he gets a bonus, which is the pleasure of John Duthie's unique company, or, if not John, perhaps a like-minded traveler who would never be caught standing in convention's line as long as his imagination and intellect were intact.

Lordy how I wish conscience was as simple a thing as I have just suggested. How can anyone whose conscience really and truly bothers him about social or racial injustice, or perhaps the terrible things we are all doing to the earth, do justice to the enormity of the problem without giving all his money away to vital causes and living a life of utter selflessness and personal deprivation? In short, how can anyone have a fully functioning conscience now-a-days without becoming a masochistic kook?

But then, who is going to pay serious attention to a kook? And what would your utter personal sacrifice really change?

If this sounds heartless you may be interested to know that when you get to be my age you tend to lose interest in the fate of humanity because it's not your world any more.

» » » » »

Midway between Albuquerque and Sturgis I started looking for a campground. The doctor suggested I only ride 100 miles that day but I had already ridden over 600. People who don't ride motorcycles can never understand what happens to ordinary human functions when a day is spent in ecstasy. Fatigue is largely a function of the brain: it is seldom called by its proper name, which is boredom. That is why it is harder to tread water for half an hour than it is to swim across the ocean.

As luck would have it there were no campgrounds, but in a hick town a seedy motel advertised rooms for $15.00. I figured it was a come on, and that the rate was only good for the hours from 3 AM to 5 AM, but no, it was legit, and I was directed to a room around back.

I couldn't believe it: around in back there were an even dozen BMW motorcycles.

Most true bikers are at heart low-life lyric poets, like Francois Villon. They prefer seedy motels because that is where the action is. They know they can learn more from the noises coming through paper-thin walls than they can from the Encyclopedia Britannica.

Ever since the day the Scarsdale Police Department confiscated my 1929 Harley-Davidson I have hardly ever raised my leg over a bike without getting the feeling that I'm a dog about to piss on something ultra-refined that would benefit from a little acid etching. Remember I'm not trying to change the system, because I consider that impossible. Besides, it's not my job, though I occasionally moonlight at it just for the hell of it, and to remind my mind who is boss, but all I really want to do is ride away from the dominant moribund system on my own system. Every Harley rider knows what I'm talking about and I'm with them 1000% on this one.

Why do you suppose Honda coined the slogan "You meet the nicest people on a Honda?" Obviously, to increase the market for their motorcycles. That slogan was not the creation of a distinguished philosopher—it was written by an ad man nobody ever heard of and motivated by economics, which is the system incarnate. This is probably why, although I have owned almost all brands of bikes, including Hodaka, Ossa and Montessa, I've never owned a Honda. I don't want to meet nice people. They're all alike. Nice. Bland. Indeterminate. I want to meet interesting people. They're all different. They're either imaginatively raunchy or they know their Mozart. They stand for something vital.

The system doesn't stand for Mozart. Just the opposite. The system uses Mozart to sell toothpaste on TV commercials, just as Honda uses a sport which, in the highest classical tradition, represents escape from the system, in order to sell the system.

If you are one of the readers who objects to my put down of respectability what would you have me do? Agree with you? Why should I? Who's writing this book anyway? I am not your problem— or your enemy either, for that matter. Your problem may be that you have been reading and believing too many magazines which, to the last greasy rag, all sell the system.

Motorcycle magazines used to sell motorcycling. As the salesman's slogan goes, they sold the sizzle, not the steak.

Today, for the most part, they're not selling the sizzle or the steak, but the anatomy.

Just a few years ago every issue of Cycle World contained a short story. In 1978 I sold them four such stories, but shortly after that the market for short stories dried up. (No wisecracks, please!) What had happened was that the more technical pieces they published, the more magazines they sold.

The age-old love of fictional suspense and conflict was replaced by the suspense of wondering what new technological goodies would be available in the future and the conflict of which company would be the first to market them.

This is a fundamental cultural problem which is no more confined to biker magazines than this book is limited to motorcycles.

What had been eliminated from all vehicle-oriented magazines in the early 1980s was the human element. For people like myself, who consider the fun of being human far more exciting than the dimensions of a crankshaft, this shift in emphasis is an indication of how recently, how swiftly, how completely and in what a deadly calculating way the raw data of technology has taken over the most intimate facets of our lives.

There is no need to belabor this point because the evidence is overwhelming: it is even evinced in outdoor magazines which one would think would still assume that a description of a sunlit meadow on opening day or the play of light at dusk in a favored fishing hole would be more appealing to their readers than technical computer-generated data about a carbon-fiber flyrod: I stopped reading those magazines because I could not make out the print through my tears.

What all this means to anyone now young enough to probably be around when technology collapses into utter boredom through its exponential excesses is that during this hiatus in strictly human evolution, mankind will have forfeited the imaginative rhetoric that has traditionally sustained him in times of crisis. As examples of language in its least and most powerful forms, simply regretting that you didn't buy the computer you wanted before the company went out of business cannot be equated in any significant way with regretting that you only have one life to give for your country.

In short, we will soon be up the creek without a paddle—that paddle being the clout of inspiring inter-human communication.

And what does all this mean to you as an individual? I can't answer that question for you but I can tell you this: having the shrewdness to buy three packs of gum for ten cents does not necessarily mean you also have the talent to pick the lock on the gate of paradise, or, lacking that, the ability to sweet-talk the guard into unlocking it for you.

» » » » »

I crawled into my fifteen dollar bed, with my ear inches away from the paper thin wall, and as I started to drift off I heard the rhythmic bed-squeaks of humping in the next room. For all I knew the lovers may only have known each other for five minutes, and they both may have been drunk, but the thought that at that moment they were as alive and as human as you can get made the squeaking of the bed as inspirational as my favorite Hallelujah Chorus, which appears in Handel's oratorio Saul.

Too weary from my long day in the saddle to make my present circumstances kinkier than that, I rolled away from the squeaks, put a pillow over my naked ear and was soon sleeping the blessed sleep of the dispossessed.

CHAPTER 22

Dawns, Doves and Self-Reliance

But even while we are talking and meditating about the earth's orbit and the solar system, what we feel and adjust our movements to is the stable earth and the changing day.

—George Eliot *Middlemarch*

The morning after my noble night in the seedy motel I was off and running an hour before dawn. This is my favorite way of starting a day, especially in the flatlands, which makes a perfect stage for the sun's triumphal entrance. I really don't think you can do justice to a dawn or any other major event unless you prepare for it properly. To get myself fully into the mood, to have my longing for it peak just as the first glowing intimations of light appear, takes an hour of darkness. I would be less than honest if I didn't admit that during that hour I am grateful for my headlight, which provides a brilliant and thrilling world of its own to travel in. However, I am not a headlight man any more than I am a leg or buttocks or breast man: I am a face man and believe the eyes are, yes, the windows of the soul. That is why my most memorable days so often begin when the first rays of the sun reveal the face of the earth.

I live for sunrises and for Joan, who—before she got her own bike, wanted me to go alone since she could no longer fit on my much-altered bike, who knew how important those experiences were to me, and who at the sound of my engine seemingly always came running out of the house and across the lawn in her bare feet to welcome me home with her sparkling eyes, each of us renewed, purified, and more in love than ever, if that's possible.

On this particular dawning a special treat awaited me. Beginning about the time the stainless steel sheen of dew became visible, I occasionally began to scare up doves which had been gravelling on the berm. No matter how often this happened, their flights always startled me afresh. I slowed down to synchronize my wingless flight with theirs, and, zig-zagging across the desolate road, I often got so close to one I probably could have reached up and pulled it out of the air. Although I have shot and eaten a great many game birds, grabbing an airborne handful of terrified dove and breaking its neck with my leathered thumb was too gross and violent an act to commit while I was so happily riding on my graceful motorcycle. This would be true even if I stopped on the spot to pluck and clean the dove in preparation for the most natural and self-reliant supper-feast imaginable. I confess to being sorely tempted, especially since I know of no law which prevents an always hungry man from catching doves on a motorcycle and eating them (which would really be the equivalent to being a cattle rancher on a very small scale). Instead, having bided my time, I am now funneling the nourishment I received from their incredible in-my-face beauty down to my right hand and, by means of a ballpoint pen slipping oilily across a yellow legal pad, I am pretending you will buy the preposterous fantasy that I am such a wonderfully civilized person I would starve to death before killing an innocent fellow-animal and eating it.

At considerable risk to my limbs—to say nothing of my life—I tried my hand at catching a few doves. They used two stratagems to escape the sudden danger I and my flying motorcycle represented. After evacuating their bowels in flight to make their bodies lighter and more nimble, they either flew fast and low or used all their energy gaining altitude and thus quicly became literally out of my reach. My opposing stratagem was to ignore the high flyers and accelerate my motorcycle until I was going about 10 miles faster than the low-flying birds. My expectation was that I could occasionally pluck a bemused dove out of thin air on the run, so to speak.

In a couple miles I managed to catch five doves. After each catch I stopped by holding the neck between my forefinger and front-wheel brake lever to cut its suffering short. Then I stashed them in my saddle bag.

At the next roadside rest stop I plucked my doves over a refuse can and gutted them by dropping the (ugh) guts in a toilet.

I now had five freshly killed, plucked and field-dressed birds ready for my camp stove; boiled in water with butter and garlic, they would be nectar for the gods—unavailable commercially at any price because it is illegal to sell a game bird.

At the next gas stop I bought a small bag of crushed ice and, after incorporating my priceless doves in it, I bungee-strapped my "refrigerator" to the back of my motorcycle beside my tent and sleeping bag. Then I used a hose to rinse the doves' droppings off my fairing, windshield, jacket, helmet and face shield. It was a nasty job—especially cleaning out the engines cylinder fins.

Anyway you cut it, death is a disgusting business. All doves can do to avoid becoming part of the nastiness is to fly high and slow or low and fast. Human beings have more sophisticated ways of finagling death: they can either listen to baroque music, make kinky love, ride motorcycles or, if you will excuse the expression, write books.

I rest my case.

» » » » »

As mentioned earlier, I have never really understood the value of the data Copernicus bequeathed to humanity. When I'm seeking out dawns in the flatlands, it makes no difference whether the sun is rising to meet my bike or whether my bike is rising to meet the sun. The intimate ambiance of the aqua-marine, high-beam indicator light on the instrument panel can blow both those concepts sky high. So can the fact that during my world-all-to-myself, pre-dawn riding, I rarely flicked on to low beam: how I set up my dawns has got to be the pertinent truth, not the conflicting mechanics of the physical process as "proved" by a mathematician who lived four centuries ago.

On a more immediate note, since it is now February in New York, Copernicus's calculations are not adding anything to the inspiring taste of the coffee I'm sipping, nor did they enhance my affectionate delight in Joan's nose-wrinkling smile as she put my 1996 souvenir Sturgis cup of amaretto-flavored bliss on my writing board just a few, still-brimming, moments ago.

In recent years motorcycles, like just about every other mechanical marvel, have become sanitized and spiritualized. They are assuming the role of religion, which is science, and the sect is Puritanism.

Their evangelists are very nice people.

Having annihilated the strictly human spirituality of the Virgin, modern scientific man has set up shop selling his own brand of spiritual values, substituting the mere complexities of the computer chip, electronic ignition and high-tech this and that for the real mysteries which were more fantastic to the Virgin because they were forever unexplainable.

Why do you suppose so many motorcyclists attend rallies to raise money for worthwhile causes? Aren't they, in effect, expressing their need for respectability and to have a bona fide spiritual dimension in their lives? Of course they are. But if this is so, why are they using their scientific motorcycles to drive home a spiritual point? Perhaps what these rallies are really telling us about the current state of civilization is that through science we are losing our spiritual values and, while this is regrettable, it is not as regrettable as doing without our technology would be. As a result, we graft what is left of our spiritual values to the machine by riding it to a Toys for Tots rally.

We have united the Virgin and the Dynamo in a shotgun marriage in a society in which the divorce rate is at an all time high. Who are we kidding?

Though easily exposed and documented, the means by which the religion of technology has us groveling on our knees is extremely varied and subtle. Its watering down influence leaches deep into our culture. The reason its trickery is not exposed more often is because it is not popular to do so, and writers have to eat. However, since I am always on a diet and don't have to write for a living, I'll document a tricky little linguistic science deception which in a bygone age would probably, in principle, have gotten me burned at the stake.

» » » » »

I remember when motorcycle journalists first started to use the word "aficionado" to describe a high-tech bike enthusiast. It is part of the journalist's job to keep up on language trends and "aficionado" was a striking and unusual word with a lot of expressive clout. As it was assimilated into popular scientific jargon, it severed all relation to its real and totally unscientific meaning.

What I am about to describe is a case of linguistic evolution which plays an important role in explaining the current state of mankind's evolution.

"Aficionado" came into popular use because of Hemingway's novel *Death in the Afternoon*, in which he used its original meaning to describe someone who loved bullfights.

It would be hard to imagine a context more out of keeping with the spirit of science than a bullfight. sorry, but a demolition derby doesn't get the job done.

A bullfight is one of the most intensely human experiences a person can have because it requires the viewer to confront death, not in theory, not by bland avoidance, but in a ritualistic format making the event specific, grim, inevitable and unforgettable. Matadors don't kill bulls, but rather people pretending to be bulls. Every aficionado in the grandstand identifies with the bull at the moment of truth, and its death serves the same function as a serious heart attack from which the patient recovers. Because the sacrifice of the bull kindles a renewed sense of aliveness in the viewer, the aficionado feels profound sympathy and affection for the bull's deliberately provoked torment.

"Aficionado" is derived from the past participle of the Spanish word "aficionar", meaning to "engender affection."

Today however, it's lost all its original meaning and is just a fancy, pretentious way of referring to a guy who digs the latest technology.

Hemingway, who was always saying things people are afraid to say, would turn over in his grave.

What happened to "aficionado" is not progress.

» » » » »

The average motorcycle aficionado reads a technical description of an ultra-complex engine in a monthly cycle prayer book and on the basis of the report, buys the bike. All the details he reads about and doesn't understand because they represent several unrelated branches of learning are fortunately covered up by acres of plastic. He is as happy as a convert in an evangelist's tent, because the packaging is not only in the latest glob tradition, but happily it hides all the mechanisms he would not be able to fix if they went kaput in Thoreau, New Mexico. Out of sight, out of mind. Thus the brave new aficionado is twice removed from the pleasures of human interplay with the essence of his bike. He has become a trusting spiritualist in a flat-out material world.

The plastic cover is the stained-glass window through which he views his sunrises.

» » » » »

I used to ride my 1932 Harley all winter except when there was snow on the road. (Even then I used to pull my sisters behind it in a Jack Frost version of water skiing called skijoring.) The bike was equipped with a large canvas windscreen and sheet metal leg protectors, like what is now called a "fairing". Wearing long johns, a few sweaters, a heavy sheepskin-lined, leather jacket and a coonskin hat—helmets were unheard of—I often rode a couple of hundred miles a day in subfreezing weather and thought nothing of it. I also rode to work everyday. Although in the Spring I waited impatiently for a really warm day when I could take the damn things off, for most of the year the windscreen and sheet metal "leggings" were standard equipment: they were the norm, and they were necessary. However their absence in the spring always wonderfully intensified the rush.

The windscreen/fairing always wonderfully intensified the rush by allowing far more sensation as well as by adding about 20 mph to my "speedometer speed." Speed is a strictly human dimension. Clocking it doesn't mean anything: it has to be felt. Copernicus would never have understood.

» » » » »

I confess to loving sensual joy. I cannot understand, for example, why anyone would prefer a room-temperature electric shaver to a badger-bristle brush of hot, scented lather on the skin, which is not only a marvelous sensation in itself, but also an essential ingrediant for full appreciation of a cooling, astringent, after-shave lotion. I have an array of beautifully masculined bottles of cologne and enjoy deliberating over which essence might best complement the morning's weather; occasionally, however, forsaking chemistry, and, with head held high, I close my eyes and think of hurricanes and tornadoes while letting my water-drenched face dry naturally.

As I have just pointed out, the windscreen on my bike was a winter necessity, but what is the *necessity* for an electric shaver? Why don't we discriminate? Why is progress always best? A guy I know uses two electric razors at once to save time. Save time for what? Is he too busy to take time out to enjoy his face? How many cocks does he use to make love? See? An electric shaver doesn't necessarily make sense just because it's technological.

» » » » »

When I first started flying it became apparent right away that the higher up you got the less sensation there was. The sensation near the ground was fantastic but this bothered me: *why should I pay big bucks per hour shooting landings when I could be getting the same rush on my motorcycle for practically nothing?* As a result of this soul searching, instead of selling my bike I sold my airplane. This was still another case where downgrading the technology upgraded my life.

For my money the elaborate fairings on the latest touring bikes directly contravene the motorcycle's greatest asset. We design technologies for the better life and then we engineer the better life out because in order to be commercially successful they must not frighten a timid public obsessed with the lust for comfort and convenience. For example, in designing airliners, the engineers deliberately placed the windows in the upper curve of the fuselage so that a passenger can't look straight down in normal flight: this of course violates the principle behind a first-class sensation. It is far more thrilling to look straight down from one thousand feet than to look obliquely out from an airliner at 35,000 feet. Any pilot will confirm this. The modern touring motorcycle designs, for all their weather protection appearances, seem to me to be an extension of the unscary airliner design principle, and I think they've got it backwards, because their wide opaque plastic frontal areas block out too much of the rush, which is the payoff for all the inconvenience and inclement weather that the bikers go through.

» » » » »

The great French philosopher Blaise Pascal once wrote "*on meurs seul*," which, literally translated, means "one dies alone." Note the tension created by his use of the word "one."

This phrase is the truest and most tragic one-liner in World

Literature.

I think it is sometimes necessary, and often a good idea, to live alone. Because I love contrasts, I often enjoy being by myself. Before and even after my hip went bad I occasionally hunted alone. I know of no better way to get a perspective on the serene glory of a dayful of time than to sit alone in a duck blind from dawn to dark when nothing is flying.

The main reason I tour alone, however, is because everybody I like to tour with is working and can't get away for the month or so that I take off. I'm sure they envy me and I like to rub it in by telling them working is the penalty they have to pay for not being old.

My first rule of thumb as a loner is this: I do not depend on the System.

The System tells me I should pack a cellular phone, but if my bike loses its sparks in the middle of a seldom traveled Nevada desert in August, I'd ten times rather have a full canteen of water than a cellular phone that may or may not pull in help because it is part of the same System that caused the electronics on my bike to fail. I know this doesn't make sense, which is why I love it. Sense can wait until I get home and update my ragged budget. Besides, if you follow the System's line of reasoning to the end of its tether, you'd end up too broke to go anywhere anyhow.

I prefer to depend on my own system. At one point in my business career my partners and I had occasion to ask a self-made man who ran a highly successful machine shop to invest in our rapidly growing business. He refused because he said when he was a young man he decided he would never invest money in anything but himself. I respected and honored his decision and was put out when my partners tried to change his mind. They had no concept of basics. How could a change in investment tactics benefit a successful, self-made man? It is scary to be in business with people who have a poor grasp of basics: I got out of the business and ended up in graduate school, and, as far as I know, my partners ended up broke.

I like to think that the successful machinist's belief in himself began in the early days of his machinist's training, when students, using only a file and measuring instruments, are required to change a ball of mild steel into a perfect square.

The long history of my life has convinced me that somewhere along the line we have lost touch with such basics and that this loss, is what, sooner or later, is going to turn us all into miserable earthbound refugees with no place to go.

My 1978 BMW is just old enough to be basically basic. Its engine is the main attraction. The machine is modern enough to be good for a dead-level 125 mph, which is far faster than I have any good reason to go. Over the years all the things that could go wrong with it have gone wrong. There weren't many, and they were all either fixable at the roadside or fixable after some limping towards help, and each time something went wrong it meant one less time I was likely to get stranded because I was that much more knowledgeable.

I set out on my 7,500-mile trip with little fear that my bike would strand me, helpless, alone, vulnerable, and prey to the first carload of crazies that came,

Ha! Then it happened.

While cruising at 75 mph two hundred miles from Sturgis, my bike suddenly hesitated and backfired. Thirty seconds later it did the same thing. About the same time it began to rain. Hard. I mean hard. I was in the middle of nowhere and you know where that is. I continued cruising, but now at 35 mph and getting sicker at heart every minute. When the same Harley riders who I had just had a great time talking to at the gas station zapped by me like I was riding out the storm at anchor and even *waved* to me to follow, I got even sicker: I wanted to be a part of their what-the-hellness.

Even though no one can tell me Harley riders aren't nuts, someday by God I'm going to get another one.

> This day however, I was forced to have other things on my
> mind.

Suddenly my bike quit altogether. In nothing flat it had
gone from a perfect square to a ball of mild steel.

Shit, Piss, and Corruption. Suddenly if I wanted to go to Sturgis
I'd have to hoof it 200 miles, cane and all.

I pivoted the sidestand out and sat in misery for half an hour
waiting for the downpour to let up. Torturing myself with
reminiscences of full days I'd spent riding alone in light rain, I
knew full well there's even an art to being miserable.

» » » » »

Oh how I love to ride on drizzly summer days tucked in behind
a misty windscreen, insulated from the moist windchill by a
rainsuit, listening to the song of a well-tuned engine, absorbed in
the rush of my solitary world—lonely, unassailable, aching with
day-long joy as I watch the earth renew itself around me.

» » » » »

When the rain let up I did some preliminary diagnosing. The
trouble was obviously electrical. The nerve center of the electrics
was in the headlight shell with one set of wires for the right
handlebar, one for the left, one for the lights, and one for the
motor. Since my lights and turnsignals worked, there were only
two sets to check out. If my electronic ignition had gone bad, I
had the original points and condenser carefully packaged in my
tool tray and could put them in and return the ignition to stock.
Basic.

I removed the headlight lens and went directly to the connection
which experience taught me was most likely to be the culprit. It
was a solder joint made when the same thing had happened in
Florida fifteen years before. When I stressed the joint, the ignition
lights came on and I was back in business.

Love, Music, and Hallelujah!

The BMW shop in Sturgis redid what turned out to be a cold solder joint and I was homefree.

Could I have solved this simple problem (using irrational rhetoric to match the growing irrationality of technology for its own sake)? If in my formative years I had decided to become a machinist and in the course of my studies had been handed a ball of mild steel in a box which I could send away, along with a check amounting to the sum total of my life's earnings, and get a beautifully streamlined, perfectly square mild steel block by express mail, what would I have done?

CHAPTER 23

STURGIS!

You know the feeling you get when you're late to the short track races, and while you are standing at the ticket window, you hear the roar of the bikes starting the first heat?

That's how I feel when I get within twenty miles of Sturgis and start seeing too many bikes to wave to'em all.

Have you ever had a wet dream or the female equivalent where the scenario is you've died and gone to heaven which turns out to be populated with beautiful or handsome virgins crazy to find out what sex is like—and you're the only person of the opposite sex there?

That's how I feel when I hit Main Street and start cruising for a place to sidestand my scooter.

Not that it matters if I don't find one right away.

Lordy! Lordy! Lordy!

I'm in my element.

I'm home.

» » » » »

The first thing you do when you get to Sturgis is go looking for good buys on tee shirts. Not me. I didn't like any of them. There were too many buffaloes, too many Mt. Rushmores, too many Harleys, and not enough BMWs. Too many had sayings that could only be read once with mild amusement or marginally accepted as oversimplified wisdom, and wearing any of them only proved that you'd bought the System as it is currently sustained by the tee shirt industry.

What I wanted was an honest-to-goodness work of art. You know, something like a one-off, *Louvre* quality eagle's head airbrushed on the back of my Hein Gerecke red leather jacket.

I wanted an original work of art purely for its own sake, not as an investment based on the popular belief that an artist's output will skyrocket in value after he's dead. As an artist who paints pictures with his ballpoint pen, I could never lower myself to dicker with a fellow artist as a pretense when what I'm really doing is trying to figure out how soon he'll go slack and make me rich. You'll never catch me finding an excuse to slap an airbrush artist vigorously on the back to see how sturdy he is or check his fingers for evidence of heavy cigarette smoking: if I had my way all artists would live forever.

I leave the above ways of capitalizing on the art of Sturgis to the investment bankers who trailer their Harleys from Wall Street to Wall Drugs, South Dakota, where they off-load them and head straight for the temporary tattoo tent as their relaxing reward for the rigors of riding seventy miles from the drug store parking lot to Sturgis.

What is more revealing of the poverty of having too much money than "touring" to Sturgis in a car while pulling a toy $20,000 motorcycle on a trailer behind it, like an afterthought.

And what is more revealing of our inability to stop our runaway culture before it self-destructs than the thought of trying to talk a trailerist into becoming a motorcyclist.

The way we all rationalize what we want tickles me. I had many more miles to go and really didn't want to spend the money for a legitimate work of art, but since I was celebrating my stretched-out birthday, I was more inclined to what-the-helling my decision than reasoning out my finances. If money got critical on the way home I could always sandwich my grape nuts and powdered milk for breakfast, eat five-for-one-dollar Oriental dehydrated soup for lunch, and rely on a can of beans for supper in between million dollar rides on my not-for-sale-at-any-price bike.

Actually I ended up proud of myself, since I was able to get what I wanted by the following rational thought processes.

I paid $30 for my airbrushed eagle. Underneath it, "Sturgis" was rendered boldly in motorcycle-appropriate calligraphy. But beneath it were the kickers: '85 '87 '90 '92 '93 '94.

By the very nature of their business, it's unlikely that tee shirt manufacturers will learn how to make a thinking man's or an art connoisseur's tee shirt during the intervening twelve months, so next year I can go directly to an airbrusher's booth, and for a lousy two bucks have him airbrush in a '95 next to the '94.

The advantage of the airbrush route was strictly economic. At two bucks a throw, it will only take me an additional four years to make my eagle's head cost effective with four tee shirts: at that rate I can't afford not to ride to Sturgis in '96, '97, '98 and '99.

And Sturgis '99 would bring me within hailing distance of my life's ambition.

Let me explain.

The first thing I did when my grammar school teacher taught me to subtract was to put this knowledge to practical use. I took the year of my birth (1919) and subtracted it from the year 2000. The result was 81.

That was how I arrived at my life's ambition: I would try to live until the year 2000, when I would be 81. This goal has always been the nut into which I screwed every stage of the body conditioning and maintenance process, using it like a "go, no-go" gauge. Unfortunately this simple mechanical process is not taught in public or private schools.

You have to do your own wrenching, which is a vital form of self-education.

It's comical. All everybody really wants to do is live to a ripe old age, yet there isn't a university in the country that offers a course in longevity or even in living the good life while you're *about* it, if it comes to that.

Luckily, since I will have to be in Sturgis in '99 to make my airbrushed eagle's head cost-effective with tee shirts, it will only be a hop, skip and jump to Sturgis '00.

Yes, the more I think of it, the more certain I am that I'll be in Sturgis in 2000 on my 22-year-old bike, celebrating the attainment of my life's ambition by getting flocks of full-bodied eagles airbrushed all over a new leather jacket.

If, over the years, that project turns out not to be cost effective with tee shirts, what the hell—let 'em sue me.

» » » » »

The first time I rode to Sturgis I headed straight for Mt. Rushmore. I'd been on the road for a month, observing the dominant culture during the tourist season and thanking my lucky stars at every stretch of twisty road that I was riding the product of a disreputable subculture and sleeping on the good earth under the gross poorman's stars.

When I rode into the Mt. Rushmore parking lot and looked up at where What's-His-Name spent twenty years of his life defacing a God-made mountain with blasted-out replicas of American presidents, I couldn't believe my eyes. What I saw wasn't the spirit of liberty. It wasn't art. It wasn't done with an artist's arm making graceful sweeps, it was engineered with calipers and dynamite, using specifications arrived at through solid geometry. What I was being asked to bow down to wasn't the Bill of Rights, it was scientific ingenuity and our obscene preoccupation with bigness.

By any standard I can think of Mt. Rushmore sucks.

Although that mountain existed ages before Columbus discovered America, it apparently never occurred to Mr. What's-His-Name to include an Indian head, nor, for that matter, an artist's head, or the head of a man of letters or the heads of fun people, like Mr. Harley, Mr. Davidson, or Joe Petrali.

However, the most amazing lack of all was that there wasn't the head of a spiritual leader. Why aren't we embarrassed to have people come from all over the world to see this triumph of the spirit of humanity only to see the heads of local, *American* leaders blasted out of usurped rocks?

Though still not right for everybody, I thought surely Jesus, Buddha, Mohammed, Zeus or Apollo would have been more appropriate.

Since the name of the game is not art, but tourism, my vote would have been for a single figure—a humongous, full-bodied Venus.

Quick, get me some ladders, calipers, computers and dynamite! What's-his-name started at age 60—why shouldn't I start getting my licks in at 75?

In my artistic vision I plan to create Venus on her back, naked, with her legs spread, so visitors from around the world can appreciate our grossness in all its glory.

» » » » »

For a full week I took traveling time out from my birthday ride to wrap myself up in the mystique of motorcycling. The highlight came unexpectedly at two A.M. when a guy rode his Harley into a stripper bar and, rapping the throttle, filled the joint with blue smoke without interrupting a single bump or grind on the stage: bikers just opened windows and doors. That's Dedication with a capital "D" and Life with a capital "L," and no mission to Sturgis is really accomplished unless you're present at one of these passionate, ancient and earthy rituals.

It was as close to a moment of grace as I could ever expect to get in a secular society.

Bike weeks at Sturgis and Daytona are like family reunions where, if I could remember them all, and looked hard enough, I could probably see an example of every sister and aunt and uncle and cousin bike I ever owned.

But not my earth-mother bike—not the 1923 Indian mom gave me with her heart stopping smile and almost imperceptible nod to my father across the breakfast table sixty-three years ago.

Not even Sturgis can come up with that bike.

"Why are not old men mad?" Yeats once asked in an unforgettable poem.

Because then they take your motorsickle license away, that's why.

You know the feeling you get when you arrive at the short track stadium and find the races were last night?

That's how I feel when I notice vendors are pulling up tent pegs.

PART IV

*Options for People Who Hate
to go to Work*

CHAPTER 24

Public and Personal Bottom Lines

Let not to earn a living be your trade, but your sport.

—Henry Thoreau

I first heard the phrase "the bottom line" when I was buying a new Harley in the late forties. The salesman and I reviewed the options, such as saddlebags, white sidewall tires, chrome this and chrome that, etc., and when all these sums were added to the base price the total was staggering. The salesman noticed the shocked innocence on my face, but never batted an eye, even as I started to protest.

"Hold on a minute," he laughed. "You haven't heard the bottom line."

"The bottom line—what's that?"

"Where have you been?" he asked rhetorically. "Relax. The bottom line is only twenty bucks per month for the rest of your life."

As quickly as I could write Herbert Foster Gunnison on the bottom of a contract, I had bought the equivalent of three packs of the juiciest of Juicy Fruit for five dollars, convinced I had just made the smartest decision of my life to date.

We all know that extended time payments roughly double the cost of what we buy. We also know that the reason we know this is because laws had to be passed to make bankers reveal the extent of their profits. What we cannot seem to get in our heads is what those laws tell us about our vulnerability to the system.

We submit to this obscene process for a very simple, human and poignant reason which has nothing to do with business: *we want what we want now because we are aware of our mortality.* That is why technologists and bankers who, unlike artistic types, are relatively free of this problem, are able to work hand in hand, devoid of poetic or perhaps even friendly impulses, to extort money from poets who want bikes for no other reason than that, as the Arlo Guthrie song goes, "I don't wanna die, I just wanna ride my motorsickle."

It should be clear to everyone except money people that if we wish to profit from the bottom line in more than its superficial economic sense, we have to redefine this phrase.

In my experience and observation the most profitable definition for life's bottom line is a single word: imagination.

What follows is a rundown on how it works.

Almost anybody who wants to make money looks within the system to figure out how to do it. It is common knowledge that you start at the bottom, kiss everybody's ass, start a savings account, buy three packs of gum for ten cents, never buy anything on poetic impulse or time payments, and work your way up. This is time-consuming, boring and a waste of human resources. It can be done, but it usually takes a lifetime and leaves you too decrepit to benefit from your lifelong denial of the good things.

My father had a friend who accumulated an immense fortune at an early age simply by using his imagination. For example one evening, he was mixing a drink and, while shaking bitters into a glass out of a bottle with a small hole in the top, he had what is known in the formal study of creativity as a "closure." Since we're concerning ourselves with the benefits of imagination rather than the process itself, let's just say that he did nothing more profound than put two and two together.

The next morning he called his lawyer and asked him to

negotiate the purchase of the company that manufactured the bitters.

A few months later he owned the company.

A few weeks later his bitters were being quietly sold in a bottle with a thirty percent larger hole in the top.

Over the next few years the profits increased twenty percent and were still rising when the new owner worked up a prospectus and sold his rapidly expanding company at a huge profit.

He told my father that just for the hell of it he'd figured out that from the time he had the closure to the time he sold the company, he had earned one hundred dollars for every hour he had been alive, including sleeping and many months of vacationing.

Using his imagination was what he did for a living, and I have limited his closures to this one example because this is not a book on how to get rich, at least not in the sense that term is generally used.

Such is the potential power of the redefined bottom line when your primary impulse is to buck the unimaginative system.

On the evidence of the above success story you'd think that anyone should be able to make a million dollars. However, there is a problem: that kind of imagination is extremely rare.

Try it.

You'll see.

If you are suddenly thinking in terms of ketchup bottles you have missed the point.

» » » » »

After my sophomore year at St. Lawrence University I spent the summer vacation working for the R.H. Donnelley Corporation. Unbeknown to me, my father paid my salary out of his own pocket.

That was the kind of man he was.

The Donnelley Corporation was a high-powered place where lots of money was made, perfectly legitimately, catering to the human need for promised but ever-elusive happiness.

I worked as a judge in a contest put on by the Roy-Tan cigar company. They gave a new Chevrolet away every day for thirty days to the person who finished the line "Man-to-man, smoke Roy-Tan cigars because . . ." in twenty five words or less. There were about fifteen judges, and all were college students majoring in English.

Most of the entries were dreadful: my heart bled hundreds of times a day. But the overwhelming broken-dream tragedies came from those who thought that creativity was an end in itself, that all you had to do was have a brilliant idea and the System would whisk you off to paradise. Their tragic flaw was that they didn't know that creativity has to be focused, that it has to have specific meaning and technical substance: in short, that even if you are gifted with imagination, you still have to learn to think your way through to its bottom line every time you call it into play. This takes an ungodly amount of discipline.

One man shipped Donnelley a ho-hum entry inside a magnificent doll house. Recorded entries, some with, some without the necessary phonograph, were common. One man sent in a "proposition": If Roy-Tan let him win the contest he would have Roy-Tan painted at his expense all over his car and drive it across the country handing out cigars also at his expense (less, of course, the usual factory discount).

We all laughed at these entries, but when I got back to Scarsdale I felt more like weeping. I used to lie awake at night thinking perhaps of the man with the "proposition." He lived in the same time zone and I could imagine him also lying awake, looking out at the stars, thinking how clever he was, hoping against hope that the Roy-Tan Cigar Company was perceptive enough to appreciate how clever he was. At first he thought he might get a phone call from the president of Roy-Tan Cigar Company congratulating him on being different from run-of-the-mill people and telling him about a gala national promotion, and he visualized photographers taking pictures of the president handing him the keys to his already Roy-Tan emblazoned car.

But the phone never rang.

And the mail was all pulp and the bill he was dreading.

And there was tomorrow and then a lifetime of tomorrows filled with not knowing why and suffering the bitterness of his perplexing martyrdom.

» » » » »

The idea of the contests in which a company slogan was to be completed in twenty-five words or less originated with a brilliant Donnelley account executive named Henrietta Davis. When I first met her I was stunned by her beauty, but whenever she demonstrated her command of the king's English, I became a basket case.

The contest business was profitable and Donnelley had it all to themselves, but one day there was a knock on the door and a voice said, "This is the government. Open up!"

It seems Uncle Sam figured Donnelley was operating an illegal lottery.

Mrs. Davis was expecting this turn of events and was prepared. By means of a series of blind tests she proved conclusively that some people can express ideas in writing better than others, that this is a skill that can be graded by qualified judges, and that consistent results can thus be obtained.

The government dropped its charges, but every once in a while an entry would come in with a P.S. like this: "I know you pick the winners out of a hat, but I'm just doing this for laughs anyway." Every one of those letters was answered.

Picking on advertising companies is a popular pastime, but in my opinion lotteries are a far more legitimate target. Lotteries are taxes on dreamers: all the contestants who entered Donnelley contests lost was the price of an envelope, a stamp and their dreams.

I have never bought a lottery ticket other than for a benefit or a private organization I was committed to. In later years when I was living in Canada and writing my book on music, I used to

have manuscript pages copied in a stationery store where people—
mostly native Canadians living on a nearby reservation—were lined
up buying lottery tickets. I was glad to be investing money in
copies of myself because I knew the odds in my personal lottery
were much better. I was far from being smug about this: what can
one do when investing in yourself would only get you miserable
odds through a fault which is not your fault?

The net result of the Roy-Tan Cigar Company contest was
that more people enjoyed smoking cigars and thirty entrants got
new cars.

Who can quarrel with that?

One of the contest judges was a lovely blonde-and-built girl
in her junior year at Vassar. I tried my zoology antics on her but
she wasn't having any. I was crushed in more ways than one.

One day my father came down from the 18th floor with Mrs.
Davis to see how the judging was going, and one of the judges
whispered, "That's Mr. Gunnison—the *President*—look busy!" I
didn't have to be told: I'd whiffed the aroma of his expensive Havana
cigar while he was still in the hall talking to Mrs. Davis and never
looked up from my work the whole time he was in the room. A
day or so later the Vassar junior asked me casually if I was related
to the president, since he had the same name.

"He's my father," I said.

The softened, welcoming look on her face hit my memory
filter like a hollow-point bullet and has been imbedded in my
brain, like a poisonous mushroom, ever since.

Woe works both ways dearie—and by the way, is that what
the Humanities Department teaches innocent little girls in
Poughkeepsie?

Another of Mrs. Davis's bottom-line ideas was based on an
ingeniously perceptive insight. About 1938 she realized that
technology had reached a new plateau. Mass production was
turning out cars that all looked alike and selling them to people
who all wanted to be different. Aftermarket accessory stores were
doing a land-office business catering to people who all thought

being different could be bought by buying identical accessories. And because being different meant you were not just anybody, this foolishness extended to accessories which made you appear to be somebody even if you didn't have a pot to piss in. For example, you could buy a fake aerial to make people think your car had the radio you couldn't afford.

In order to capitalize on this trend Mrs. Davis sold the Sun Oil Company on the idea of selling through Donnelley's direct mail branch a Sunoco logo which could conveniently be mounted above a license plate with one of its bolts.

Now why, you may ask, would anyone pay good money to advertise the Sun Oil Company on the back of his or her car?

That's where the Mrs. Davises of the world enter the picture with their bottom-line imagination.

When you get your metal Sunoco advertisement in the mail, it had your initials on it. In bold lettering.

They sold like hotcakes.

Donnelley made a killing.

But again, one day there was a knock on the door in the form of a telephone call.

It was the purchasing agent at Sunoco.

He informed Mrs. Davis that he had a gentleman in his office at that very moment who was willing to furnish Sunoco identical logos for one-third what they were paying Donnelley.

"Look," Mrs. Davis began, "we're not in the tin sign business. This is an advertising company."

Sunoco never gave her the slightest trouble after she got finished explaining the facts of life to the purchasing agent, or perhaps she titillated the president of Sunoco with the prospect of still other advertising gold mines the Donnelley Corporation was about to offer him.

» » » » »

I thought Mrs. Davis was the cat's meow. I would have followed her to the ends of the earth. I knew she was happily married, near twice my age, and infinitely smarter than I was, but I also knew you didn't have to enter one of her contests to be a dreamer.

I saved a lot of stamps and envelopes on Mrs. Davis, if you know what I mean.

All my life I have considered Henrietta Davis the personification of what Coleridge described as "the ascendancy which people of imagination exercised over those of mere intellect."

In the context of this book the group with "mere intellect" would have to include the great majority of college professors in whose care the world happily awaits extinction.

» » » » »

In the early months of the Second World War I again spent my vacation working at Donnelley's, once again at my father's expense.

Donnelley had been taking on war contracts which dovetailed with their clerical expertise; one such job was compiling parts lists and service manuals for military vehicles. They ran into considerable difficulty with this one because auto companies did not want anyone, not even military personnel, to know about the enormous numbers of parts in their top-of-the-line cars which were interchangeable with their lowest priced models.

I thought it depressing and not a little pathetic that such civilian conflicts should be part of the war effort.

My job was to supervise the packaging of sutures for army hospitals. Suture material was shipped to Donnelley's in large spools. It then had to be cut into two foot lengths, hand wrapped into coils and slipped into plastic envelopes.

Cutting it to length was accomplished by reeling it onto a different size spool which had a two foot circumference and then cutting it off. Bunches of individual sutures were then rubber banded between two rectangular pieces of cardboard, and from these packs an operator pulled out a suture, coiled it around the index and middle fingers and inserted it in the envelope.

There were fifty men and women working at desks and the set-up was similar to a large classroom, with my desk in front facing the rest.

For the first few days my job was excruciatingly boring because there wasn't anything for me to do. I just sat there twiddling my thumbs while fifty identical human beings picked identical sutures out of identical packs and wrapped them eight times around identical index and middle fingers and slipped them into identical plastic sleeves.

Hour after hour after miserable hour was thus pilfered from fifty eternities.

My presence was simply to insure that everyone was working: I was moonlighting as the System's scarecrow.

Not wanting to torment fifty bored fellow humans by earning my living while brazenly sitting in front of them enjoying a book, I contrived a way to do this surreptitiously.

As it happened, at that epoch in my life I was deeply engrossed in my Pickwick Papers project, and since it was a thick book I had cut the pages out and collated a day's supply between the pages of a large black-and-white mottled ledger book I opened each morning with an audible sigh as if the fifty-first albatross had separated from the room's flock and had just alighted on my weary shoulder.

» » » » »

When I read *Pickwick Papers* I not only discovered that Dickens had a marvelous sense of humor but that the explosive spark of his wit was usually triggered by what might be called the "technical manipulation of his imagination."

I was not reading Dickens for entertainment, but for knowledge. This came about partly because of the concept of self-education which was well entrenched even in my college days, but also because I admired the writers I read so much I wanted to emulate them, and I soon realized the knowledge gained from the emulation was more important than the short-term, page-by-page entertainment.

It is hard for me to imagine a writer worth reading who doesn't read for technical information and write for entertainment.

Early on in my sessions with *Pickwick Papers* I began to pick up on certain techniques which Dickens created to precipitate his bursts of hilarity. And since I always read with an editing pen in my hand (and detest narrow margins in books with broad concepts), I soon began to document his techniques in the margins. Almost all of them were based on sharp contrasts. For example, he would use elaborately formal rhetoric to describe a ridiculously informal situation. Comic episodes were treated as tragic ones and vice-versa. Noble impulses were lavished on fatuous projects. Points of view were expressed by boldly stating the reverse.

Occasionally a genius joke flew in out of the blue in the form of an outlandish, astonishing and seemingly unclassifiable word or conclusion.

Oh how I admired that book!

My *Pickwick Papers* project consisted of reviewing my marginalia and reclassifying them into broader areas which were not necessarily related to writing but were simply borrowed brainy techniques for resolving any problem crying out for a creative solution.

Ultimately I arrived at devices which fell under generic headings such as "reversal," "halving," "doubling," "continuum," "unexpected detail" and strictly literary spinoffs from the above, such as "when to leave well enough alone," "when to go for broke," "when to look it up," "when to take a deep breath and redline the phrase of the day," "when to ask Joan for help" and "when to blow your brains out."

Although the above categories appear to be general, this was far from the case: each technique embodied rich personal associations gleaned from my extensive reading.

Here is an elementary example of this process taken directly from your living experience just a few moments ago. Do you recall the parenthetical remark (and [I] detest narrow margins in books with broad concepts)? That succinct, time-saving phrase was the result of the routine technique of "reversal"—in the case at hand of the word "narrow." Although this is not as easy as it looks, there was nothing creative, clever or even imaginatively startling in the resulting succinct phrase. It was simply a routine procedure which has become so routine I get little pleasure out of the process. Fortunately, however, the overwhelming number of bookworms read for entertainment and this prevents the anatomy of a writer's hand from betraying its ball-pointed legerdemain.

Painstakingly, over many rough, frustrating years I somehow managed to cobble together a slot machine in my head. It has many borrowed parts and a few which were bought for practically nothing from writers who didn't know what they had. Some, I confess, were acquired while scrounging in junkyards, but as far as I can tell my intellectual slot machine works well enough to get the job done, though, never satisfied, I am always tinkering with it.

Whenever I need something to keep the two of us happy with what we're doing at the moment I pull the handle on my slot machine. Instead of cherries or lemons or beechnuts stopping at the moment of truth, I get "reverse it" or "double it" or "halve it" or an assortment of variegated "whatevers" in the window of my mind. All I have to do is keep pulling my one-armed bandit's arm until I hit the jackpot which represents, God help me, the best I can do.

The delight I get from whatever creativity I may or may not have no longer comes, as mentioned earlier, from pulling the lever— it comes from tinkering with the machine's innards to increase my odds, my range, and wherever possible to involve my heart and sense of humor.

If I had more time I'd like to tell you about my Célene's *Journey to the End of the Night* project, but because that would throw this chapter out of balance, perhaps we should get back to our narrative.

Besides—

A little creativity goes a long way because, if it goes too far it becomes the norm, and life as we wish it were ceases to exist.

» » » » »

What was obvious about what was going on at those fifty desks in the Donnelley "schoolroom" was so horrible I don't want to think about it, much less write about it.

At the time, I occasionally diverted myself from thinking of the reason why all those sutures were suddenly and desperately needed by thinking about what I might do to increase Donnelley's profits and, far more importantly, *to please my father.*

I looked out at the fifty occupied desks which represented the System. Everything had been working with apparent perfection for about four days when I decided to apply what I had learned from my *Pickwick Papers* project to the situation at hand.

I pulled the lever on my home-built slot machine and hit the jackpot on the first try: three "halves" appeared in the windows. I walked over to the nearest desk, took a cardboarded packet of sutures back to my desk and implemented my jackpot. By cutting the two rectangular cardboard slabs in half, the packaged unit could then be folded in half. Now, instead of straight suture ends sticking out of both ends, loops were fanned out of only one end. This made the sutures far easier to pick up and they only had to be pulled out half as far. Finally, eight turns around the fingers were no longer needed to make the coil—only half as many.

Within hours, the production of fifty workers had doubled.

I was elated because I knew my father would be pleased and began to wonder how he would show his appreciation; however, as it happened, I was a beyond-suturing casualty in the war against inefficiency.

I found myself in the position of the Roi Tan contestant with the "proposition." All my father and I had in common was that we lived in the same time zone. For the first expectant few days I used to look out at the stars at night wondering what marvelous reward my father was dreaming up for me—perhaps a car of my own—but then there was tomorrow and then a lifetime of tomorrows in which I could never summon up enough confidence even to say,

"Dad, won't you even give me credit for the business sense of what I did? You know, dad, *business?*"

To his dying day my father never mentioned my little contribution to the Ruben H. Donnelley Corporation's profit margin.

» » » » »

As mentioned earlier, when I was a kid my father sent me to the Keewaydin Camp in Brandon, Vermont, on the shore of Lake Dunmore, which sparkled in sunlight and was even more beautiful at night when the sparks were magically transformed into occult glints.

Keewaydin was a way of life and I loved it like you wouldn't believe.

Being young and impressionable, I believed everything the counselors told me, which wasn't much because they all had the reverent taciturnity that goes with mirrored, birchlined shores and the piney-aroma of daybreaking fog which descended from heaven when the old man of the mountain was smoking his pipe somewhere in the mysterious prominences just behind our campground.

For two weeks out of every six weeks summer encampment the counselors put a bunch of kids in canoes and led them down Otter Creek into Lake Champlain and thence by portage into Lake George.

The ever-laconic counselors occasionally gave necessary instructions and sometimes barked stern commands, but they never preached.

"Look around you, kids, what do you think?" was all they seemed to say.

I can't speak for the other kids, but I looked around me and felt like crying it was all so beautiful; however being too old and self-conscious for that, I secretly dissolved myself in the mists of time while being careful not to miss the obligation of a single paddle stroke because although I suspected I was alone with my thoughts, I was not alone in the canoe.

Today Keewaydin's lonely outpost of eternal values on the shore of Lake Dunmore is one of the supreme accomplishments of mankind. Even in the 21st century it is still trailing 18th, 19th and early 20th century clouds of glory from the magnificent Age of Romanticism and—contravening all the technological logic in the book—they still, by God, use wood and canvas canoes.

(I send them money whenever I can, and if this book does well they will be in for a pleasant surprise.)

In 1928 or thereabouts I was voted Keewaydin's "best camper" and proudly brought home a gorgeous three-handled silver trophy about a foot high with my name engraved under the names of former winners.

My father placed it on a desk in the library where it remained until I had to return it the following summer.

Several years later when my father and I were complaining about each other I remarked that nothing I did ever pleased him, and conjured up the best camper trophy as an example. He had never even mentioned its existence, much less congratulated me.

"There was a good reason for that," he responded. "I didn't want you to get conceited."

"But dad," I said, "do you think I would have won that trophy if I had a tendency to conceit?"

From an unknown part of whatever I was I felt the sweet ascendant rush of self for the first time: I had bested my father in the area I admired most—his intellect, or more specifically—his deductive reasoning. The crafty king had been checkmated by the lowly pawn.

I waited a few moments for him to concede the game. My heart was beating like a triphammer.

And I waited.

Then I studied his face.

It was not arrogant.

It was not defensive.

It was just uncomprehending.

Clearly our problem was psychological. When I recalled the above traumatic exchange on the occasion of my suture escapade's dénouement I suddenly realized the childish game my father and I had been playing would not only never end but was potentially lethal. He couldn't help this and neither could I, but I had more to lose than he.

It was time to part while we were still friends.

The reason I have gone into all this detail is so my father, at long last, will know my side of the story. This is based on my conviction that he will take this book out of the library and also that the library exists.

It is inconceivable to me that a heaven could exist without a library containing this book.

» » » » »

In order to spare my father's feelings, I trumped up the excuse of a job opportunity and moved far away from him—800 miles, to be exact, to Louisville, Kentucky.

Operating on the belief that one should never lose sight of the bottom line, I had given a great deal of serious thought to where I would move and picked Louisville because I understood the duck hunting on the Ohio River was fantastic.

CHAPTER 25

The General Electric Limousine and the Fate

of Happiness in the Twenty-First Century

Progress is our most important product.
—General Electric advertising slogan

Progress is our most important problem.
—sign in General Electric engineering department

» » » » »

With just a handful of notable exceptions such as model airplane engines, pump shotguns and motorcycles, I think most technology is potentially boring, and my guess is that this is because it isn't alive.

This chapter states my case.

When I lived in Louisville I worked for eighteen years as an industrial salesman and made frequent calls at Appliance Park, the huge General Electric complex where all their major appliances were manufactured. GE provided a limousine and chauffeur to take visitors from one building to another because they were too far apart to make walking cost-effective for busy salesmen, though I was rarely too busy to take a little hike between buildings on a warm spring day or a snowy wintry one. That's how I kept in touch with the real world: that's how I kept my sanity. Besides, even from a business standpoint my theory of selling was that it wasn't how fast you got around, but how fast you were thinking *after* you got around and were sitting in a purchasing agent's or an engineer's office: that's what got results. Note that I said, "fast," not "slick". I was selling a fine product for a fine company and was proud of what I did. But what bothered me almost all my working life was that I had to spend so much time at it that could have been better spent, as Thoreau suggests, inspecting the color of the first crocus in spring or the quality of a snowstorm.

I particularly remember one bitterly cold, snowy morning when I had to stop and put chains on my company car. I was lying on my back in the snow under the car trying to hook up the inner chain links. The damn clasp was bent and my hands were so cold I kept dropping the chain in the snow so I could blow on my fingers. All sounds were muffled as the snow fell silently upon itself, creating a new world, inch by inch, just outside the complex anatomy of steel girders, bell housings and exhaust pipes which comprised my haven for the moment. Cold and miserable as I was lying in the snow in my good clothes, clothes so inappropriate to the purpose, it occurred to me that I was happier—far happier— being where I was and doing what I was doing than I would be a half-hour later sitting in a purchasing agent's office discussing money, aware that if I so much as hinted at the religious experience I'd just had I could have blown the whole deal. (This conflict between what I was and what I pretended to be eventually landed me in a mental hospital, but let me save that for later.)

For now let's get back to the GE limousine. It was a marvel of technology, but the only parts of the marvel I ever saw were the glamorous parts. It was loaded with power this and that. The windows were sexualized with a cosmetic tint. The latest music was always whispering a barely inaudible love lament which came from the heart of an audiocassette. The limo was a virtual entertainment center on wheels which the chauffeur could steer with one finger!

If, through some science fiction gimmick, that limousine and chauffeur could have been transported to the Acropolis around the year 400 BC no doubt Plato would have written *The Technocracy* rather than *The Republic* and Aristotle would have written a limo owner's manual rather than the *Poetics*.

But now let's forget science fiction as a literary genre and consider the fiction of *science* as the fact it actually is.

» » » » »

I am well aware that some readers are getting a little tired of my constant swipes at technology. Some even may consider me ungrateful in view of the pleasure I get out of many triumphs of technology (though I must say that gratitude is utterly wasted on machinery). Be that as it may, perhaps some readers are wondering what my qualifications are for setting myself up as an authority. Some may even consider my education invalid. I have no quarrel with that, since higher education initially created our dilemma.

My credentials as an authority on world woes and personal joys are not based on the intellect but came about by chance. The only advantage I have over you is that of an accidentally acquired perspective, and even this is only true if you are less than about 70 years old. The first twenty-six years of my life were lived in unmitigated joy and innocence. At the risk of being misunderstood I admit to worshipping beauty and finding it everywhere. Then one morning I had a traumatic experience. I was forced to witness the rape, torture and murder of a beautiful woman with a miraculous smile.

Yes, my mother.

The age of innocence was gone forever. Humankind had raped its own earth-mother at Hiroshima on August 6, 1945. My only claim as an authority is that I have lived on two earths, in two worlds. As of August 6th, 1945, I have lived my life with a worldview sadness that nothing can obliterate. We blew it, are still blowing it and there is no end in sight.

Perhaps all this will be inevitable. Perhaps there is really no such thing as innocence, but unless you have lived for a quarter of a century with nothing more to fear than getting run over by a cement truck because of your own stupidity, you can never really understand how sweet even the illusion of innocence can be, how this fact alters your concept of the quality life, and why you become out of synch with a culture that diverts itself from its self-induced fear with more of the technology that created the fear in the first place.

Meanwhile the latest spook on the block is the computer, whose self-generating complexities will soon be capable of outwitting world-class accountants as well as world class chess players. At the most inopportune time in human history, this may one day leave you staring at a blah-green screen behind which there resides a null-space or sub-space or vector space which, under infinitely complex and arcane transformations, is equal to the zero. This is all that remains of a non-human culture which, after outdistancing the collective human mind, was found not to be viable.

The brains which created the computer are colleagues of the brains which created the nuclear bomb. One is the sire of mega-destruction and the other of mega-confusion, and if you want to add a personal dimension to such juxtapositions, the guillotine makes the perfect image for the ultimate impact of science. What all these inventors have in common besides feverishly high I.Q.s is a curious lack of concern for eschatological consequences: the inventor of the guillotine was himself guillotined.

As Thoreau said, once you understand the principle . . . .

And as Robert Pirsig said in effect: Thoreau? Oh, that was another set of circumstances, another time—he had nothing to say that we can use.

» » » » »

If I claim that the limo is fiction—an illusion—because we play around with the idea that it is alive when it obviously isn't, you may well ask what all the fuss is about. After all, what is wrong with a little harmless word play on the fantasy that limos are alive?

If we anthropomorphize a puppy dog we are of course being ridiculous in pretending that it is human, but we are not being ridiculous in our assumption that its life impulses are identical to ours, that it has hopes and fears and responds to affection.

But how do we justify anthropomorphizing machinery which is incapable of responding to our affection because we created it out of inert materials? Isn't there something less than human in our tendency to give our cars tender loving care, to pat them affectionately on the hood, to speak to them—"c'mon, baby!"—and then abandon them to the used car lot or crusher without a second thought when they no longer suit our purpose? For this reason it seems to me the GE limo may be considered a fiction in the sense that it is not by any stretch of the imagination a natural companion for a strictly human relationship which includes such things as love, gratitude or joy in an early-morning snowstorm.

There is a cruel and ironic humor in the remark that when a teenager is making love to his girlfriend in the back seat of his car, it's not the girlfriend he's in love with, but his car.

I once asked the limo chauffeur a loaded question, and while I thought I knew the answer, I was nevertheless startled by the attitude accompanying it. I had long considered the limo, which operated only within a two-or-three-mile network of roads on General Electric's property, as a striking metaphor for the limited scope of twentieth century man despite all science's promises.

"What's it like to drive this fancy limo around all day, Dave?", I asked.

What follows I inferred from what his response:

It ruined Dave's day. It was unbelievably boring. He would far rather shovel coal all day. He no sooner got started than he had to stop. He no sooner stopped than he had to start up. The limo could go across the country at high speed but all he ever did was drive it slowly round and around a narrowly restricted circuit. The graphics were limited and unvaried. He had to make simple motions over and over. Despite its glamorous appearance and self-creating functions the limo wasn't doing anything, all by itself, to please him.

What he did say was "I'm not driving this limo down the street, Herb, it's driving me up the wall."

At this point the limo represents technology on a day-to-day level when the subtle enticing showroom smell of newness has evaporated, when it has worn out the welcome generated by the promises, and when it is unable to do something exciting *and unexpected* for us entirely on its own. Its limitation is identical to the musical limitation of a CD in which all the nuances of a live performance of music are forever cast in concrete: a pattern is emerging—life is systematically being replaced by a subtle and ingenious form of death.

Now let's give technology a break by asking a bunch of twelve-year-old kids if they would like to take turns driving the limo around the G.E. grounds on weekends. Wouldn't that be a blast for them? Of course it would. But for how long? At what point would the sophistication of their nervous and motor functions amount to overkill when applied to the simple repetitions of their driving movements? At what point would the sameness of the scenery pall? My guess is that is would be extremely unusual for a twelve-year-old kid to want to do that every weekend for six months, let alone five days a week fifty weeks a year for the rest of one's life, like Dave—if you want to get personal and serious about the magnitude of this disaster.

On the other hand, four years later when the kids get their licenses, they'll be begging for the family car until they can finally wrangle one of their own. Unaware of their fate, they will begin to repeat in principle the same deadly cycle which will get progressively worse as engineers make driving simpler and simpler, until, thanks to electronic tracking on super highways, it is completely automated.

At that point Dave's daily nightmare, by comparison, will seem like a Caribbean cruise.

In all the examples cited thus far note that the limo has hardly changed at all, give or take a new model or two. I structure my life in the technological world around the fact that I find this extremely important, because my life has been changing in significant ways ever since I can remember: you would only have to compare the first draft of this chapter with this end result to sense the truth of this.

Conversely, the life of a machine is not edited: if it develops too many untenable concepts or split infinitives it is hauled to a junkyard and crushed.

O.K. Suppose we rent the limo and chauffeur out to transport a bride and groom from their wedding reception to a swank hotel in another city. Now at last the limo is not only not boring but, in fact is so excitingly glamorous they remember their ride for the rest of their lives. Why? Because for the bride and groom the limo was not the main event. The main event was what was happening to them on a strictly human level while just happening to be in a limo.

This is the bottom line of my obsession to make technology work for me.

CHAPTER 26

What You Can Learn about Yourself by Trying

to Break the Coast-to-Coast Speed Record

on a Motorcycle

I enjoyed my 75th birthday more than all the rest combined, but I vividly love these jewels also.

The greatest single moment was when I rode out of my garage on my Dodgem like a wide-eyed kid with an inexhaustible supply of quarters in his leathers.

The greatest ten minutes was when I rode my dynamo for long incredible moments over the naked bodies of screaming virgins on my fateful way to Tucumcari.

The greatest month was when I rode 7,500 miles, one glorious tenth of a mile at a time, without ever looking back.

The greatest four months were when I wrote the first rough draft of this book, one crisis sentence after another, and in spite of my cat, Beemer, who insists on climbing up on my writing board and spreading himself across my manuscript as he is doing right now, just as he does every morning at about eleven o'clock. As I try to get a ballpointed word in edgewise, or rather paw-, nose—or tailwise, in that occult ways Siamese cats have, he tells me that I've got it all wrong and am working too hard and too long for one day.

There's nothing like a sybaritic cat to help you determine if you're taking your work too seriously.

» » » » »

For my 45th birthday celebration I took a two-week vacation to try to break the coast-to-coast speed record on my motorcycle. I really can't tell you why I wanted to do this except to say that I have always dearly loved competition, greatly missed playing team sports when my college days were over, and had been toying for several years with the idea of competing with the greatest adversary of all—Father Time.

In retrospect my record attempt probably also had something to do with a less grandiose challenge: I wanted to be as good a motorcyclist as my father was a businessman.

In 1964 the record was held by John Penton, who was also a legendary National Champion enduro rider. Although we weren't close friends, I knew him, rode on the same number with him on several national enduros, and discussed my plans to try to break his coast-to-coast record with him.

He was extremely helpful. He told me, for example, not to use an aftermarket exhaust system because a loud motorcycle will make the fuzz think you were going faster than you are. He also told me not to take the time to re-jet the carburetors when I rode over the Rocky Mountains but simply to disconnect the air filter. He told me things like this not only because that is the kind of guy he is but also because the bond among enduro riders is even greater than that between long-distance tourers, if you happen to be a touring biker and can imagine such a thing.

My project required an enormous amount of work. The first step was to get a complete physical, which I passed with flying colors. Then, when my doctor found out why I wanted a prescription for medication to keep me awake, he told me that what I was about to do was the most dangerous thing he could ever imagine anyone doing.

It's a funny world.

The most dangerous thing I could ever imagine anyone doing is going off an Olympic ski jump.

The reason I didn't consider my record attempt dangerous was because I didn't intend to go fast. I looked at it the way a tortoise looks at a hare. Also in the six years since John Penton's 1958 record, the route had been considerably shortened and was now almost all superhighway.

If we assume for the sake of simplicity that the new distance from New York to L.A. was 3,000 miles, I only had to average sixty miles an hour to do it in fifty hours, breaking John Penton's record by two hours, eleven minutes and one second.

The key to success, therefore, was not raw speed, but consistency, and for that I simply had to keep wide awake for fifty hours. While, however, keeping in mind John's serious problems with lack of sleep; he in fact had to stop for a considerable time because of double vision. The idea of using amphetamines bothered me because I was trying to prove what I could all by myself, not what could be done with an assist from the science of chemistry. For this reason I went to the library and researched the phenomenon of sleep.

The first thing I learned was that you can't store it up. If I had gotten ten hours sleep a night for a couple of weeks before the record attempt, it would not have done me any good.

What did me an immeasurable amount of good, however, was learning how the urge to sleep works. The human body uses many tricks to get what it wants. When it wants to sleep it releases a hormone that sends a message to the brain which makes life miserable until it gets what it wants. However, since the body can't think and because the reason the brain is not giving into sleep may be circumstantial, rather than willful or self-indulgent, the Creator wisely arranged the process so that the body does not release all its sleep hormone at once: the first shot is the biggest, but subsequent shots become weaker and weaker because the sleep hormone is produced far slower than it is used up in a lengthy sleep deficit caused by a prolonged survival crisis.

What this means is clear: if you force yourself to ride a motorcycle or drive your car far longer than you should without sleep, after about eighteen hours you are going to get drowsy, and not long after that you are going to be flat-out miserable. If you are cruising on a superslab at 75 mph you are in a life-and-death situation. There is no doubt about it. You cannot, under penalty of serious injury or death, think of *anything* other than staying awake. You must assume that there is a gun with a hair trigger at your temple which will go off if you so much as nod your head. This torment, this utter, unbearable, hell will last for approximately half an hour.

John Duthie told me that he had miraculously escaped serious injury. Once, while concentrating on staying awake late one night in his pick-up truck. He passed a curve where a few years before he had come across the wreck of a fire engine that had just over turned and exploded the stimulus of that recollection was so powerful that it broke his concentration, and as he started to day-dream about the burning fire engine, he instantly went to sleep and ran off the road.

In addition to what I learned at the library I also did a little medical theorizing on my own. For example, I decided that when the urge to sleep had me by the throat, it was beneficial to exercise by repeatedly standing on the pegs and sitting down because the increased circulation would probably help to flush the lethal hormone out of my system. I also doubt if anyone can go to sleep while exercising.

When the half-hour crisis is over you return to normal and feel great. The benefits lasts for about six to eight hours, and then—whamo!—you get another shot of hormonal misery. This time it is not as severe and it doesn't last as long. Now the chief danger is that you will relax your vigilance and assume you have it made. You don't. You will be playing Russian Roulette with a double-barreled shotgun and until they finally stop entirely they reoccur every eight hours or so.

Once I had a full understanding of the physiology, chemistry and psychology of sleep, I began to wonder if my body had any other sneaky tricks in store for an innocent guy trying to milk all the fun he could out of his 45th birthday ritual.

It occurred to me that I often got drowsy after eating a big dinner. I also remembered that it is hard to sleep on an empty stomach, and that the first thing an insomniac does when he gets up in the middle of the night is head for the refrigerator. I couldn't find anything in the library on this so again I did some freelance theorizing about various body parts, such as the stomach and the brain.

I have always been fascinated by the fact that human beings are half brain and half viscera. Not "about" half, but half. 50-50. If you don't think this is a fact, it may not be true in your case. However, since I'm writing this book I get to make the rules and one of the delights of this perfect set up of mine is that nobody, not even my cat, can tell me what's true and what isn't.

This is not to say I try to take advantage of my readers. If you are a college professor and insist that your brain-to-viscera ratio is 90-10, I'd be inclined to go along with you and perhaps be even be more generous and put your ratio at 99-1.

If you are a professional body builder and feel your ratio is 10-90 I'd go along with you too, though not before squeezing your biceps and asking you who wrote *The Transposed Heads*, which is Thomas Mann's allegorical study of the question.

The point I'm making is that we all tend to favor either the brain or the body. Our culture almost demands that we do this: it is rare for someone to earn a living with equal contributions from each.

Although the tendency to capitalize on either our physical or mental assets is natural and understandable, there is what I consider to be a profound synthesis. It is expressed in *mens sana in corpore sano*, or "a sound mind in a sound body," which you may recall goes way back to my Berkshire days.

That concept was by far the single most important benefit of my classical education.

I knew my bike would make it because Butler and Smith, the

BMW importer in New Jersey, generously donated a complete inspection and tune-up for my record attempt, so all I had to do was to prepare my body with the same dedication I lavished for my dirt bike riding. I took a weekend jaunt from Louisville to Montauk Point on Long Island and another to Key West, each time stopping for just four hours of sleep before coming straight home. Those trips convinced me breaking the record would be a piece of cake.

However, since I would be awake more than twice as long as I had been in either of my shakedown trips, and as the result of my freelance theorizing on body parts, I decided to play a little trick on my stomach. I assumed that if my body was hungry it would give me a shot of "awake hormone" because it would "know" that if I went to sleep it wouldn't get fed. To this end I mixed up my favorite formula for the high-energy gorp I ate on backpacking trips and kept it in a leather pouch tied to the handlebars. When my stomach started to grumble I let it grumble, on the assumption that the grumbling was the sound of the awake hormone being secreted. When it stopped making a fuss I took a couple of mouthfuls of gorp, but I made a point of letting my body be hungry the whole trip. I don't know if this helped me with my sleep problem—I suspect it did—but I never took any precious minutes out to eat or defecate the whole time.

There was one final body problem to deal with. Often I got "sick" a day or so before a big enduro. It wasn't anything I could put my finger on but I was sure I was ill. There is a name for this now but I didn't know it then. It's called pre-race anxiety. What's really bugging you is that you may be seriously injured the next day. That's why before enduros radios play soft music all through the night in the campgrounds as technology substitutes for mother-in-the-next-room.

My worst attack of pre-race anxiety came just before the 1952 Little Burr National Enduro when I got so sick I decided not to start, but at the last minute started anyway, figuring I could always quit after the first checkpoint if necessary.

Joan was waiting for me at that checkpoint.

"How do you feel?" she asked anxiously.

"Never better," I replied. "Why do you ask?"

That was the last time my body pulled that psychosomatic trick in an attempt to keep my brain from putting it at risk, or at least the last time it came within a country mile of succeeding.

» » » » »

I don't know how it works now, but back in 1964 you documented your record attempt by punching a time clock at the Western Union office in New York and getting it initialed. You bought your gas on a credit card and had the receipts initialed and your trip ended at the Western Union office in L.A., hopefully with a brass band and champagne.

As I walked out of the Western Union office in New York City at 5:00 A.M. my brain had the following dialogue with my body:

> Brain: Boy, body, old buddy, are we going to have fun!
>
> Body: Yeah, but at whose expense? If we wipe out you may go to heaven but if my heart stops pumping I ain't goin' nowhere.
>
> Brain: Your heart ain't—I mean isn't—going to stop pumping. Trust me. We're just going to take a leisurely 60 mile an hour trip to L.A.
>
> Body: What if I need sleep?
>
> Brain: I've covered that.
>
> Body: What if I need food?
>
> Brain: I've covered that too.
>
> Body: I don't like it. Besides, I'm sick.
>
> Brain: You're not sick. You're bluffing.
>
> Body: What if I have to go to the bathroom?
>
> Brain: I'll let you, I promise.
>
> Body: Well suppose I refuse to cooperate?
>
> Brain: Look, if I tell you to put the binders on, you damn well better do it pronto—it's your ass as well as my ego.

Body: I still don't like it. Don't I have any rights at all?

Brain: Of course you do, old buddy. Haven't I taken excellent care of you for 44 years, 363 days?

Body: Yes—

Brain: Then what are we arguing for?

Body: Because what we are about to do is dangerous. Do you remember the time you ran me into that rock on the Jack Pine? My foot *still* hurts.

Brain: That was a dirt bike competition in the woods and this is all superhighway.

Body: Yeah. That means we'll just be going that much faster when—

Brain: Look, I don't have time to argue because I've already punched the Western Union time clock. Now please walk me over to my bike.

Body: Make me just one concession and I will.

Brain: I'll do better than that. I'll make two. Do everything I want for the next 45 hours, and then I'll buy you a steak dinner and get you laid at the first opportunity.

Body: You will? (He starts walking me over to my bike.)

Brain: Of course I will, as long as that last concession is approved by my superego.

Body: What's a superego? I know you have a super one, but exactly what is it?

Brain: It's the brain function that has to do with conscience, you brute.

Body: Brute eh? Boy oh boy, brain, have you got a lot to learn.

» » » » »

I hadn't been into the run an hour before I was in trouble. Riding 3,000 miles at a numb-steady 65 miles per hour was boring boring boring. It was the last way I wanted to spend the two days I'd been waiting 16,424 days to turn into a fantastic celebration.

That son-of-a-bitch body of mine was trying to trick me by feeding me low energy stimuli, figuring I'd realize I wasn't having any fun and stop and buy it a steak lunch and fix it up with the waitress. What pissed me off was that, although it couldn't think at all, it thought it was smarter than I am, and was always humping for 10% more than its fair share of us.

I have to say that my basic record-attempt miscalculation was that averages really don't interest me. If I want to cross a river and someone tells me its average depth is three feet, I don't want that to mean the depth varies from six inches to four feet, because those are just statistics. I don't care how deep it is otherwise, but somewhere I want that sucker to be over my head. I want to have to learn to swim or hollow out a tree. If a river isn't deep enough, somewhere, to make me take lessons and practice doing something important I don't know how to do, I might as well start walking the long way around.

I was carrying enough gasoline so that my first stop was to be a parking lot just off the turnpike in Cleveland, Ohio, 486 miles from New York City. The local BMW dealer was to rendezvous with me there at 12:00 P.M., seven hours after my 5:00 A.M. start, but he agreed to get there an hour earlier just in case. I felt like hugging him when I showed up at eleven-thirty and found that he already had everything spread out and ready for my pit stop.

In addition to an open tool box, he had placed a basin, a bar of soap, a wash cloth, a towel and a large thermos of warm water on the hood of his pickup. I'm not into hugging guys I've just met, but I'm not ungrateful either. Despite the fact that I wouldn't ever have considered abluting at a time like that, I didn't want to hurt his feelings, so I washed my face and hands. Also, under the circumstances it seemed like a smart move to try to parlay cleanliness into Godliness.

At my second five hundred mile fuel stop an incident occurred which turned out to be a predictable reaction on the part of gas station attendants. I will get to it in a moment but first let me set it up with a reminiscence which will also be an example of how I amused myself during the long hours in the saddle with no TV.

» » » » »

Back in the days when I was heavy into antique automobiles, my friend Bill Chescheir had a 1924 Stanley Steamer. It looked like an ordinary car, but instead of an engine under the hood it had a humongous boiler with gate-valved and asbestos-wrapped pipes going all over the place. It was fired by a kerosene heater. Because the engine was very small, it was mounted between the frame rails under the seat, and since it ran on steam, it had a thirty-gallon water tank under each running board. What looked like a radiator up front was actually a condenser where the steam exhaust was cooled down and partially returned as water to the two tanks.

When Bill was low on water he liked to pull into a gas station and ask the attendant to top off his "radiator." The guy would get a water can and empty it in the condenser and then he'd get another. And another. Then he'd get a hose. After the hose had been going five minutes or so, he'd walk over to the spigot and twist it to make sure it was turned on all the way. Then he'd get down on one knee and peer under the car to see if the water was leaking out into the street where he couldn't see it. Nine times out of ten the attendant would go through this routine without comment, although each stage of his metamorphosis, from curiosity to bewilderment to consternation to dread, was clearly recorded on his face.

When the ten-gallon condenser and two thirty-gallon tanks were full, Bill would tell the poor guy he wanted to buy a gallon of kerosene.

"Sorry, sir," the attendant would say, "we don't sell kerosene."

"That's okay," Bill always said, "but will you please check the oil?"

Now, dear reader, do you know enough about my friend Bill Chescheir to understand why on our way back to Louisville from

Topeka I wouldn't let him ride the same 1963 BMW I was riding in my cross country record attempt?

At my third five-hundred mile stop for gas the attendant got down on one knee while I was refueling all the tanks through the main tank.

"What's the matter, son?" I asked him.

"There's something wrong, sir," he replied anxiously, "no motorcycle will take this much gas."

On the theory that it is better to be wrong than never to have witnessed the impossible, I left him with that belief.

» » » » »

Three hundred miles from Albuquerque disaster struck. One of my auxiliary gas tanks, which I had picked up used at a farm implement store, had apparently been stored with gas in it, which apparently evaporated and left a varnish residue. This had finally worked its way through the two in-line filters and the valves on the port cylinder stopped working.

I had ridden 1,720 miles in slightly over 24 hours. It took me ten hours to go the next 300 miles because the bike was only running on one cylinder and because my own pushrods had packed it in as well.

Why did I give up? I think it was because there is an ingenious falling off of determination the further you go, it is subtle because it is not a direct desire to give up but rather a willingness to quit as the result of obstacles that come along. I might have gotten the cylinder to work by removing the valve cover and manipulating the stuck valves by hand with a generous application of Bardall to the gas, but instead I just gave up. Another subtle excuse to stop was that I wanted to break the record by a substantial margin, despite the fact that, even though a record is not official unless it breaks the old one by over half an hour, breaking it by ten minutes would have been a real accomplishment. The reason for giving up may seem justified at the time, but that decision may be strongly influenced by your body and your subconscious crying out, in their voiceless way, for rest, for sleep, for an end to the whole inhuman struggle.

At 8:00 A.M. I left my bike at the Albuquerque BMW shop which was run by a very capable woman who, among other things, wouldn't let her customers lallygag with the mechanics while they were working on their bikes. This is the way it should be when you stop to think about it. I hung around the shop all day reading old motorcycle magazines, with no particular desire to sleep, and spent the night at the service manager's house, talking to Jim Fauci about motorcycles until well past my bedtime, when, according to Jim, I fell asleep in the middle of a sentence while looking at my watch!

This wasn't true: I had found out what I had set about to find out and, having satisfied my curiosity, decided it was time to go to sleep.

I had been wide awake and fully functioning for exactly fifty-five hours.

The next morning a mechanic finished overhauling my port cylinder for a defect not of BMW's making, and he also installed a sexy fiberglass fairing, an extremely rare item in 1964. While all this was being taken care of, the memorable lady dealer let me borrow a small, ladylike R-50 BMW.

I rode the R-50 way up on one of the hillsides surrounding Albuquerque and witnessed the thunderstorm I described earlier, unaware that thirty years later, almost to the day, I would be celebrating another birthday, one in which I was not trying to stay awake on a motorcycle, but trying to stay alive any way I could.

There was no essential difference in the rituals.

» » » » »

About a week later around 10:00 P.M. I picked up my Ohio Turnpike ticket at the Western toll booth. I had been riding east for over 35 hours with only three quick stops for petrol and another to put on my rainsuit.

At a lonely 3:00 A.M. the previous morning, riding in wheat country, I saw a thunderstorm up ahead surrounded by vast prairie moonbeams. Dark violet whirlwinds scudded across the horizon but it was light enough to see the wheat bending and roadside puddles rippling in the wind gusts that were becoming personal and viperish. I got very excited as I always do when turning the pages of a real-life gothic novel. The contrast between the ageless storm and the sleek black 1963 miracle ghosting me across the sweet, dark, deserted earth at an ungodly speed was almost more than I could take in. I hadn't just won a million bucks, I was cashing in on a cosmic lottery and didn't know whether to laugh, cry, telephone my mother or just go mad.

Instead, I pulled into a falling-down Shell gas station, abandoned in the middle of nowhere, and put my bulky rainsuit on, like an idiot, before I had taken my leak.

» » » » »

The Ohio Turnpike was in my back yard. I had it made. As the result of my many years of enduro riding, I was a past master at keeping time in my head while riding a motorcycle at speed. With only 625 miles to go I knew exactly how fast I had to push it for the next hundred miles so that I could ride the last 525 miles well within the speed limit and still arrive at the Western Union office in New York City 45 hours after leaving L.A.

Not 45 hours and one second.

Exactly 45 hours: if I arrived ten minutes early, I'd wait ten minutes before punching the clock. Savoring those ten minutes would be the triumphant climax of my forty-fifth birthday celebration.

This may come as a surprise to you, dear reader, but I wasn't interested in breaking the coast-to-coast record. Not really. Why should I be? It would only be broken by someone else, just as I was about to break John Penton's six-year-old record.

The formal record would only be a statistic. I had already broken a more meaningful record because I had probably not only ridden a motorcycle from L.A. to the western toll booth on the Ohio Turnpike faster than any motorcyclist had covered that distance before, but I had done it under the most trying circumstances imaginable. I had been forced to ride through the mayhem of a 3:00 A.M. thunderstorm when what I wanted to do more than anything in the world was to sit with my back against an abandoned gasoline pump and watch the total storm, from the first lightning flash silhouetted against eternity to the reappearance of the first moonbeam. I wanted every last drop of that storm. I wanted to be super-saturated with humid, earthy beauty.

But I had miles to go before I slept.

I was trying to set a record for thanks and figured an exact hour's worth of super intense living for each of the 45 years I had been privileged to be alive was as much as even a deeply religious person could reasonably be expected to give.

And if circumstances prevented me from doing what I set out to do, so what? John Penton could keep his well-earned motorcycling speed record for a few more years and Henry Thoreau could keep his well-earned philosophical gratitude record for eternity while I settled for a cool one, a kiss from Joan, a soft bed and the ecstasy of feeling my total self float mystically away into the Tristanesque world of non-being—of surcease from my never-ending struggle.

CHAPTER 27

How I Became a Tycoon

I have sometimes wondered if my lack of interest in money beyond a reasonable amount was legitimate or whether the truth was that I lacked ambition.

When I was young and searching for basic answers I read the results of a survey in which people were asked if they were satisfied with their net annual incomes. Regardless of the income, in almost every case the answer was that no, they were not, but that they would be *if they had just a little bit more.*

I thought about my situation and decided that was exactly the way I felt.

This was another of the great revelations in my life. For starters, it bothered me that I felt the way everyone else did because that made me a statistic rather than a self-determining human being with fingerprints and a brain to match.

Nevertheless the more I fretted the question the more convinced I became that my knee-jerk response was not me talking, it was the System, shouting.

Clearly, as the survey proved, if people in every income bracket would be satisfied if they just had a little more money, except for brief periods just after they moved up to a higher bracket, they would always be suffering a nagging discontent. I felt this was an unacceptable way to spend one's time on earth because not only was the happiness-ratio bass-ackwards, but in order to get yourself in that predicament you had to work your ass off.

The wording of the survey question also bothered me. Considering the value my mother taught me to place on this living adventure, almost from the beginning I wasn't interested in just being satisfied. There is a world of difference between being satisfied with your lot and being positively happy, so I was always on the lookout for ways to rejoice, yes, damn it, to exult.

To reach such states there was almost no limit to my ambition. Besides, my happiness functioned independently of surveys.

If Jim Strader woke me up out of a sound sleep at midnight with the news that the ducks were in at Cloverport, I'd be at his house at 4:00 A.M., duckboat in tow. And if the thermometer was in the teens and it was windy and spitting snow these were bonuses: this is the stuff a duck hunter's exultation is made of.

A box of store-bought shotgun shells cost roughly the same as a ticket to the movies, but mine cost about half that because I reloaded my own. Not only was the cost trifling, but the reloading was fun and gave me deep satisfaction because it was part of the ritual.

Was I happy with my income?

You're darn tootin' I was.

» » » » »

Ever since the night of the day Tony's dying horse squirted blood on my side, life has exceeded my expectations. Since that night I have been aware every day, sometimes every hour, sometimes for minutes on end, that life is not only beautiful but the earth on which I live it out is trancendently lovely as well, and that not only is there such a thing as paradise, but I am living there every moment—even as I write this sentence—a process which I am therefore deliberately stretching out beyond the limits dictated by style and which, by a supernatural coincidence, will be concluded with the information that the woman I love just bought me a bowl of oatmeal and dried bananas—with the affectionate, nose-wrinkling smile I can never see too often—and I am eating breakfast now as I write and it is nectar for the Gods.

Such moments give me reason to suspect that the forces controlling the galaxies and their myriad sheets of raindrop tenants are benign. These forces may even be helpful, perhaps even to the point of arranging for additional otherworldly vacations for those who most obviously are grateful for any given paradise. (I think the possibility of this is greater than that of forcing the issue with ever more aggressive rockets.) But the possibility of my fanciful dénouement is ultimately irrelevant because I am, as I write these combinations of words which have never been written before, not only momentarily immortal, but existing in an uncloyable paradise for the foreseeable future.

I look around at my paradise.

Our tawny-necked Siamese cat Beemer is lying on the Persian rug in front of me, graceful even in sleep. The huge wall across the room is solid with books: just one of them— *Walden*—is giving me material for this and perhaps a few adjacent pages. On the wall to my left there is a photograph of its author in a gilded oval frame: *stand up and take a bow, Henry David.* Below him a TV set is squatting unused on an antique table, like a relic of a once-proud mechanistic civilization that collapsed in its own excesses, the button that turns it on, and life off untouched for four years.

On the right wall there is the head and cape of a magnificent stone ram I shot in the summer of its ninth year and ate that winter, thus eliminating for it the certainty of losing its teeth within a year or so and becoming too weak to defend itself against stalking wolves bent on eating it alive.

Below the ram's head is a photograph of me taken on my fifty-fifth birthday, holding the ram's head off the ground, not in selfish triumph, but rather at peace with the brutal facts of life and death as I had observed them for over half a century. Just behind its shoulder you can see the bloody mark where my 130 grain .308 bullet entered the ram's body in the absolute prime of its life, mushroomed through its heart and killed it compassionately in less than ten shock-numbed, seconds.

This unforgettable moment took place 125 miles into the

wilderness by float plane from the nearest isolated settlement, and 175 river miles back out by freight canoe; and the photograph was taken 2,000 feet above stratus clouds. It took a day to backpack up the mountain, a week to locate a legal ram, two mountain climbing days to pack the meat out, a day to smoke and preserve it and ten long scary days to paddle back to civilization on the swollen and rapids-infested Tuchodi River.

The above may seem like going to a heck of a lot of trouble to obtain meat just because it wasn't available at supermarkets, but my ram was special. It had not been shot with hormones to make it heavy on the stockyard scales or with lifeless substances to make its meat red, and it had not fed on green-looking stuff grown with chemical fertilizers and sprayed with toxic pesticides, and it didn't get its water from galvanized tubs filmed with dust from passing pick-up trucks, but from skywater condensed as dew on unmolested plants which grew where clouds grow.

Spending my birthday the way I did was my way of expressing gratitude for the gift of being able to do it. I'm sure the ram would have thanked me if he had studied wildlife biology or, lacking that, if he had retained memories of the sight of starving rams being eaten alive by wolves and had the anguish-ridden ability to foresee his ultimate destiny, as I can.

Suppose—not seriously, but just for laughs—you learned, after reading this book, that I had been killed instantly in a motorcycle crash. I'd rather you didn't assume it was a blessing because it was all over in a flash, like a bullet in the heart.

Why?

Because I am not a dumb animal, that's why.

I do not want, nor do I court, a technological death. I don't want to die riding my motorcycle and I wouldn't be caught dead watching TV. I want it all. I want to be eaten alive by the wolves of my imagination. I want to go off in a puff of horror or beatitude, as the case may be.

Ever since I learned from a little known and unpopular book

of Mark Twain's that there is no sexual intercourse in heaven, wild horses couldn't drag me up there.

When all is said and done, I'd settle for an eternity in which I am forever holding the scope crosshairs of my .308 on the heart-lung area of a mountain sheep, with my finger on the trigger of life and death.

Above the clouds.

Alone.

In a paradise of my own making.

» » » » »

For about twenty-five years after college I earned my living pretty much as I would have if I had been an orphan.

Except for two things.

The first was that I had a college education. I could not have gotten the well-paying job which I had for eighteen years without it. There is no doubt about it, knowledge is money. That is why it always grieves me to see kids dropping out of high school, believing they have a lock on smartness, convinced they're getting a head start in the business world, when in fact they are making a major decision when they're too young to see the whole picture.

I feel I owe some of my readers an apology for what I have just written and admit that my situation was different. In my case it was assumed that I would go to college, and it was also assumed that I would go to law or medical school if I wanted to. In not taking advantage of these opportunities, what was I but a high school dropout in principle, though on a higher level? Surely if I had become a lawyer or doctor I would have earned more money.

The difference, I suppose, is that I made my decision when I was much older, had observed the happiness quotient in rich, not-so-rich and downright poor families, and concluded that wealth and poverty were both best avoided because they tended to destroy personal freedom and were anxiety-producing. Within the above parameters, I could not honestly say that I saw a direct connection between the amount of money a person had and his or her happiness.

And as far as being a lawyer or a doctor was concerned, they never tell you the truth until it's too late and you've already become one. The only kind of law that wouldn't be as boring as reading a dictionary in a language you didn't know would be to be a criminal trial lawyer, but I could not stomach legally defending a murderer I knew was guilty even though I do not believe in capital punishment, as for being a doctor, who wants to look at naked bodies all the time and be on call twenty-four hours a day? It wasn't the extra learning that turned me against law and medicine, it was the feeling that my work would dominate the living I wanted to do. Desire to help others never entered into my decision because there were waiting lines for doctor jobs and besides if I carried this "do-good-principle" to its logical conclusion I could have with equal virtue become an undertaker.

When I got out of college I didn't stop learning. If I were to distill the essence of what my four years at St. Lawrence did for me, I'd say that they taught me the delights of the learning process. Practically all the literary allusions I use in this book came from books I read after college—books I read purely for the pleasure of acquiring knowledge and because there was nothing I would rather be doing at the time—no, not even making money. Each book taught me at least one thing worth remembering.

I once heard a movie critic remark on the radio that if a movie contains just one unforgettable scene it is a great movie. This struck me as an important truth, because there is so little worth remembering in our pathologically active culture.

Books are part of a diametrically-opposed culture in which they have traditionally been considered so important they are made available to everyone free in public libraries.

You don't watch books. A book is a process that takes place entirely within your mind. Your eyes are just innocent bystanders. I rarely read a book that doesn't have an unforgettable concept in it, or edge material, or that doesn't teach me something about writing. In a book you can slip through a time warp at the limit of ordinary experience into a world you could never know by any other means. Books are reminders that life is a process: you stop turning their pages at your peril. They are an affirmation of the belief that the human mind does not have to change just because it is a well-established fact that computers are better for the economy than ballpoint pens, and in that connection a good book is like a fertile island beyond the horizon in a world gone mad, surfing Miami Beach for grains of sand.

» » » » »

The other condition that made the earning of my living different from that of an orphan was that I knew at an early age I would one day inherit money. I had no way of knowing how much but had reason to believe it would be a considerable amount.

This is a touchy subject. Its taboo-rating approaches that of incest. The only reason I can see for this is because the need for love is always at odds with the lust for money. Isn't it reasonable to assume that if a man denies some of his pleasures to leave money for his son when he dies, that as part of that beneficent process he would sit down with his son and explain how much money he can expect to get, and discuss openly and practically what impact it will have on later life? Wouldn't such things as the life expectancy of the father and the age of the son enter into the planning of the son's career? If such factors were discussed openly, all sorts of benefits appear. Suppose for example a well-to-do father had a son late in life who was a talented athlete and who wanted a well-paying career in sports which would end when he was in his late thirties: wouldn't the knowledge that he would have a livable income after his sports career was over spare the son anxiety over his future as his days as a professional athlete inexorably closed in on him?

When my father retired from the Donnelley Corporation he was given two retirement benefit options. The first one was to get a single, very large lump sum. The second was to get a much smaller annual income for as long as he lived. My father, a whiz at finance, made all the actuarial and financial calculations. Then he entered a human factor into the mathematics. He went to two doctors and asked each one how long he could reasonably be expected to live. They both told him he probably had a long time to go. He then opted for the lesser annual income, lived well into his eighties, earned a great deal more money than if he had taken the other option, and no doubt enjoyed life more and suffered less anxiety because of a well-researched decision he made when he took early retirement at 64.

The difference between the way my father planned his retirement when Donnelley held the purse strings and the way I had to plan my career when my father held the purse strings lay somewhere in a cultural no-man's-land. No one attitude is right for the simple reason that they are constantly changing. However the taboo against a son discussing his inheritance openly and frankly with his father never *was* right and is long overdue for change. The error probably began with the religious scam that money was evil unless it was given spiritual value by donating it to a church. It seems to me quite clear that this is a form of coercion by guilt. If a son asks his father about his inheritance he is accused of being guilty of loving money more than his father. But suppose this is in fact true? Suppose the father, realizing his son loves his money more than him, disinherits his son? Isn't the father guilty of a similar transgression? Isn't money in both cases the cause of the lovelessness?

I don't know whether my father loved money for its own sake or not. I'm inclined to think he didn't, that in fact he got his deepest pleasure out of many things it doesn't take wealth to possess. I also think he was driven by the *fascination* of business, but only up to a point. He was a hard worker, but by no means a workaholic. He once remarked that workaholics were people who liked to work more than they liked to think about more efficient ways of getting what they wanted. In his later years he told me that as you get older it gets harder and harder to get out of bed and go to work.

Perhaps this is significant: when the work itself no longer was fun, he quit—a year earlier than necessary.

Sometimes I wonder what my father would think if he knew that at the age of eighty I often shut the alarm clock off a few minutes before it is set to awaken me at 6:00 A.M., and that I bounce out of bed and can't wait to get started doing what I am doing right now, not for you, dear reader—with all due respect—but for me, for the pleasure of retrieving odd scraps of information from the convolutions of my brain, dusting them off, and offering them to you with no goal in mind other than that they might make you chuckle, or raise your eyebrows, or perhaps wonder if you have missed out on some activity that is still within reach. Money doesn't enter into what I am doing this moment: if it did this book could never have been written.

Be all this as it may, I couldn't bring myself to say, *even with a smile*: "I love you, daddy, but I've got to know how much money I get when you kick off so I can plan my life." As a college graduate with a BA in literature, it would have been uncouth, lacking in taste and sensibility. On the other hand, it might have transcended both formal literary education and our moribumd static culture and reached my father's heart through the fine, gold-braided wires of the imagination—through the obviousness of its ironic excess. It might have been my way of demonstrating my worth, of matching the imaginative excess I admired so much in my father's conversation.

The reason I never brought up the subject was because the taboo was simply too formidable. That frigging taboo cut my love for my father and his love for me right down the middle: it did not permit us to communicate on a level which would have brought us all the benefits of loving someone honestly. In retrospect, I know it was not a limitation in either of us. Instead, it was simply not in the stacked-deck cards of our common culture, so we just shadow boxed with each other.

» » » » »

When I first started my working life my inheritance didn't figure into my calculations at all. It was too far in the distant future. Then as I moved along from job to job, it became apparent in a few short years that I could easily make more than enough money to be happy, particularly because I preferred tents to large houses. I had no desire to be president of anything, because I felt if I were I wouldn't be my own boss. Work was a necessary evil that I put up with because that was simply the way things were.

I define work as *doing one thing when I'd rather be doing something else*. My problem was, however, that I couldn't think of anything I liked to do that would bring me an income commensurate with the standard I assumed my father expected of me. There is no money for an average person like me, at least, in reading, listening to music, hunting, building model airplanes or taking canoe or motorcycle trips.

However, after a few false starts I finally wound up in a job that, in some ways, and as long as I was young, was the perfect compromise.

I had been selling farm implements in the Louisville area and enjoyed that job because my work took me out into the country, but I wasn't getting where I thought I ought to be: I was only where I wanted to be. However, I was vaguely restless and increasingly aware that I lacked ambition.

One day I registered with an employment agency and the next day they called me about a rare opportunity coming right up and that I qualified for it because I was a college graduate. The company interviewed applicants for two days, and I was one of the six who had their expenses paid to Chicago for more screening, and I ended up with the job.

After a seven-week training program I was given a company car, a respectable salary, a commission and an expense account. The night before leaving for home I went out to dinner with some seasoned salesmen who were in Chicago for a sales conference and the subject of expense accounts came up. They gave me the lowdown on how to make extra money padding an expense account. They also told me how to handle the flack when you got caught with your fingers too deep in the till.

I took it all in. I even made notes.

When I got back to Louisville I cheated on my expense accounts from the very beginning, except that instead of cheating my company, I cheated myself. I stayed in the seediest motels I could find. I bought the cheapest gas. I charged half as much for my meals as I had paid for them. I took customers out to lunch and didn't put the bill on my expense account. I forgot to charge the company for minor repairs on its car.

After a couple of months I got a call from my district manager in Cincinnati. He was very upset.

"Herb," he said, "you've got to do something about your expense accounts. They're too good. You're making all of us look like criminals."

For the next eighteen years I financed all my hunting trips, my antique car rallies and my motorcycle trips from the overages accumulated from my expense accounts. Many of them were so bald-faced wicked I was a little concerned about finally getting nailed. Nevertheless they were never questioned.

Why? Because once a reputation for honesty is established it is hard to refute, or because most businessmen, unlike artists, lack imagination, or because they don't read books containing first principles; perhaps it was a combination of all three of the above.

How did I know a reputation for honesty is hard to refute? By reading books dealing with the making and breaking of reputations. Thomas Hardy's *The Mayor of Casterbridge* is such a book: it is subtitled "The Story of a Man of Character."

How did I know businessmen lack imagination? By reading the "Bawl Street Journal", the April Fool's edition of Wall Street Journal, in which corporations insert cliché ridden, banal and downright unfunny ads to prove they are human and wind up proving they don't even understand irony, the first principle of imagination.

How did I know businessmen don't read books containing first principles? Because such books never mention money.

How did I come up with the principle behind the idea that was to finance my recreation for eighteen years? It was in one of the books I read after college dealing with the creative process, and while my friends were stealing peanuts on their expense accounts, they were all telling me I should improve myself by watching the Discovery Channel.

» » » » »

Having thus arranged for the financing of my recreation, the next step was to turn my full-time job into a part-time job so I would have the time to recreate myself.

I knew my job had the potential for what I was after. My territory was Kentucky and Southern Indiana and the company was located in Chicago. I rarely ever had any contact with it. They didn't know whether I got out of bed or not, and it was clear that they were not the least bit interested in my personal life. I was just one of about 125 red pins on a map of the United States. All I had to do was give them what they wanted. Their sights were low: all they wanted was money.

For the first five years or so I worked hard, built up my territory, and gave them what they wanted. Predictably, I kept getting raises, my commissions increased, and I was hooked into a profit-sharing program. Everything was great.

Then General Electric decided to build all its major appliances in Louisville, and the packaging of those products consumed prodigious amounts of the product I was selling.

For me and for everyone else selling what I was selling, this was like manna from heaven. As the enormous plants went up, year after year, it was obvious that GE would use far more of our product than the rest of my territory combined, instead of working hard, for the next few years I worked at white heat, and, one after another, I got all of the business in each plant as it began operations.

Then it happened.

One day I got a call from the sales manager. He was upset. A customer of mine who used $100 of our product a year, had been having trouble reaching me and had called the main office to complain.

"Herb," the sales manager said, "you've got to realize that our smallest customer is as important as our largest one."

I was tempted to ask him if he came to that conclusion because of the smallness of his brain. I mean, I was *really* tempted. I'm sure I could have gotten away with it because after all they only wanted money and they were getting truckloads of it from their red pin in Louisville.

Fortunately reason prevailed.

Instead of telling the sales manager what I thought of his grasp of first principles, I took my wife, my $100-a-year customer and his wife out to a fancy dinner at the Brown Hotel. Although the bill came to $65.45, I rounded it off to $100 when I put it on my expense account, with full knowledge that a pat amount like that would look fishy. This was the riskiest expense account caper I had pulled up to that time but I believed in poetic justice too much to deny myself the pleasure.

My expense form was approved without a hitch: obviously my expense accounts had never been filed among those which had to be checked with a fine-tooth comb, so armed with this knowledge I gave myself a 10% weekly expense-account raise for the rest of my tenure with the company.

I had found my niche in life. Without offending my sense of moral responsibility, I was as free from the System as I could reasonably expect to get.

From then on I worked hard—around the clock, when necessary, but including my two-weeks, paid vacation, I managed to take 75 days off each year. (This was far short of the three months' work per year it took Thoreau to get the basic necessities of food, shelter, and clothing, but then Thoreau wasn't into dirt bikes, hi-fi's and antique automobiles, to say nothing of a wife and kids.)

This arrangement suited me fine. I knew the difference between what I could do and what I was doing might keep me from being called to Chicago for a management position, but I also knew they probably wouldn't want to risk taking me away from a proven record in the field for a management position I might not be able to handle.

It didn't seem to me to make much difference in the long run whether I gave the company my all or just the part of me that didn't matter.

» » » » »

I marched happily, if somewhat out-of-step, to Thoreau's drummer for several years, and then in the space of a few short months the orchestration changed to that of Berlioz's "Fantastic Symphony," specifically the episode known as 'The March to the Scaffold,' which ends with a slithering orchestral rendition of the falling of a guillotine blade.

My troubles began when I was called into Boris Pressman's office on an urgent matter. Boris had been chiefly responsible for enormous savings in packaging as the result of the use of a revolutionary design of corrugated carton. The carton was being closed and sealed with our product, but changes in the way major appliances were designed and assembled would shortly result in an increase in assembly-line speed.

Boris told me that preliminary time and motion studies showed that our manually tensioned machines would not be fast enough to handle the increased production speed.

What, Boris wanted to know, could I do about it?

I knew that no one in our industry had an electric tool but that our engineers in Chicago had been developing one for several months.

My first step was to call the home office and get the latest scoop, but instead of useful information all I got was flack.

"You salesmen are all alike," the head of the engineering department fumed. "You're hired to sell what we've got, not to stand around with your finger up your ass while we design products for the future . . . . Look, I don't care how big your account is or how much is at stake. We're not about to let you have a prototype pneumatic tool . . . . No, I can't even tell you when they'll be available. Every salesman we've got keeps hounding me for these tools . . . . Look, you're just going to have to stand in line . . . ." CLICK. He'd hung up.

Thanks a lot pal.

In an ironic way, I meant it. Without realizing what he had done, our chief engineer had just solved Boris Pressman's problem.

I had been aware for some time that the assembly line speed was about to increase and that our machines would soon become obsolete: I had done time-and-motion studies on my own. The answer was obviously to have a machine that tensioned our product automatically, rather than manually. I tried to figure out how it might be done but without success, because I was thinking in terms of a bulky electric motor.

The key word in my call to our engineering department was "pneumatic."

As soon as I hung up I dialed a friend who sold pneumatic tools.

"Hey Joe," I said, "could you let me have the loan of a pneumatic tool for a week or two? I can't promise anything but I'm into something that could do you some good."

"Sure, Herb," he said, "how many do you want? Want me to drop 'em by your house?"

"Oh, that'd be great. How about tomorrow? I only need one."

"Can't make it tomorrow, Herb. Gotta take the kids to the State Fair. How about Sunday?"

Sunday it was.

That's how guys in the trenches talk to each other, and they don't even work for the same outfit.

I was at a machine shop when it opened on Monday morning, and, tense with excitement, I rushed to explain my problem to the owner before he had even unlocked his shop door.

Tense with excitement, I began to explain my problem to the owner of a machine shop Monday morning while he was unlocking his door.

"Wait a minute. Wait a dad-boned minute," he said, "for Christ's sake let me go inside and take off my coat."

He was an old guy, but I noticed the suggestion of a smile: he knew what it was once like to be eager.

I put our tool and Joe's pneumatic tool on his desk.

"Can you take the handle off this tool and adapt the pneumatic tool in its place?" I asked.

He chucked our manual tool in his rough hands and turned it around as if he were admiring a glass of fine wine.

"Yes, I can," he said.

"When?" My excitement was increasing.

"Two, maybe three, weeks—I'm kinda busy right now."

"Would it make any difference if I told you that if you can do it, and it works, you would almost certainly get an order for twenty-five more, just for starters, from GE?"

"How soon do you need it?" he asked.

"How soon do you want an order for twenty-fivefrom GE?" I smiled.

"I really can't have it for you until Friday," he said with finality written all over him.

"A.M.?"

"No, P.M."

"Noon?"

He shrugged. "Noon," he said.

And then: there was a touch of father-and-son in the eye contact above our grins, cutting through that stunted aspect of my life like a knife.

At eleven o'clock on Friday I stopped by to see how things

were going.

The new tool looked great, and, though it took some getting used to, it worked perfectly.

While all my hunting buddies were down in the country for the ritualistic opening of the dove-hunting season, I spent the weekend in my garage using an air compressor Joe dropped off, I practiced with the pneumatic tool until I was blue in the face.

As I worked hour after hour with the new tool, the accumulated guilt of my years of expense-account larceny gradually evaporated and left me morally cleansed. I was once again an honorable but dull and predictable member of The System. Still, I felt inferior: I could never match the many months of larcenous, unnecessary busywork which high-priced engineers were systematically billing to our common employer.

Monday morning Boris and I went out on the line and I demonstrated the new tool.

I could hear him behind me sighing with relief, and when my demonstration was almost over I looked over my shoulder and whispered with the backs of my fingers against my mouth, "whatsamatter Boris, won't this line go any faster?"

This time our grins were like those of two brothers.

There's a lot to be said for the life of a salesman.

When things go right, that is.

And when you're young—oh yes—when you're young.

» » » » »

Later that week Joe called to thank me for all my help. He'd gotten an order from the machine shop for twenty-five pneumatic tools.

It was quite a week.

In fact, it was very close to being the peak of my career as a salesman.

The actual peak came a few weeks later. It was a subtle thing, traumatic in an unexpected way, and the significance of the experience didn't even sink in at first. However because of its subtlety, in order for you to understand what happened, I have to fill in some background.

Just as I am not a guy who likes to ride motorcycles, but a motorcyclist, I am also not a guy who likes to hunt ducks, but a duck hunter. Duck hunting is a terrible obsession to have because you can only do it a few weeks out of the year. Nevertheless, because of my "arrangement" with my employer, I got to do more duck hunting than most guys whose jobs restricted their intensely-loved sport to a pitifully few weekends.

I was lucky.

Boris Pressman was not a guy who liked to hunt quail. He was a quail hunter. He trained his own hunting dogs and lived for the open season. We understood each other, and I had invited him to go duck hunting. However, I hunted out of a duck boat and he was afraid of being on the Ohio River in freezing weather, and so he had to turn me down.

Boris decided which suppliers of packaging supplies got GE's business, and he was very responsible at it. I knew that if I or my product did not perform to his satisfaction, he would turn me down, but as reluctantly as he turned down my offer to take him duck hunting.

However, I also knew that there was a bond between us that counted for a great deal over and above our professional association. An important part of my job was to cultivate such relationships whenever possible partly because they could be my ace-in-the-hole during a temporary run of bad luck.

One afternoon after discussing a technical matter with Boris while we were taking a coffee break, I mentioned that the duck hunting season opened the next day.

Later, as I was leaving his office and had my hand on the doorknob Boris called "Herb?"

I glanced back.

Boris laughed. "Since we probably won't see you again until after the duck season—GOOD LUCK!"

I winked, smiled and closed the door gently behind me, feeling like a tycoon who had just signed a contract to buy General Motors or some other damned thing.

I was forty-three years old.

Without a drastic restructuring of my life, there was no place to go but down.

That was where I went.

PART V

Lordy How I'm Going to Hate It When the Music Stops

CHAPTER 28

What I Learned From Having

a Nervous Breakdown

Knowing who you are is good for one generation only.
—Carson McCullers
from *Everything That Rises Must Converge*

My father once told me that often when faced with a difficult business decision, he would remember conversations with his father, and he would ask himself what his father would have done if he were in *his* shoes.

I never had such discussions with my father, partly because I was away at school or summer camp most of the time, but also because I simply wasn't interested in a business career. The real reason, however, was probably that my father was a second-generation go-getter—a hard act to follow—while I was an intimidated, third-generation loser: what would a cowering infidel have to say that would interest a God?

However, our problem was even more complex than that even though I respected and admired him to a degree that bordered on love, I can't honestly say I ever loved my father. I know it probably was not his fault because his mother died when he was very young. Anyway, this remains the greatest lost happiness of my life. Perhaps without knowing why, I secretly and desperately wished I could have been like him because, in the culture I was fighting every inch of the way, the most admired trait a man could have was the ability to make money.

With disarming sincerity, Adam Smith once expressed the view that "the unprosperous race of men commonly called men of letters" get their reward in "public recognition." He concluded from this that "admiration and monetary reward are of the same nature and can become substitutes for each other."

Long before I read *The Wealth of Nations* I anticipated Adam Smith's truth. Therefore my emergent philosophy of life was simply the notion that if I could sell other human beings on the idea that the taste of Juicy Fruit gum was more important than the pennies to be saved when buying it, their gratitude would be equivalent to, if not greater than, a million dollar bank account.

Almost certainly without realizing what he had done, one day my father unwittingly but extremely effectively created an imperishable and inflamed desire in me for "public recognition."

When I was about eleven years old our family spent the summers on a farm my father bought in Harrison, New York. He worked in Brooklyn and came up on weekends to spend most of his time riding horseback with my mother.

One Sunday evening before driving back to the City Dad singled *me* out from the rest of his family by honking the horn on his spiffy car and waving me to him. This was unexpected and big: he told me that if I would set up a little target range he would show me how to shoot a .22 rifle the following week-end.

I was in heaven all week, hobnobbing with Gods. I badgered my mother for tin cans and anything else she was about to throw out that would make an unusual target. I surveyed our property for a backstop and found a suitable bank on Monday. On Tuesday I decided it might not be high enough since I had never shot a .22 and my bullets might go wild, so on Wednesday I shoveled three feet of dirt on top, which took most of the day because the ground was hard and full of rocks. On Thursday, to make sure I didn't get in trouble, I added another two feet to the backstop. Friday I nailed all the interesting objects my mother had given me to a heavy plank resting on two forty-gallon drums half-full of water which I had to roll a hundred yards uphill. This took some engineering because I had to devise my own chocks to keep them from rolling back down the hill when I stopped pushing. Then around the stage I made a wooden frame and suspended objects from strings so they would move when hit and make the follow-up shot more challenging.

I thought of everything, I even painted everthing, including different colors for different target objects.

When it was all finished, I stood back and leaned on my shovel, enjoying my handiwork. The set-up looked great and I knew my father would be pleased. Then I took the next step and tried to imagine what form his appreciation would take: perhaps he would buy me my *own* .22 rifle. I could see life opening pleasantly. All I had to do was use my head and not be afraid of work and perhaps throw in a little imagination and my father and my teachers and eventually my boss would all be pleased and I'd be especially happy because all these exciting future events would be the direct result of my understanding, starting at an early age, of how to avoid indifference and the bad and seek out desire and the good.

Friday night I didn't sleep a wink.

Saturday morning I walked on air to my target range with my father and his gun, feeling like a successful adult for the first time in my life.

What happened next stunned my young being: he took one look at my labor of love and said, "Oh, this isn't what I had in mind at all—wait here, I'll be right back."

He returned with a gunny sack of assorted empty bottles, ripped the frame I built with all the targets dangling from strings (which instantly became ridiculous), turned my plank over and lined up *his* bottles.

Although I have loved guns and hunting all my life, I have no memory of the first time I shot a rifle.

I've often thought that Saturday morning was when I got the idea—which dogged me for about the first half of my life—that the reason I was so stupid and therefore had to work so hard was because my memory was poor.

Despite the above whistling in the dark about the duration of my torment, I'm not kidding myself: I know I'll go to my grave desperate for "public recognition." The excessive desire for recognition is a terrible curse that has to be fought every inch of the way. It becomes more of a problem in old age, where, despite constant vigils, it is almost impossible to escape an occasional lapse into curmudgeonhood, which may happen simply because your joints are cranky. This circumstance, which resulted from a boyhood trauma, puts you, dear reader, in the catbird seat, since by viewing my lapses compassionately you have a chance to reveal your humanity.

Can you accommodate me by giving me a little public recognition? I mean, of course, if you have any of it lying around that you don't need.

» » » » »

Like me, my father's brother's son, my cousin Foster Jr., was having self-image problems because of *his* father, whose intensely dynamic personality and whirlwind success story (which we'll get to shortly) must have been intimidating beyond belief. Consequently Foster did nothing in particular with his life, at least when you compare him with his dad. Shortly after getting a master's from Columbia University, he became a recluse in the classic, bizarre tradition. His inner life was always a mystery to his friends and family. Like me, he was in and out of mental hospitals, but spent more time in them and was there for more complex and serious reasons than I was. While my relations with my father were strained, they were understandable: we were simply two fundamentally different types. But Foster's run-ins with *his* father had a Kafka-esque unreality from which there was no hope of awakening.

Instead of getting his Ph.D., he got a second masters in a different subject, not for any particular reason, but simply because he enjoyed the learning process. He was a fascinating conversationalist. Although his small talk was tiny and stiff, in a split second it could explode into a revelatory concept garnished with oddball delicacies and meaty facts which I should have known but somehow didn't.

Foster Jr. was always doing things one simply doesn't do. A notable example occurred during a family Thanksgiving dinner when he was eleven and I was fifteen. While everyone looked on in amazement he took three Oreo cookies from a serving plate, carefully shaved the sides off each one with his knife, rolled their white interiors between his fingers until they looked like pieces of chalk, and ate them. Then he reassembled the spare parts, put them back on the plate and folded his arms as if to say, "Well?"

We didn't do anything about it. In fact no one even spoke for a couple of minutes. I finally broke the tension by asking my sister to please pass the gravy. I felt sorry for Foster, and although I heartily approved of what he had done in principle, I thought his performance was a little too prissy and that he should have gone off by himself in the dark of night and gunned down some Scarsdale streetlights. I would have been glad to show him how to do it. However in the 1990s, when the double-centered Oreos came on the market, Foster's performance proved to be sixty years ahead of its time, and I am now suffering the retrospective indignity of having been upstaged by my kid cousin.

Once when we were both in our late twenties, and drinking together in a tavern full of people with problems, he remarked with a sudden peculiar hesitation in his voice how frustrating it was to be expected to top or at least duplicate his father's brilliant career. Instantly I sympathized with him, but while I admitted I had essentially the same problem, I could not in good conscience say I was *expected* to follow in my father's footsteps. Aside from his tendency, especially during my adolescence, to criticize me for not finishing things I started before I had time to finish them, he left me pretty much alone. My problem was simply that I had been born into a family that got things done and I hadn't really been able to do much of anything.

In the latter third of his life Foster Jr. lived alone in a posh condominium apartment in Hartford, Connecticut. To my knowledge he never invited a friend, relative or anyone inside. I knew something weird and mysterious was going on and often wondered about it, but I never asked him about his personal life because I didn't feel even being a close relative gave me that right. From time to time we learned he had bought other apartments in the same building, but aside from that there were no clues as to what was going on. He didn't own a car and rarely went anywhere.

Although he wrote columns—sporadically—for various newspapers, and started several offbeat societies, he never had a regular job. He was also an eloquent defender of lost causes, such as the right to smoke.

When the gay liberation movement was in its organizational and policy-making stage, he became actively and prominently involved, as chronicled in Martin Duberman's book *Stonewall*. Considering his retiring nature, it must have taken great willpower for him to mingle actively in the outside world's affairs, but he did this regularly and even delivered speeches, surely the ultimate challenge to his profoundly introverted nature.

When he died suddenly at the age of 68, my aunt Florence's daughter Elizabeth was in charge of disposing of his estate. The family had assumed he had been living off the fortune his father left him, so the astonishment was great when we discovered he had quietly and cannily amassed another fortune in his *own* right by playing the stock market.

And what had been going on in those vault-like condominiums all those years? I'm sorry but I cannot betray what I know my dead cousin would not wish to be disclosed. It was nothing illegal or immoral, but I can tell you this: if one could make a business career out of bizarre and original activities, you might say that Foster Jr. was a fantastic success.

In retrospect, even though metaphorically I owned General

Motors or some other damned thing at the age of forty-three, clearly I was the low man on the Gunnison totem pole. But even from that low vantage point, I could never figure out why Foster Jr. spent so much time amassing a fortune of his own when his father had already left him one. I can't imagine anything more ridiculous than owning two fortunes: if you don't know what to do with the first one, why spend a lifetime acquiring a duplicate?

» » » » »

My ongoing problem was that I was reading the wrong books— books that taught me how to gladden my soul. Thoreau, for example, said in effect—and this cannot be repeated too often— that if you arise in the morning full of enthusiasm for what you are about to do, *that is your success*. I have found this to be true all my life.

Getting out of bed in the morning has always been something I dearly love to do. Take today as a random example. I have been up since 5:45 A.M. My alarm was set for 6 A.M., but I knew today I'd be starting a fresh chapter and was so enthusiastic about choosing one, just *one*, out of the infinite ways there were to start it, that I was awakened by the alarm in me that warns me not to sleep when I could be up and about doing something stimulating and exciting that I have never done before.

Every sentence I write is as different as the blank paper I write it on, but unlike this particular sentence, all the rest have to make sense, and that isn't easy to do when you're living happily in a civilization on the verge of suicide.

Well now, my problem at the age of forty-three was that my job was too easy. There were not enough challenges. There were no surprises. All there was was money. Don't get me wrong, I wasn't getting rich, but I wasn't afraid to open the mail the first of the month either. Granted, if a friend called to ask if I wanted to fly to the Bahamas for the weekend I had to turn him down, but if someone called to say the mallards had arrived from the North I was ready, willing and able to work 'em over that weekend, and Monday and Tuesday as well. And if there were no business calls at my answering service I might spend a few weekdays working on the restoration of my 1909 Packard roadster, or ride my R69S Beemer to the U.S. Air Force Museum in Ohio because it would soon be too cold to ride, or take a canoe trip on Kentucky's exquisite Green River. To combat the guilt I was beginning to associate with my three or four-day weekends I began—with highly significant irrationality—to take an occasional Thursday off. Obviously, however, this only compounded my anxiety-guilt problem.

I finally reached the point where even the two or three days a week I was working were becoming an awful nuisance.

One Friday I had a call from Frank Morris at my answering service. He wanted to see me right away. There was nothing ominous about that: Frank was a friend of mine. Besides, he always wanted things "right away."

Though I didn't know it at the time, that call triggered a nervous breakdown. I got in my company car and drove out to General Electric. After signing in at the central registration office, as I had done hundreds of times, I drove to the appropriate parking area, as I had done hundreds of times, and started to get out of my car, as I had done hundreds of times.

I couldn't.

I mean, I *literally* couldn't.

The weird thing was that I could put my hand on the door latch, but I couldn't pull it.

I tried blowing the horn: it worked.

I decided to drive my car around the lot and park it in a different place to see if that made a difference but discovered the only way I could make the car go was to head it towards home.

I drove home with no trouble at all.

My wife called GE and left word that I had been taken sick and would be in touch soon.

For the next three months I couldn't have gone to work if I'd wanted to.

I was locked in the psychiatric unit of Norton's Memorial Hospital on Monday morning.

Coincidentally, the day before in the "Louisville Courier Journal's" Sunday Magazine there was an article called 'Motorcycle High Jinks' about the scrambles races our club sponsored in Lebanon Junction, Kentucky. On the cover there was a great photo of three riders going over a jump which was subsequently published in several national motorcycle magazines. I had staged and taken the shot with a 400 mm Kilfit lens on my Nikon F with an electric back. I shot up two 36-exposure rolls of high-speed Ektrachrome and developed them with the E-2 process, and got lucky. Inside the magazine there was a picture of me and my bike, and word quickly spread around the psych ward that a motorcycle racer had just been admitted.

I was famous.

On the psych ward.

The trouble was, I wasn't a motorcycle racer. Not a professional, that is, and not even what you'd call a winner.

That was why I was in the hospital: I wasn't amounting to anything. Hell, I didn't even own General Motors. That was wishful thinking.

When they lock the door behind you in the loony bin the first thing you get to do is go to the craft shop. The idea is that if your hands are occupied your mind becomes absorbed with what you're doing, and since it is impossible to think of two things at once, you get a respite from what's bothering you and begin to calm down. As I had often discovered at home in my recently neglected model shop, this idea works.

The craft shop supervisor introduced me to Mrs. Keirce. Mrs. Keirce was going to make a cocktail table top by gluing small squares of tile on a piece of plywood. The piece she had was too long, and the supervisor handed me a saw.

"Mr. Gunnison, would you please cut the end off Mrs. Keirce's plywood?" she asked.

I looked at Mrs. Keirce. Wow! I'd cut off anything she wanted.

As she handed me the plywood, I noticed that her arms and body were as beautiful as a pair of swan's neck handlebars on a Moto Guzzi V7 sport bike.

I began my cut.

"Aren't you the motorcycle racer?" she asked in a husky, sexy voice as I stroked back and forth on her plywood.

"Not really," I said. "That's kind of why I'm in here."

I didn't elaborate, being unfamiliar with the protocol in such places.

When I was about half way through the plywood I stopped sawing because it was resting on a wooden chair.

"I'd better check to make sure I don't saw into the chair," I said, worried that perhaps I'd already done so.

"It doesn't matter," Joan answered, winking, an instant before turning her day-making smile loose on my until-then unacknowledged loneliness.

In just a few heartbreaking but irresistibly heartwarming moments she began to put me out of my misery.

My life had been changed forever by a single divine stroke of luck. But oh what I wouldn't have given to have had God or somebody with unmistakable authority tell me a week in advance that a woman was about to transform the rest of my existence! If this is the best of all possible worlds, why was I forced to meet Joan casually? Why wasn't I allowed the bliss of a week's anticipation and the sublimity of entering the looney-bin's craft shop to discover that the joke is true, that God is indeed a Goddess?

Why do we have to fight so hard for happiness and so often at other's expense? Why do we so often stumble onto it? Is it because if we were always satisfied our Goddesses would not be able to do what they do better than anything else on earth?

Joan was, and is, a bottom liner to the core.

And she knows that if she dies before I do, I will put one of her bottom lines on her tombstone. She said it in a fit of minor exasperation during one of our rare cross-purpose exchanges: she suddenly shook her head, held up her hand and uttered it.

"Love is the bottom line," she said.

» » » » »

I told my shrink all about my childhood, family history, and job.

"You are an alcoholic," he said, "why didn't you mention that?"

"I'm not," I retorted.

"Then you're gay."

"Wrong again."

"Well then," he continued, "if you're not either of the above then you're a workaholic."

I burst out laughing.

"That's funny. That's *really* funny," I laughed, barely able to slip the words in amongst the spasms.

"Well," he continued after I'd settled down, "if you aren't any of the above, you must be crazy."

At that my laughter resumed but this time it was more like a drowning man gasping for air.

I was very sick: the doctor exhumed a motorcycle episode I'd had a month before that was so grim I don't want to think, much less write, about it. Laughter was a release. My shrink and I laughed a lot together, but there was nothing funny about the sickness which landed me in the hospital.

Not being able to get out of the car was not why I was there. That was merely the point where the remaining fragments of my psychological defense mechanism joined forces and were able to pull the plug on my potentially lethal shenanigans. Their way of protecting me from myself was to simply make it physically impossible for me to function in the area where for eighteen years I had been acting out a role that was not only *not* me, but was diametrically *opposed* to my nature.

I was by temperament an introvert, and, although not as reclusive as my cousin Foster Jr., I was still far from being the extrovert my job demanded of me. For example, I frequently had to entertain and drink with customers I often had nothing in common with: also I really didn't like to drink. The morning after one of those sessions when someone asked me what I did for a living I surprised myself by blurting out "Oh, I'm just a professional friend."

That was an early warning sign: I take friendship as seriously as love.

I was a successful salesman but a poor closer. Fortunately I was not in the kind of sales where being a good closer is the salesman's most important asset. I had a flair for the technical aspects of my job and was able to fake the personality of an extroverted salesman, but it was the faking that slowly, over an eighteen-year period, ate me alive.

One day when I had taken a couple of engineers out to lunch, the subject of Liberace came up and one of them told this anecdote: when Liberace was once asked if he was bothered by constantly being canned by classical musical critics. He responded, "Of course I am bothered. I cry all the way to the bank." That was the origin of the phrase "to cry all the way to the bank," and I laughed as hard as the engineers, but I was crying for real inside, where it counts.

I have always been a classical music lover, but this is what I am, not what I pretend to be. My interest in music was so serious in later years I wrote a book about the pernicious effect of recordings on the art of live music, in particular, opera. What the hell was I doing spending my life among otherwise decent people who thought the greatest of the arts was a joke? But it wasn't just music: I had a liberal arts temperament that I suppressed and sometimes I even ridiculed my feelings by saying things I didn't believe because they helped me make money.

The doctors agreed that I had been forcing myself to live a lie for eighteen years. The erosion of my defenses was gradual but inevitable. And all that time I thought I was cleverly setting up a good short-work-week-life for myself when, in fact, I was fighting a delaying action against the very real threat of suicide.

Following my release from Norton Hospital there was a rough period of readjustment. Deeply affectionate ties had to be broken nevertheless I knew it was a matter of life and death: thirty percent of those who suffer from what I suffered from commit suicide.

Although I didn't realize this until it was too late, I don't believe there is any way a divorce can be handled with honor or without damage. Thirty-eight years later I still feel pangs of regret at the outcome of my youthful promises and expectations which, for a few incandescent moments, made me feel that an altar not of my own making had something going for it, and that the irrational intonations of hopelessly noble vows carried less weight than affectionately insouciant words and shameless hands.

How I wish I could have left something tangible of myself behind for Dorothy—a supplicating hand, perhaps, or a lovely vial of tears.

CHAPTER 29

Self-Education from the Top Down

I never let schools interfere with my education.
—Mark Twain

Joan was a Duke graduate and had written her master's thesis on Robert Frost at Purdue, and since I figured it might be hazardous to be married to a woman who was not only prettier than I was but was also fourteen years younger and better educated, she had no trouble talking me into going to graduate school. Fortunately my St. Lawrence marks were high enough to make me eligible for the Master's Program in English at the University of Louisville.

It was a weird feeling to be back in college after a twenty-four year hiatus, and my very first class made me wonder if I had made a grave mistake. It was a course in Victorian Literature which began with Dickens. All graduate classes begin with the assumption the students have studied the subject on the undergraduate level.

The first words I heard in my graduate school career were those of the professor asking the class what it thought the chief characteristic of Dickens's work was.

"Didacticism," a student said confidently.

Hoo boy! I thought. What is a 44-year-old man like me, who once owned General Motors, doing in a class like this, where in the first ten seconds a fellow student uses a word I never heard of?

Fortunately though, after looking up "didacticism," within the hour I decided I knew more about Dickens than the guy who used the fancy word.

I was off and running.

After I got my master's I was offered a position teaching part-time while I completed the course work for my Ph.D.

It is generally assumed that when you get a Ph.D. in Literature you will spend the rest of your life teaching on the university level. Allowing Ph.D. candidates to teach is not only a way of giving them an income to defray graduate school costs but is also a way of evaluating their ability to teach. In a graduate program in English there are no courses in teaching. There aren't even any practice teaching sessions. What happens is that if the powers-that-be get reports that you are a lousy teacher somehow you never quite get your Ph.D. Either you inexplicably keep failing your French or German exams, your Miller Analogy test or your comprehensive exams, or else you are slowly starved to death: your dissertation runs into endless road blocks.

Graduate school is often a brutal, inhumane arena, even in the humanities: I have witnessed many sickening examples of this.

Fortunately I didn't have any of these heartaches. My problem was I wasn't sure it would be in my best interests to teach for the rest of my life. If you have ever considered going to graduate school, try the following anecdotes on for size.

The evening after my class in Victorian Literature I attended my first class in Chaucer. The professor was marvelous. He told me many things about Chaucer that went far beyond my limited undergraduate middle English studies. His word choices were delightful, he could turn a phrase like nobody's business and he had a deliciously whimsical sense of humor.

Apparently because of an error in the scheduling of my classes which resulted in a conflict, my Chaucer class was changed to the following morning.

The next morning I discovered that I was about to hear the professor's first lecture a second time.

He delivered most of it verbatim.

Hmm, I thought. How long did it take for him to run Chaucer

into the ground: is this what I want to do for the rest of my life to my own favorite authors?

I once taught a course in Ibsen, Shaw, Tolstoy and Strindberg, and after teaching the same works for two years, I asked if it would be all right if I broadened my scope by teaching *War and Peace* instead of *Anna Karenina* the following year.

The head of the Humanities Department said no, it wasn't.

Hmm, I thought. Do I want to teach *Anna Karenina* for the rest of my life in a system of higher education where my offer to spend what would amount to six weeks of my own time in a meticulous study of *War and Peace*, (which would enormously broaden the impact of my life as an educator) was rejected *out of hand*?

I thought of my experience trying to get a student who hadn't done his homework to understand the difference between patriotism and nationalism, and it occurred to me that this was because he had not been taught this vital difference in high school. Okay, since there are far more high school dropouts and graduates than there are college graduates, and since this is a democracy, and since wars are one of the great outrages against mankind, what prospect did I have of setting the world straight on this vital problem?

Hmm, I thought. Do I want to beat my head against this wall for the rest of my life?

Because I'd worked hard and had earned the right, I thought it would be cool to get a faculty parking sticker for my motorcycle. However, I ran into an unbelievable amount of opposition. It seems my colleagues did not think walking into class wearing motorcycle boots and carrying a helmet was good for the image of higher education.

Hmm, I thought. Do I want to drive a car to work for the rest of my life?

One rainy weekend I read Joseph Conrad's novella "Youth", just for pleasure, and discovered an astounding thing about it no scholar had ever noticed. (I checked this out in "The Explicator".) It wasn't a romantic yarn about being young and venturesome at all. The title was ironic: it was a figurative story about premature old age, and *I could prove my thesis.* The figures were right there in the book, but for over a century no scholar had taken the trouble to do the math, though the arithmetic was as simple as 2+2 = 4. On Monday I made the rounds of the English department, wanting to share my discovery, but nobody was interested. There was a temporary crisis in campus politics, and that's all my colleagues wanted to talk about.

Hmm, I thought. Do I want to work with people who aren't interested in the dangers of premature old age when there are already unmistakable signs that they're already far older than they realize?

One semester I had a bright student in a freshman English class. Then, in what seemed like just a few months, I had her again in a senior honors class in Existential drama and found out she was married and had two children.

Hmm, I thought. Do I want to discuss the life and death matters all great literature deals with (what life is all about is what literature is all about) among young people who change greatly from year to year and thus artificially accelerate *my* awareness of the passing of *my* years?

Instead of teaching how to use a dictionary according to the data in the syllabus I decided to bottom-line this project.

With the aid of multiple dictionaries and stop watches, and after preliminary instructions on the proper technique for speed-locating words, I set up a definition-finding contest and discovered, to everybody's amazement, that it only takes, on average, eleven seconds to look up a word! I hoped this information would shame the students into looking up words which, without this knowledge, could easily be considered too much trouble.

Everything I did was turning to dust. Shortly after this I was called on the carpet for not teaching the dictionary "the way it is supposed to be taught."

Hmm, I thought. I've managed to eat regularly without knowing that in a college dictionary, genus names as well as binomials and trinomials are italicized, but names of taxa above the genus are not. Did I want to spend my life teaching such information to students who, as the result of this stultifying academic emphasis, would spend their post-college years not looking up the word "didactic" because they didn't know it would only take eleven seconds?

Did I want to deny myself the pleasure of teaching by example the first principles of creativity to students hungering for them because such principles are not on the formal agenda? While standing on the carpet I was called on for another of my multiple transgressions; I was told, with withering sarcasm, that "the reason blackboards are there is so you can write on them."

Hmm, I thought, is that higher education or a low form of indoctrination?

One summer vacation while I was at U of L, I applied for a job at a prestigious university in Halifax, Nova Scotia. During the interview I mentioned that I had a special affinity for Chaucer and in fact had a scholarly paper published on him but that I could not speak Middle English very well.

"That's too bad," the head of the English Department replied, "because that is the *sine qua non* of Chaucer."

Hmm, I thought, do I want to work for an outfit where the official view on teaching Chaucer is that how you *pronounce* what he wrote is more important than what he wrote *means*? Did I even want to talk to people who hid their ignorance behind impressive-sounding foreign phrases?

The fact that the Latin phrase *sine qua non* literally means "without which nothing" raises an interesting point in Chaucer scholarship, because if his reputation is based strictly on the fact that he wrote in Middle English, why aren't all the other Middle English poets nobody ever heard of equally famous?

Granted, Chaucer's use of Middle English is an aural delight beyond compare, but why not leave that aspect of his genius to voice professionals and use recordings for that purpose? Wouldn't that be "giving the machine artistic work to do"—to use Louis Mumford's unforgettable phrase?

Many of the ideas and attitudes expressed in this book had their origin in *The Canterbury Tales*, particularly "The Merchant's Tale," and I had to dig most of them out by taking my own idiosyncratic pilgrimages.

The impulse that drives professors to spend long hours learning to pronounce an obsolete language is, I concluded, their way of hiding the fact that they are intellectually naked in a cold, cold world.

With increasing frequency I began to feel that I had been fenced in with what Henry James referred to as "a seminary of five hundred grazing donkeys."

» » » » »

One day a petition was circulated in the Humanities Department stating that the University of Louisville should not accept grants from the United States Government which had as their primary objective the destruction of human life.

I was about the twentieth person to read it, and as I scanned the signatures above mine, I was gratified to see that all my Humanities Department colleagues had already or would soon sign it.

However, the petition was overwhelmingly defeated by the science faculty.

It seems to me that what happened to that petition still represents the bottom line of higher education. The noble and expectant principles of the Enlightenment had been corrupted by the Industrial Revolution which in turn created the present Dark Age of Strobe Lights.

I wanted no part of it. I had gone to graduate school for the enrichment of my soul, and Yeats and D.H. Lawrence and Joyce and Tolstoy and a host of extraordinarily talented people gave me that enrichment in all its glory. That was the reward for all my hard work. Any diploma or degree I got or didn't get was as irrelevant to the effort as *officially* holding the coast-to-coast record on my motorcycle would have been. The System thrives on *official* whereas I abhor *officialdom, officialese,* and *officialism* and live my life in direct opposition to the whole *official* kit and caboodle.

Suddenly the university seemed an unlovely, contentious, even lethal place: while most professors were trying to blow up the world, others were trying to save it.

Just as if they belonged to the same species of intelligent animal, both ate in the faculty dining room.

After the petition I had signed with a full heart had been defeated, I looked at most of my science colleagues as if they were hunters of Thorpe's "The Big Bear of Arkansas."

I wrote my master's thesis on Thomas Bangs Thorpe, who was a member of a group of nineteenth-century American writers known as the "Southwestern Humorists." For anyone interested in writing, this genre is a gold mine. William Faulkner acknowledged his debt to their work, and Mark Twain represents the culmination of their influence, which was not so much in the stories they told, but rather in the skill with which they told them.

Let me illustrate this with some edge material. Everyone learns in high school that Mark Twain wrote "The Jumping Frog of Calivarias County." He did no such thing. That story had been making the rounds for years before Twain latched on to it. What he did, which was a tremendous accomplishment, was simply write up the story far more entertainingly than it had ever been told before.

Because I have always been interested in writing and had several pieces published in national magazines before my graduate school days, I developed a strong empathy for Thomas Bangs Thorpe while researching my master's thesis. I admired him. I respected him. Yes, I even loved him.

How could one not react thus to a writer so skilled in his art that he could create a novel, *His Master's House,* which was acclaimed in the South as a pro-slavery book and acclaimed in the North as an anti-slavery one?

Thorpe's short story "The Big Bear of Arkansas" was a thinly-veiled allegory about an enormous mythical "creation bear" which is obsessively tracked but rarely even glimpsed by a hunter devoting his life to killing it. After many adventures, one morning the cunning and elusive big bear of Arkansas walked out into a meadow in full view of the hunter, who, from a sitting position, killed the bear with a ridiculously easy shot.

And what was the hunter also doing when he shot the creation bear from the sitting position?

Defecating.

» » » » »

Although "The Big Bear of Arkansas" was the greatest of the many bear stories written by Southwestern humorists, they were all vastly entertaining. Many of them were embellished with outrageous dialects and grammar, as in the following excerpt:

> The bar sudden-like riz up on his behime legs and looked at me. His eyes was full of blood and dirt. I tuk aim and fired at 'em and the next thing the bar knowed, he didn't know nuthin'.

The difference between Thorpe's "creation bear" story and the above excerpt from a lesser Southwestern humorist is this: Thorpe was making an important point about the environment (a century before the issue became fashionable) which went beyond the mere killing of a bear, just as this book is designed to go beyond the mere riding of a motorcycle. Thorpe looked upon the earth with love and awe and was keenly aware, long before almost anybody realized it, that it was in the early stages of its decimation. For this reason, and also because we have a common interest in the infinite delights of language, I not only had empathy for him, but I felt I owed him something. It bothered me to think that a man who gave his heart and soul and intellect to future generations was lying like a piece of dirt in his grave, unremembered except by a few graduate students who had gone down the list of thesis subjects and settled on him because he hadn't been done too many times before.

I knew my Thorpe thesis would be put on microfilm and filed away forever and be forgotten. That was the system. It was inevitable. Still, I wanted to at least make a gesture or perhaps a point that went beyond the mere writing of a scholarly thesis in order to give the idea that was burning a hole in my heart an audience. That idea was that education has no real value unless it is related in a tangible way to the hopes, fears and loves of the individual student's life, and, by extension, to mankind.

At the end of my thesis I added the following remark:

"Because I developed a strong empathy for Thomas Bangs Thorpe while researching this thesis, I plan to visit his grave in Brooklyn, New York, where he is buried and where I was born."

When a graduate student completes a thesis he or she has to defend it orally. Professors ask questions, probing for inconsistencies and flaws in the scholarship. The purpose is to test the student's ability to respond extemporaneously to challenging questions, as he or she will soon be required to do in the classroom.

I defended my thesis successfully and was congratulated on completing the University of Louisville's Master's Program.

As I was gathering up my notes my thesis director told me as a kind of afterthought that the final note about visiting Thorpe's grave would have to come out before the thesis was microfilmed.

"Why?" I asked, incredulous.

"Because it's not scholarly," he said, "take it out."

Out it came, and out I knew I would ultimately go as well.

» » » » »

One morning while my class was forcing me to make a difficult extemporaneous defense of an untenable offhand remark I'd stupidly made, I got a welcome reprieve in the form of a knock on the door.

I went out in the hallway. A woman representing the Student

Council apologized for interrupting my class and explained that I had just been chosen U of L's most outstanding faculty member for the year. She wanted to make sure I would attend the year-end awards ceremony the next night.

I thanked her and then returned to my desk wondering if it might be possible to extricate myself from the flack I was getting from my students by making use of the information I'd just received.

Fortunately my mistakes for the day were limited to the first one.

Ten days later I received a curt notice in the mail that the University of Louisville would not rehire me for the fall semester. I had not been fired, I just wasn't rehired.

I left university life with no regrets whatsoever because my disillusionment with the teaching profession was far more than offset by what I had learned from the literature and poetry I'd read while preparing myself for a job I really didn't want.

Nietzsche was by no means alone among the world's most influential thinkers in his belief that if a philosopher expects to deserve our respect, he must teach by example, and it was the examples I'd found wanting not only at the university but in popular pseudo-academic philosophy as well.

» » » » »

When a Zen-oriented philosopher describes riding a motorcycle many miles with a dangerously worn rear tire or changing his oil by dumping the imperishable, used-up slime on the ground beneath an elm tree behind, of all metaphorical places, an abandoned schoolhouse, or taking his helmet off on reaching the first state without a helmet law, I believe what he has written.

However, using Nietzsche's parameter for earning our respect, if the above seer's thesis is that technology will lead to a safer, cleaner and more spiritual world, then I must reject the thesis because if its proponent is not aware that technology is dangerous, that a helmet is *de rigueur* and that a worn-out tire on a motorcycle absolutely cannot be used with impunity, or if the philosopher desecrates the earth with the yucky by-product of scientific progress, he disproves his thesis by his actions. Indeed, he has so little awareness of the absurdity of his living ambiguities that he actually describes them in a public document. Who but the coterie of limited academics, who delight in claiming to understand what no one else understands, would reserve praise for Mr. Pirsig's gobbledegooked affronts to the intellect?

» » » » »

Since Thoreau's two-year sojourn at Walden Pond filled in spades the requirement of teaching by example and because the experiments I too had made in the art of living all confirmed Thoreau's first principles, I immigrated to Canada with the expectation of expanding my horizons through a day-to-day occupation and preoccupation with life in a simple, basic and semi-wilderness form.

Although I knew I would miss discussions with those of my students who agonized over what life *really* was, this was no longer my concern. Besides, I had a life to get on with. I felt I had given my two cents worth to the betterment of mankind, but the powers that be accepted it as a tax earmarked for defending the system against motorcycling infidels.

When I began my Canadian experiment in wilderness living I was often accused of copping out like a hippie. However, by what stretch of the imagination can reading great works of literature— Ibsen's "The Doll's House", for one, and getting a feeling for, say, Ibsen's commentary on the tragic consequences of needless sacrifices, be construed as a *lack* of understanding of where your basic commitments should be? If the struggle to come to terms with the immense responsibilities of being an individual human being with a life of its own to sort out is considered a cop out by people who have bought the system, then one may well assume that blindly buying the boilerplate system is the ultimate cop out.

» » » » »

Joan and I lived over twenty years in a log house we built together in a remote part of the Canadian Rockies. Our nearest neighbor lived over a mile away. We cooked on a woodburning stove, heated with wood and used propane for lights and refrigeration. The lack of modern conveniences was more than offset by the view, which was breathtaking in almost every direction. We conducted many experiments in the art of living while existing in our grandstand, which faced all the visual beauty I could handle at one time. Some of our experiments were successful, others weren't, but the learning process never stopped. Our only concessions to the modern era were our hi-fi, powered by a small propane generator, guns for food, a radio telephone, a chain saw for each of us, a pickup truck to haul wood and water, and of course three motorcycles, two for me and one for Joan.

Even to touch on that life would take me too far afield: I also know if I got started, I wouldn't be able to stop.

Those uncluttered years were glorious beyond measure and I couldn't have been happier if, instead, I'd saved a world that has never shown the slightest inclination that it would ever put up with being saved.

CHAPTER 30

Bucking Broncos and Rattlesnakes

My route from Sturgis was drawing me relentlessly West to the setting sun. Sturgis had been my goal but now that I had achieved. The prospect for the rest of my trip confronted me as nothing more exciting than long, dead-engined, downhill coast. I glanced at my speedo and smiled ruefully at the coincidence—75 MPH: one mile an hour for each year of my existence. What had I done with my life besides go to motorcycle rallies? What was I, this instant, speeding away *from*? What was I eternally *hurtling* towards? And where in hell *was* I? Montana, for Christ's sake. They called it Big Sky Country, but all I could see was gophers.

Usually when I'm touring alone in the wide open-spaces I feel solitary, a deliciously off-beat and perhaps even ungrammatical state of being. It almost never degenerates into loneliness because my thoughts keep me company like long-lost brothers. For the first time on my birthday trip I was suddenly lonely.

Perhaps rubbing elbows with a quarter million deliriously happy motorcyclists during my stay of execution at Sturgis was too much of a contrast for my now aloneness. Perhaps it was a bit much even for an ardent lover of contrasts to handle. I wanted to ride back, to regain my lost happiness, to say "hello again" instead of "goodbye forever." But Thomas Wolfe cannot be quoted too often: "you can't go home again." The short track races were always *last* night—oh lost!—and where have *you* been? I felt like a loser, a user, a worse than nobody. I was burning up irreplaceable fossil fuels, polluting the atmosphere with a pre—catalytic converter bike, scrubbing off on asphalt what was once a lovely rubber tree, and in my retirement years, at least, paying for my parasitical pleasures with money which for the most part was earned by my father.

It was a blistering August day. A very pale moon, fit only for poets grasping at straws, was pasted on the sheet-lightning sky; however by mid-afternoon I came to a festive bannered town where a rodeo was in progress and, suddenly desperate for diversion, decided to stop and play my little game.

My little game consists of spending a couple of hours in a small town. I park my bike and then walk around as if I had lived there all my life: I look at the boys and wonder which of them I would have played mumbletypeg with; the girls, and which one I might have been lucky enough to marry; the business men and which one among them had miraculously escaped the bondage of money; and the old men and which of them had no regrets. I smile and nod at all of them, and they all smile and nod back, the way everyone does in small, heartwarming towns.

When I leave town I amuse myself for the next fifty miles or so by wondering how different my life might have been if I had lived my years out in that spot and knew no other towns except the surrounding ones. Such fantasies evoke contrasting moods of sadness and elation: sadness because I can't live a lifetime in each of the towns I fall in love with, and elation because even in the dreariest of them a single life, given half a chance and a local library, could retain the glory it had the day it was born.

The rodeo in this town, however, led me to change my game plan, and I turned into the fairgrounds. The parking area was hot and dusty, so I side-standed and covered my bike under a large elm tree with no dead branches. Debating whether or not to lock it, I locked it but not without an audible sigh, and I cursed my inflexibility in the matter.

Then, cane in hand, I hobbled to the rodeo with the air of an old resident who had helped build the grandstand half a century ago.

The bucking bronco event had just started when I sat down. There were six contestants, but only two were the kind of men people build grandstands for. The other four didn't seem to be trying hard enough and bit the dust almost as soon as they left the gate. Still, I could identify with them because once when I lived in Canada I had been thrown from a bucking bronco and broke my shoulder on the frozen ground. I could easily have done without this recollection in my downer mood, but despite this temporary relapse, I enjoyed the rodeo immensely and stood up in front of the crowd as the proceedings came to an end, and, in my imagination, announced in a loud voice that I had enjoyed living my life with them and would see them all again the next life-time through. I dearly love this sense of being a part of every life that ever was or ever will be, and especially the sense of sharing a particular time out of the eons that were and will be available.

» » » » »

While I was removing the cover from my bike an ancient babbler strolled up to me with the imperishable confidence of those who have forgotten the art of listening. I hadn't talked to this one two minutes before he fell with a vaporous thud into the category of old guys who are obsessed with local politics and use the word *ilk* a lot. I felt like crying out with impatience and heartbreak but tipped the poor beggar twenty polite minutes out of my priceless day's hoard before scrambling off to new adventures.

Later that evening, while my bike and I were throbbing through Montana a hundred miles nearer West, I had an unpleasant feeling that something I had seen at the rodeo had been traumatic. I couldn't put my finger on it, but knew it was something to be avoided at all costs.

I put it out of my mind, whatever it was.

Around midnight, while sleeping on my back with my head and shoulders outside my tent directly under the stars, something I dearly love to do—I felt the delicious sensation of wake-up-raindrops on my face. Nature was doing for me what Montaigne occasionally asked a servant to do: to wake him up in the middle of the night in order to shorten the nothingness period of sleep's non-life, which would give him a brief dark escape *to* consciousness followed by the pleasure of drifting back to sleep. This is not the kind of information to be found in a dearly-bought owner's manual, yet I possessed it for practically nothing. Almost all my joys spring from my love of books dealing with the art of living, like Montaigne's *Essays*. The reason I was reveling in the fact that the big sky was tossing me bonus minutes of the good life in the midst of the long night's nothingness was because many years ago Montaigne had alerted me to this rare delight.

I looked around at my paradise. My bike was facing me at a shallow angle, canted on its sidestand, so I gave my hopelessly childlike eyes permission to play with it for a few moments. Every night I park it at a different angle to my tent: (one shouldn't leave such pleasures to chance! Hell, this pleasure in itself is enough of a reason to avoid motels.)

But soon, realizing the rain cloud meant business, I hunched my sleeping bag back into the tent, readjusted my closed cell mattress and zipped the rainfly shut.

Before I drifted back to sleep it began to rain hard and since I can no more sleep to the sound of rain drumming on my tent fly than I can to Handel's "Water Music" suite, I put my hands behind my head and enjoyed the concert.

Then it hit me.

What had been traumatic that afternoon was this: in close and dramatic contrast I had witnessed the sight of success and failure.

» » » » »

I once owned a priceless bucking bronco and it was one of the great treasures of my life. About two feet high and black as the ace of spades, it had been sculpted by Frederick Remington.

The horse was rearing at the sight of a rattlesnake and the

rider was leaning forward in the saddle with his whip arm raised. Wearing chaps, a cowboy hat and a cartridge belt with a Colt revolver in its holster around his slim waist, he had the bearing of a determined man in full command of a dangerous situation.

The cowboy was a man of action in the thick of life, just as Frederick Remington had been, but Remington was also an artist of astonishing sensitivity. It was in this human totality, beneath its black exterior, that the statue's priceless quality struck home like a thunderbolt: it seethed with static energy.

My Remington statue was not something that I could have afforded at any period in my life without unreasonable sacrifice, but I not only got it for nothing, it even had *my full name* inscribed on the base.

Presented to Herbert Foster Gunnison
Founder of the Brooklyn Municipal Club by his Fellow
Members

The statue was willed to me by my grandfather, who was the owner and publisher of "The Brooklyn Daily Eagle".

The "Eagle" which was a fine newspaper in its day, competed successfully with "The New York Times", "The Tribune", and "The World". Walt Whitman, who could not stay at any job very long in his early days, was the "Eagle's" drama critic for a while.

My grandfather started out on the "Eagle" at the bottom and worked his way up until he owned the newspaper outright. When he controlled its editorial policy the "Eagle's" reputation for taking forthright stands against injustice was so great that if a referee made an unpopular call during a hockey game at Madison Square Garden the crowd used to shout "We'll tell the "Eagle"! We'll tell the "Eagle"!"

Because there were no syndicated cartoonists, each major newspaper hired its own comic strip artists, and one of the "Eagle's" artists had created an extremely popular comic strip called 'Hairbreath Harry'. Harry was the good guy and Rudolph the bad

SEVENTY YEARS ON A MOTORCYCLE

guy who was always trying to abduct Harry's girlfriend, Belinda. Each episode took up a whole page and they only appeared in Sunday's paper, and since every 'Hairbreath Harry' episode ended in a crisis for Belinda and Harry, kids used to play guessing games to see how Harry would rescue Belinda from Rudolph's clutches the following Sunday.

Because my father worked at the "Eagle" I often visited the room where the comic strip artists worked, and since they had to produce cartoons many weeks in advance in case they got sick and their output lapsed, I was able to read episodes that were weeks away from publication. Armed with this information, I easily acquired an unearned reputation as a clairvoyant when kids were discussing how Harry was going to rescue Belinda. Armed with this spectacular information, I easily acquired a reputation as a clairvoyant when kids were discussing how Harry was going to rescue Belinda on the following Sunday.

One day 'Hairbreath Harry's' creator was finishing up an episode which took place in a sausage factory and because he noticed that I could not take my eyes off it, he got what I remembered later as a peculiar look on his face. Then, stating he could just draw another one, he gave me the original, which gleamed with wet-sheened, hallucinatory colors the printing process hadn't yet dulled.

That evening I lay on my stomach on what was to become a hallowed part of the living room rug and was soon obsessed with my pristine, dripping-with-color episode of 'Hairbreath Harry', unaware that I was about to have my first encounter with the delusion of graphics substituting for life. Rudolph had abducted Belinda and was trying to force her to marry him. He had tied her up and placed her—on her back—on a conveyor belt which was moving her body towards the maw of a sausage making machine. (For some reason I couldn't get comfortable and kept squirming around with my stomach on the rug.) While Harry was trying to break down the factory door to rescue Belinda, the artist gave his audience a full view of the sausage machine. On its left there was

Belinda, blonde and red-lipped, with ropes criss-crossed between her breasts and only inches from the machine, and on its right finished strings of sausages were falling into a tub.

At that sight my sex life began.

In later years I often had occasion to reflect on that moment. It was the most natural life-episode I had ever experienced and was clearly precipitated by the desire to perpetuate life and beauty (Belinda) and to drive death and ugliness (Rudolph and the tub of sausages) off the face of the earth.

All I had done was to spontaneously donate my adolescent two cent's worth to the cause of life and beauty, and if that is generally considered something to feel guilty about, then sexual morality is probably based on the desire of people who are afraid of life to protect those who aren't from fears they don't have.

My grandfather's noble stands against injustice were all well and good and I'm not knocking them, but the greatest favor his newspaper ever did for me was when it got my sex life off to a rip-roaring start with that unforgettable psychedelic sado-masochistic comic strip fantasy.

However, when a few weeks had gone by and I had discussed my experience with Belinda and the sausage machine with other adolescents, I no longer felt like a privileged clairvoyant. Instead, I was just another self-indulgent kid getting off on the comics every Sunday. As a result of all this a few weeks later when I was asked how Harry was going to rescue Belinda from her latest predicament, I felt uncomfortable. I began to squirm and said I didn't know.

Then in a flash of inspiration I told the truth about my "clairvoyance."

My adult life was off and running: from here on out it would only be natural to the extent that it dealt with the truth as I experienced it. There would be no middle ground. When I began to write I realized that all writing that falls short of perceived truth is rudimentary and serves only to process information.

» » » » »

My grandfather was clairvoyant.

Back in his day reporters were always trying to get the scoop on each other, because when a big story broke, the first newspaper to get kids on the street shouting "EXTRA, EXTRA, READ ALL ABOUT IT!!" got all the business. For that reason reporters telephoned hot news to their papers, and because in those days you only got a few minutes' telephone time for a nickel, reporters always carried pocketfuls of nickels around with them so they could monopolize perhaps the only telephone booth in the vicinity of the news event. The industry joke was that you could always tell a reporter because his pants were falling down from the weight of all the nickels in his pockets.

It was obvious that cooperation was better for everybody than chancy cutthroat competition, and so my grandfather became one of the founders of the Associated Press, but the irony in that was that the news services were eventually to spell the downfall of many local newspapers. My grandfather was clairvoyant because he sold his paper to the Gannett chain before this development became obvious, and a few years later The Eagle, along with The World and The Herald Tribune went out of business.

When my grandfather sold his newspaper, my father, because he was out of a job, placed a full page ad in "The New York Times" announcing his extensive business experience and availability. I don't recall the full wording of his ad, but the lead-in was: DOES YOUR BUSINESS NEED A TRANSFUSION?

He then bundled his family in our Buick and drove us all to Boca Raton, Florida, where he relaxed on the beach for a couple of weeks reading juicy offers from many major companies before finally choosing a vary prestigious position as Vice President of the Donnelley Corporation.

» » » » »

Years later, when I went to my grandfather's funeral, I had a cold and during the service I got a tickle in my throat that made me cough. I didn't have any cough drops and since it was embarrassing to be coughing on such a solemn occasion, I tried so hard to keep from coughing that I got red in the face and tears streamed down my cheeks.

After the service several people told my parents how moved they had been at the grief-stricken sensitivity I had shown at the funeral.

Many years later I read Camus's *The Stranger*, a pivotal existential novel in which the protagonist, Meursault, is executed for a crime he did not commit because among the damaging evidence against him was the absurd charge that he did not cry at his mother's funeral. This story reminded me of my oppositely absurd reputation as a weeper at my grandfather's funeral, and I felt the full-circle brunt of emotional interplay and the pity that the most intense moments in life are often so hard to deal with honestly in real life. They come to life only in the greatest art and literature, where people like Camus, Yeats and Wagner sometimes lay their understanding hands on my shoulder.

As the result of a variety of experiences, such as the above, I became convinced at an early age that the culture I was born into was too preordained, inflexible and unimaginative, and that if I was going to live a happy life I had to analyze my role in it, not in terms of what was expected of me, but of what I expected of myself.

Being born into a wealthy family is not always the bed of roses those who were not probably assume it to be. This is particularly true if you happen to be born into the third generation of wealth.

Many Americans are aware of the saying "shirtsleeves to shirtsleeves in three generations." This scenario has occurred so frequently in our society that it is more of a rule than an exception. There is abundant historical evidence that is by no means limited to the United States but is a widespread and deeply entrenched psychological problem.

This is what happens: in the first generation an ambitious man works his way to the top and leaves his money to his son, who starts much closer to the top, increases the net worth of his inheritance, and works his way to a still higher top. The second generation successful man then leaves his money to his son, who squanders it in a few short years and is forced to roll up his shirt sleeves and start at the bottom, just like his grandfather had to. But the difference is he does this *without ambition*, and therefore with no prospects of success.

I don't offer the following observations as a preamble to a sociological or psychological treatise but strictly as something for second generation go-getters with problem sons to consider: the problem may be bigger than both of you.

There are apparently obscure psychological reasons for this phenomenon. For example, in Greece as far back as the seventh and sixth centuries B.C., during what is called the Age of Tyrants, the third generation loser problem was a well-established fact of political life in all the Greek city-states. The *tyrants* were not tyrants in the usual and pejorative sense but were in fact the first examples of the great age of individualism in European history. They strengthened the power of the city-states, built imposing public works, promoted trade and encouraged literature and art. In short, they were highly capable men, men we justifiably admire, in contemporary culture as "go getters." Curiously enough, however, although there were many of these men (because there were many city-states, or towns of about 8,000-10,000 souls) none of them ever established a dynasty because by the third generation the driving force of the original go-getter and his son had mysteriously evaporated, and the governments were quickly taken over by fresh, highly motivated go-getters, and after three generations these city-states were taken over by fresh, eager *tyrants*.

Because the lottery of birth spit me out in the role of a third generation loser, I have always been fascinated by what causes the shirtsleeves to shirtsleeves syndrome and the accounts of my often traumatic experiences with it that follow are designed to shed some light on the subject from the point of view of the *self-made victim*.

I suppose there are many causes for all the heartaches. I observed one example recently in, of all places, a motorcycle shop. There was a large machine shop in a neighboring town that had been started by a man who kept increasing the business and adding new machinery and floor space, and when he died his son took over the business and increased its net worth by a considerable margin. The second generation son had just died prematurely and his widow was in the motorcycle shop buying the good life for her three sons. It was clear from their conversation that her only object in life was to make her sons happy, but it was also clear that her sons didn't have the faintest idea how happiness works. All they knew about motorcycles was what they had read in magazines. Their judgment consisted simply of adding up all the hi tech features on the assumption that the more of them they had between their legs the better riders they'd be. Although with each such feature and with each "indispensable" accessory the price rose disproportionately, that didn't faze the mother one whit. She wanted her sons to have the best and money was no problem.

It doesn't take many motorcycles now-a-days to go through a fortune. It was a first rate tragedy: even the salesmen were raising eyebrows at each other as they pushed the bought bikes aside.

All I could think of was the two poor guys who bent over machinery all their lives with micrometers in their hands, and for what?

Visibly moved, I cleared out: the motorcycle shop had suddenly become an unlovely place.

A half hour later I realized I'd forgotten my credit card and went back to retrieve it.

Mom was now buying her darlings jet skis and trailers.

The tears I'd wept at my grandfather's funeral may not have been earned, but on that unforgettable afternoon I surprised myself by shedding a legitimate tear as I looked at the four happy human beings with money to burn and thought of the misery that would inevitably follow.

Was this just a family, or was it perhaps a nation?

» » » » »

Looking back fifty, sixty or seventy years to the time when I was trying to find my place in the sun, I didn't yet see the relationship between what my father did every day and the benefits resulting from his work. I think my problem therefore, which may be common among kids born into similar circumstances, was that I took the benefits of wealth for granted. Let me turn the father/son relationship around to try pinpointing the source of trouble.

Suppose, for example, that I decided at an early age to be a writer. Let's say I worked hard at my craft, became successful, made lots of money and enjoyed the ego trip, a legitimate bonus in any earned success story.

Now assume I have a young son who has no idea what I do in my study every day. He goes off to camp in the summer and to prep school the rest of the year, all he is aware of is that he is privileged. He probably doesn't even know how lucky he is, and the more he becomes immersed in what he considers his God-given opportunities for recreation, the more alienated he becomes from my work.

He has no way of knowing, for example, that on this particular day because I am doing a major edit on this chapter, I am getting great satisfaction out of expanding on the third generation-loser syndrome: there are many, many wealthy men who are having serious problems with their sons, and my hope is they may benefit from this day's writing.

(Also by developing this market for my book I could be increasing my royalty checks!)

However, when I said my imaginary son had no way of knowing, it could only be because *I* had never shared the joys of my work with him, and looking back, I suspect that is the bottom line of most failing father/son relationships.

Because my father told me very little about his business life, he never told me about how he got completely out of the stock market months before the 1929 crash; I learned that only years later from my uncle Foster.

When I was old enough to understand, suppose he had told me how he felt on the commuter train as he watched other businessmen studying the financial pages and making notes for new investments while he was convinced they were all making a horrible mistake. Suppose he had communicated the drama, the tension and the moneyed excitement in his daily life to me: suppose he had told me how tremendous he felt on Black Friday. Suppose he had cued me in on all the fascinating and highly imaginative wheelings and dealings that went on at the Donnelley Corporation every day.

Who knows, I might have gone in the advertising business and become rich and happy, instead of just happy.

» » » » »

There are other tricky aspects to the father/son relationship. Children born into any walk of life probably take their nitch for granted. However, there is probably a greater incentive to break free on your own if you are born into poverty because misery and exploitation comprise your world. I have known at least four men in various stages of breaking free of humble and abject circumstances of birth and who had to learn everything from the ground up, including how to talk and how to hold a knife and fork. My heart went out to them and I supported them any way I could, and although financially I was unfortunately not much help, their trust and friendship meant a great deal to me—yes, damn it, it brings tears to my eyes to think of them, perhaps because I never had a son or because I deeply respected the effort it took to overcome the obstacles they faced through no fault of their own. Perhaps, and more importantly, it was because their determined efforts were individual examples of man's capacity to exceed himself and ultimately, perhaps, at least to alleviate injustice, prejudice, and war.

One of these men lived in my hometown in Canada and one in my hometown in New York, and part of the joy of writing is knowing they will be reading this from across the gulf that separates our origins and our destinies.

» » » » »

Another problem I had as the poor son of a wealthy father was that when I observed the privileged class, I could not honestly say I thought they were as happy as they should have been. The only difference was they bought yachts instead of canoes and duckboats, but I'd far rather freeze my ass off in a duckboat I built myself than be at the wheel of a $100,000 cruiser with a highball in its gimbal and nothing in particular to do other than drink it.

The rich play tennis at country clubs instead of public courts but the game is the same—what good does all your money do if your spectacular overhead smash goes into the net while your secret young mistress is watching from behind a palm tree? What these observations added up to is that I was unwilling to do what I, perhaps mistakenly, thought I had to do to get rich, assuming, of course, I had the ability: the sheer amount of work seemed disproportionate to the rewards, and this complex conclusion doesn't even take into account the integer of my Low self-esteem.

Because my father's work always struck me as mysterious and super-brainy in an almost occult way, I was intimidated by the business world and, because I knew I would one day be forced to find my niche in it, I developed at a very early age what I assumed to be a completely justified inferiority complex.

I definitely felt I could not be a successful businessman because I was too stupid. But if I couldn't be a businessman, what was there left to be?

One evening at the dinner table when I was in my early teens I innocently asked my parents what an inferiority complex was. By their sudden, convulsive starts, the sound of a knife dropping on china, their looks of alarm and then elaborate and overdrawn ridicule of the very idea of anyone having an inferiority complex, I knew that whatever it really was, I had a whopper. My inferiority complex was a lump of arsenic in my brain. It took half my life to absorb it into my blood and eventually to my kidneys and bladder and ultimately to the toilet, where it belonged in the first place. I figure it cost me more in unearned potential than all the money I've received from my father's estate, and if I were wealthy and had a son—knowing what I know now—I'd buy the best professional advice I could find on how to bolster his self-esteem without breaking his spirit.

» » » » »

When I graduated from St. Lawrence my father, mother and I went out to dinner to celebrate. While I was reaching for a piece of bread my father grabbed my arm with one hand and removed my wrist watch with the other. Then he slipped a new watch on my wrist and said, with a warm smile, "this is your graduation present— now get a job." Dad had a gift for saying a lot in a few words. What had he just told me? The smile told me he loved me. The grabbing of my arm told me that life was a wrestling match and that force and energy ruled the world. The slipping of the new expensive watch on my wrist told me he was glad he had been able to send me to college and was pleased that I had the sense to study hard and graduate. Then, in only four words—"now get a job"— he not only paid me the compliment of assuming I understood the complex usages of irony in language and that I would appreciate the histrionic and literary finesses of his imaginatively conceived sledgehammer blow. What he did was lay out the rules and regulations under which I would have to live out my life with the handicap of the heritage of being a third generation loser. I got his message loud and clear. My father had done his level best to prepare me for life in the real world: from here on out, if I wanted something I had to get it myself, as he did and as his father had done before him.

I had been toying with the idea of going to work for the Donnelley Corporation, but my father never brought the subject up and I knew partly instinctively and partly as the result of my training as an English major that it would be a mistake to ask. My father had just said, "Now get a job." He hadn't said, "Now get a *relative* to give you a job."

Years later my mother told me that when my father graduated from St. Lawrence, his father (also a St. Lawrence graduate), went through essentially the same routine with him, and so my father, wanting to be a newspaper man, got a job as reporter for "The World". After a couple of years he began to get by-lines, and shortly after that he received a phone call at work from his father, who addressed him as Mr. Gunnison. His father explained that he had been reading his by-lines and thought they had merit. Then he said, "Mr. Gunnison, I wonder if I could entice you to come to work for the "Eagle?"

» » » » »

In short order after I graduated I got myself a job, got myself a wife, and got myself in trouble.

Perhaps there's something about getting a wife after living so long on Hancock Street that upsets your equilibrium, but before I realized that supporting two people took approximately twice as much money as living alone, I had run up a considerable debt: $1,400 was major money in 1947.

Furthermore I was acutely aware that I was displaying all the symptoms of a third generation loser.

Although I was making a decent living working as a wage analyst at Western Electric's Point Breeze plant in Maryland, my work was torture. I had to take the beautiful, and unpredictable English language, the language of Shakespeare and Pope and Dryden and murder it by writing concise and clinical descriptions of various boring job duties to be later used for dickering with unions over wage rates.

Unhappy at work, all I wanted to do when the bell rang was pleasure myself. Thus about $1,000 of my $1,400 debt had gone for repairs on my motorcycle, a Stevens speaker for my hi-fi, and flying lessons. I had every reason to be ashamed of my extravagance and lay awake nights trying to figure out how to get myself out of my predicament.

While still in the bloom of youth during that desperate time, I had the misfortune to read Gogol's short story "The Overcoat" about a loser who had a low paying job copying other people's manuscripts and who needed a warmer overcoat to ward off the bitter Russian winters. In describing how he planned to save money from his meager income to pay for the coat, Gogol inserted a detail that I'm sure has sent shivers up the spines of many aspiring creative writers.

The poor devil decided to be careful where he put his feet down while walking to work: he was going to try to walk only on smooth surfaces in order to save shoe leather.

How better could one describe the tragedy of a man struggling to achieve basic comfort while the poor guy was being held captive by the shortness of his mind's reach?

My education had given me a deep appreciation of literature, but the thought of trying to earn a living by writing was preposterous. I was no Gogol, and the reason I knew that was because I spent a week trying to equal Gogol's shoeleather caper and gave up in despair.

Perhaps the limitation of my mind did not involve out-Gogoling Gogol, but I didn't realize I might have been able to make a comment about his short story that went beyond shoe leather—like this one.

You don't have to be a Gogol to earn money writing. And incidentally, to talk shop for a moment, the idea of equating economics with shoe leather and three packs of gum for ten cents came from Gogol's story.

Isn't it amazing how often literature and life touch the same bases?

» » » » »

Gradually, sickeningly, I realized I could not bail myself out of debt and would have to ask my father for help.

I hated doing it. I just hated it.

My father listened attentively to my woes. Then he asked pertinent questions. He took a small notebook out of his pocket and asked for the figures again. He wrote them down, added them up, and asked more questions.

Finally he said, looking me in the eye, "Okay. Now, if I give you $1,400, will you be clean—will that take care of all your debts?"

"Yes," I said, looking him in the eye.

"And if you are free of debt, will you be able to *stay* debt-free on your income?" he asked.

"Yes," I replied.

"What are you going to do if your motorcycle breaks down again?" he asked, deliberately, I'm sure, equating it with my washing machine by the tone in his voice.

That blow smarted like hell.

What we were now talking about was not my debts or even economics, because my father was vindicating his way of life to me and I was making a feeble stab at preserving mine, I felt deep down that he was absolutely right and I was pathetically wrong. After all, he had the money that would solve my problem because he'd earned it by hard, thoughtful work, while I had an excruciating problem because I looked on money simply as something that had to be exchanged for something else in order to give it tangible value.

Forever after that moment, whenever I put myself in my father's shoes, I saw myself as a disappointment to him, as someone who did foolish things, made frivolous choices and had no ambition beyond the pleasures of the moment. The fact that my mind might have had a marketable artistic twist meant no more to him than classical music or poetry because it was not in his nature to appreciate such things. This, however, didn't change my awareness that I was a disappointment to him, and even though I knew it was not in my power to change my way of life, I was still saddled with a heavy weight of guilt.

My father won our little contest hands down. He had every right to equate my joy-of-living motorcycle with my utilitarian washing machine, but the blow still smarted like hell because it summarized what seemed to me to be my utter inferiority.

"If my motorcycle breaks down again, I'll push it in the garage and leave it there until I can afford to fix it," I answered him, meaning every word, but I was sick at heart as I tortured myself with thoughts of a broken-down bike in the springtime.

Game, set and match: with that my father presented me with a check for $1,400.

In later years I sometimes felt that a lesser man would have told me, flat-out, that on the basis of what I had just told him I was now completely on my own and could not expect any more help.

My father never lectured me: it wasn't necessary. Besides, what he *didn't* say packed more of a wallop.

He probably wrote off the money as the cost of sending me to graduate school at the University of Hard Knocks and as graduate schools go he got a terrific bargain for 1,4000 bucks.

I stayed clean and out of trouble for more than twenty years and ironically, when I got seriously in debt again, I was in the final stages of graduate school. I had my master's degree and was completing my final semester of course work for a Ph.D. in American Literature, determined to maintain my A average while also studying for my comprehensive exams and teaching part-time.

» » » » »

Between the writing of the last paragraph and the beginning of this sentence ten minutes have gone by. During that time I lost a battle with the legitimate, literary side of my personality. Intellectually I knew I should strike out the detail about the A average, on the grounds that it wasn't necessary: the reader will form his opinion of my ability from reading this book, not from any statistics I throw at him to make me look good. Indeed, an alert reader would probably pick up on the A-average detail and give me an F in good taste for mentioning it.

On the other hand I worked hard for those A's because I don't have a natural talent for learning and have to fight the process every inch of the way. However, my scholastic record is part of what I have done successfully in life, and as a potential third generation loser, I am proud of this accomplishment and want you to know that because, among other things, it is what this book is all about.

This kind of information is particularly important to me right now because this and the following chapters deal, as you will soon find out, with what I have always considered to be the greatest and bitterest failure of my life.

» » » » »

The most I can say to defend my second experience with indebtedness was that I didn't get into serious debt lying on a beach somewhere eating lotus leaves.

I was changing careers and had been sinking all my accumulated resources in graduate school which was draining me dry. As result Joan and I had to exist primarily on what she earned teaching poetry part-time at the Indiana University Center across the Ohio River from Louisville.

One Monday morning, after studying all weekend for my Ph.D. German examination, I got a call from the bursar's office telling me that if I didn't pay my overdue tuition charges by the end of the month I would be denied admission to classes. I was in a crisis situation and had to come up with a few thousand dollars pronto in order to complete my Ph.D. coursework. (Once that was over I planned to get a full-time job while writing my dissertation.)

My three-year-old, trail weary Triumph dirt bike was only worth about $450. If my hi-fi and particularly my classical record collection had been new, they would have gotten me off the hook, but in the used market they were worth less than half of what I had invested. Besides, they were not material possessions, but part of my soul: I was unwilling to sell my soul for a Ph.D. on the grounds that this would be counter-productive.

My ten-year-old Chevy's transmission had recently become problematical, and the only thing I possessed that would get me the needed money was the Remington Statue of the bucking bronco. However, I didn't own it. It was owned by my *family*. I was just taking care of it (and often wondered how to handle it in my will, since both my daughters loved horses).

Did I have a moral right to sell it? Unlike my grandfather, I hadn't done anything to get it, so I knew if I sold it I'd feel like a prodigal grandson—a wastrel, a worse than nothing. Also, considering the respect I had for my heritage, that would be a heavy lump of failure to carry around for the rest of my life.

I was faced with a difficult, difficult, decision.

However, because I was determined to achieve my Ph.D. goal no matter what, I began to rationalize methodically: I dug out my notes for an ethics course I once took, but this was worse than useless. Besides, there is something wrong with the outlook of a system of higher education that considers ethics a subject that has to be taught.

Since my grandfather was dead, I was convinced he would not be upset if I sold the statue.

My father? Oh boy. That was the toughie. That was catch-22 in capitals and Roman numerals because the problem inherently denied the solution.

Fortunately at that time I had an experience coming within an ace of convincing me that the creator of the universe had a personal interest in my education.

A new acquaintance, who happened to be a commercial photographer, stopped in for a visit, and since photography, although not a fine art, is at least an art. We began exchanging opinions about what art is and what it isn't.

In the course of the discussion I had occasion to walk over to the Remington statue, which he had not commented on, and ask him what he thought of it as a work of art. He scanned it for a few seconds, then shrugged his shoulders and said it didn't do anything for him.

"You know," he said, "I have a friend who creates marvelous works of art by welding hub caps together in bizarre patterns—they're really far-out."

Eureka!

My Remington statue did not belong to me or my descendants at all. It belonged to the dominant culture, and the dominant culture had no more use for it than it had for the classical records on my music shelves.

Frederick Remington was out: welded hub caps were in. Mozart, Wagner and Handel were out: Schoenberg, Stravinsky and John Cage were in.

The game was over.

There was no permanence to Art, to Families, to the World itself!

The cavalcade of human aspirations was nothing more than sheets of newborn raindrops being blown onto shimmering asphalt on a stormy Brooklyn night in ever-present proximity to a sewer.

Would mankind ever find out what it really wanted—or more to the point—what it really *needed*?

It was every man for himself and one day at a time until the evening sun goes down and the morning sun doesn't come up.

That evening I wrapped Frederick Remington's statue in a heavy blanket and bungee-strapped it on the back of my Triumph dirt bike. It was the only vehicle I possessed that I could be reasonably sure would take me to New York and back without breaking down. I felt I had to take the Remington to a prestigious New York art dealer in person in order to maintain control over the transaction. Just shipping it there was out of the question: it would be an admission that I was taking the easy way out even when I was disposing of my inheritance. The truth was, however, that I would never really know whether I was acting from a responsible impulse or just needed an excuse to take a long motorcycle ride: sometimes personal honesty is harder to come by than global truth.

Before daybreak the next morning, on February 14th—Valentine's Day—I took off for the 1,900-mile roundtrip ride to New York City with Remington's statue bungee-strapped behind me and my future up ahead, winking and crooking her forefinger at me, like a diseased hooker hanging out of a window.

And instead of the trials universal tires I used in the enduro off-season, I had shod my mount with full knobbies, in case I ran into snowstorms or rattlesnakes.

CHAPTER 31

The Descent into the Abyss

My avowed love of contrasts fell far short of appreciating the contrast between a priceless work of art bungee-strapped on the back of a $450 motorcycle, particularly since both of them were whizzing at 88 feet per second over winter pot-holed roadways.

There was a desolate inconclusiveness to what I was about to do. Alone, sick at having to surrender the statue and never really warm, as the miles ticked off I began to question my sanity. Early on the first day I hit a nasty chuck hole and felt the statue momentarily part company with the seat, and at the very next opportunity I bought another bunch of bungee-chords. As I was stretching them over the bucking bronco, I noticed the blanket was filmed with oil. A check revealed the engine was almost out of oil. How could that be? Another check identified the cause: the air cleaner was adrift. Apparently when I took that spill on the last fall enduro it had been knocked loose. And yeah, I ate a lot of dust that day, and it doesn't take much enduro dust to turn an engine into an oil burner.

As night began to fall my world fell apart with it. With the setting of the sun the temperature dropped and I began to shiver— was this the first stage of hypothermia or was it because of acute insecurity brought on by lack of intelligence?

Even with replenished oil, the engine seemed to be making weird noises amplified by the moist blackness of night. These bizarre noises reminded me of Swedenborg's unique gibberish and that reminded me of Blake's crack that Swedenborg acted as if he were the only writer who ever broke a net.

Was I breaking a net or entangled in a net of my own making? Or even worse, was I—this very moment—pulling together from deep within my irresponsible self, the taughtened ends of its drawstring? Obviously it was the latter because now Swedenborg made me think of Berlioz, and the episode in "The Damnation of Faust" which Berlioz filled with Swedenborg's wonderfully bizarre language.

Faust and Mephistopheles are galloping on two black horses— oh God!—black as my bucking bronco—with a hideous beast, baying, pursuing them. In my mind's eye I saw the huge night birds that swarmed around Faust, uttering terrible shrieks. I saw the earth writhe before me—hup! hup! hup!—I heard the thunder roll beneath my wheels—hup! hup! hup!—and just as it began to rain blood the fantastic chorus of demons and the damned cried out "Has! Irimiru Karabrao! Has! Has! Has!" The Prince of Darkness asked Mephistopheles if I had freely signed the fatal document which consigned me to the fatal flames. "No, No!," I shouted—"I will turn around and bring my heritage statue back home!" But I could no more turn my bike around than get out of my company car that fateful day at GE.

"He freely signed," confirmed Mephistopheles.

I was doomed: I could not go back: I had sold my heritage to the devil.

As I was swept away by the genius of Berlioz's imagination I heard the chorus of Demons and the Damned singing triumphantly

Diff! diff! Meronder, meronder, aysko!
Has! has! Satan! has! has! Belphegor!
Has! has! Mephisto
Has! has! Kroix
Diff! diff! Astaroth!
Diff! diff! Belzebuth!
Sat, sat rayk ir kimour.

The power, the energy, the diamond-forming heat of Berlioz's music blew me away, the missing audible substance of it more than offset by the thought of how terribly Berlioz, an incurable romantic like me, suffered in a world dominated by money and power. I felt closer to him that night than I have ever felt to any of the tormented artists who have enriched my life beyond measure— and who are forced like me to live in a world in which even higher education is ruled by the bursar.

» » » » »

The next morning, thanks to the catharsis of Berlioz's "music," I assessed my situation with an astonishingly clear head. The Triumph was burning oil at the rate of one quart per 100 miles. Something expensive was wrong, but the problem had stabilized. As a result I was able to maintain a steady 50 mph pace, and my only problem for the time being was that the whole back of my bike was coated with oil—including the sides of the rear tire. I bought a piece of 6 mil plastic and covered the blanket, even tough I was pretty sure the oil had seeped through to the statue. However, rather than check I preferred to live with the hope that it hadn't. I also put on my rain jacket, as the back of my leather jacket already had a light film of oil on it.

With the engine oil topped up and several quarts on board I resumed my trip, banking from side to side every once in a while to keep oil from accumulating on the sides of the rear tire to the point where it would be dangerous if I suddenly had to swerve. Although this became dreadfully monotonous, the stakes were too high not to do it.

I was in good spirits. Why shouldn't I be? After all, I was riding a motorcycle. And then—what do you know?—I saw something astonishing: a Gunnison Home.

It was an early model, all by its lonesome in the middle of a lovely field, and suddenly the floodgates of many happy memories opened.

That house had been built by my father's brother, my uncle Foster.

» » » » »

Let me tell you: Foster was something else.

When Foster was born it wasn't a normal parturition: it was more like letting a tiger out of its cage.

The first of many stories that made the rounds about Foster took place when he was about thirteen, living with his father, brother and sister, my dearly beloved aunt Florence. Occasionally Foster would be late for breakfast, and his father would send Florence upstairs to find out what was keeping her brother. Invariably she would find him sitting on his bed, with a sock on one foot, and twirling his other sock in his hand as he gazed out the window, his eyes, shall we say, fixed at an indeterminate point above the horizon.

Florence would come downstairs and announce "Foster is twirling his sock again."

Foster was a dreamer, a visionary, but at an early age he was caught in a vicious bind.

My grandfather once remarked that children weren't interesting until they became adults. Since my father was six years older than his brother, he was the first to interest his father, who took him to Europe on "Eagle" business trips, discussed management problems and strategies at length with him, and treated him like royalty. He even bought him a canoe and one of the first cars registered in St. Lawrence county when he was in college.

Meanwhile, the younger Foster got very little attention.

I have often thought that Foster was not consumed with ambition so much as obsessed with proving he was the equal of the father who had rejected him when he was a child and could not defend himself.

In any event when he graduated from St. Lawrence he got a job selling lighting fixtures for a manufacturing company in New

Jersey. He was not a natural-born salesman because at first he lacked confidence: when he knocked on doors he hoped they wouldn't open. But he was determined to succeed. He told me he used to go in men's rooms and fill a sink with cold water and submerge his head until he had purged himself of his lack of confidence. Apparently it worked because he developed into a supersalesman, and so in a very short time he was making barrels of money.

The lighting fixture company was owned by two men on the verge of retiring, so Foster approached them with the proposition that instead of paying him in commissions, he be paid a modest salary and that the commission money go toward stock in the company. The two partners agreed.

At that point Foster had the bit in his teeth. There was no stopping him.

When he learned that Radio City Music Hall was about to be built in New York City, he approached the architects with the idea of having the largest lighting fixture in the world in the foyer. It was consistent with the concept that bigger was better: it would make a significant contribution to the hoopla.

They bought the idea.

Foster designed the lighting fixture.

The company he now owned built it.

At the opening ceremonies at Radio City Music Hall news photographers produced a twenty-five foot ladder and had Foster climb to the top to have his picture taken next to the largest lighting fixture in the world.

When they were through they called "you can come down now, Mr. Gunnison, we've got our pictures."

But he didn't come down. Other rungs had been the lightning fixtures he sold to the Waldorf Astoria, Chrysler Building and the Empire State Building. However, now he was literally at the top of the ladder. The way he told it to me he looked around him, smiled and enjoyed his success. And when he finally started down the ladder—in his own time he knew that he had sold his last lighting fixture, and that he wanted to move ahead.

As I said, that's the way he told it, but I don't think he was smiling and enjoying his success at the top of that ladder.

I think he was twirling his sock.

Shortly afterwards he sold his business, and after paying off the original owners and taxes, he netted a cool million dollars.

This was in the early thirties—in the darkest days of the Great Depression.

He was 29 years old.

» » » » »

As the result of his negotiations with the Radio City Music Hall architects, Foster became interested in architecture, studied it on his own, and during these studies he got the idea of building houses in a factory on an assembly line.

Marine plywood had recently been developed and he decided to make his houses out of that, but the only available press large enough to make panels the size he needed was in New Albany, Indiana. Since the press was too large to move without enormous expense, and since New Albany was just across the river from Louisville, which was the geographic center of the United States and therefore the perfect location for the nationwide distribution of his prefabricated houses, Foster moved to New Albany and began operations.

As they used to say in those long-gone days everything was swell, until one day the Ohio River swelled out of its banks and went in one end of his factory and out the other, wiping him out.

A week after losing his fortune Foster got dressed up, had a large lunch at Louisville's venerable Brown Hotel, bought a couple of two-dollar cigars, and strolled down the street to the biggest bank in town.

"I would like to see the president," he told the receptionist.

As you know, this isn't the way you do it. The receptionist's job is to see to it that every Tom, Dick and Harry doesn't get an audience with the president.

But the man named Foster was not Tom, Dick or Harry.

Foster, dark and handsome as a movie star, was also intensely dynamic, with a resonant voice and a spirited wit.

The receptionist ushered him right into the president's office in unreceptionist-like confusion.

After glaring at his receptionist, the president extended his arm and said, "How can I help you, Mr. er"—he glanced down at the receptionist's card—"Mr. Gunnison?"

They sat down.

Foster offered a two dollar cigar to the bank president, who shook his head.

Then Foster lit his cigar.

He blew out the match.

Holding it up, he looked around for the ashtray.

The president slid it over to him.

Foster disposed of the match.

Then he took a puff and blew the smoke ceilingward.

He paused, then suddenly looked the president straight in the eyes, and smiled.

"I've come here to borrow a million dollars," he said.

» » » » »

From that point on no natural or circumstantial disaster could stop Foster. During the Second World War when there were housing shortages, he used to get orders for hundreds of his prefabricated houses from subdivision developers.

Unlike his competitors, he turned them all down.

Instead, he quietly established dealers all over the United States and rationed his houses with strict impartiality. He established the Prefabricated House Institute, which set standards and gave certifications so that the harmful influence of fly-by-nighters could be minimized. He set up another institute where dealers from all over the country could come to learn how to conduct the business of selling Gunnison homes from the ground up. Ever the shrewd manipulator of human nature, he kept a list of call-girl numbers as an inducement to lure dealers to New Albany for refresher courses.

Years later, when United States Steel decided to enter the prefabricated house business, it made a detailed study of all the major companies and bought Gunnison Homes because, among its many assets, it was the only company with a well-established network of successful dealers.

Although he did not have a degree in architecture, he was so knowledgeable that he was often asked to give talks at architect conventions and took great pride in those offers.

Considered the father of the Prefabricated House Industry, he is enshrined in the Architect's Hall of Fame in Washington, D.C.

He was a good friend. I miss him. Writing this tribute to him is making my day. I could devote an entire chapter just to anecdotes about him, but what follows will have to suffice.

Foster was more than a master of social situations—he created legendary ones. In order to appreciate the following example, please bear in mind that it happened a long time ago when, as the saying went, no one would say shit even with a mouthful.

A very proper friend of the family had bought a house and carefully supervised the interior decorating. She was proud of what she had done and during the housewarming was showing guests her decorating accomplishments. The woman, wife of the president of a large and prestigious corporation, knew that Foster was a highly skilled interior decorator and was anxious to get his input. He warmly approved of her tastes and offered a few minor suggestions. For example there was a lamp on an end table made from an antique flintlock pistol braced in an upright position with the shade on a rod about a foot above the muzzle. Foster gently turned it 90°, remarking that "the pistol is more graceful if one sees it in profile."

Finally the woman came to the mantelpiece and I could tell from the look on her face that she considered it her *piece de la resistance*.

"Well, what do you think?" she asked proudly.

Foster had been glancing reflectively around the room. "Everything is great, you've done a wonderful job."

Then he turned and, noticing the mantelpiece, added, "Except that you fucked up the mantelpiece."

The hushed room began to fill with arched eyebrows and dropped jaws. Soon they were accompanied by pervasive smiles, which Foster blithely ignored as he went into the details of the botched mantelpiece, for to acknowledge the success of his coup would have been to deprecate it.

Foster was the anecdote incarnate.

What most amazed me Foster was that, although he had an enormous range of interests and pursued them with unbridled zest, he never let his outside interests interfere with his working life. If he stayed out till four in the morning, which he sometimes did, he'd be in his office raring to go at eight A.M. He was well-read, loved foreign movies, favored classical music (especially Mozart), and at one time was hooked on stock car races. Once he called to tell me I shouldn't miss a certain exotic dancer appearing at a local carnival. I never had a dull conversation with him. His imagination was boundless. He was my idea of perfection in a man.

However I sometimes felt awkward when I was with him and felt sorry for my cousin Foster Junior.

It wasn't because of his manner—he was always warm and friendly toward me.

The stress came from what he represented. The odds alone were overwhelmingly against a repeat success story in any branch of human endeavor, and I have always been glad I had enough sense not to beat my head against that wall the way I did in weak moments with my father, even though in Foster's case I felt his life was richer than mine, which was not really the case with my relationship with my father.

» » » » »

My reveries about Uncle Foster entertained me until I got to West Virginia, and once on the Pennsylvania Turnpike I felt as if I were in the outskirts of New York City. The weather was holding steady. I was thriving in an equilibrium between being cold and being too cold. Although I have been in an advanced state of hypothermia several times, when I had to concentrate painfully to keep my wits about me, I have never caught a cold or gotten sick in any way as the result of riding a motorcycle. Many years ago, while riding over Eisenhower Pass west of Denver while it was spitting snow, I got so cold that when I finally came to a restaurant I was shaking so hard I could only look helplessly at my cup of coffee. I couldn't touch it without spilling it, and by the time I stopped shaking, the coffee was so cold I had to order a fresh cup.

That second cup is one of my fondest caffeine-rejuvenation memories.

» » » » »

As I resumed my reveries I recalled that I once had a dentist who bragged that he lived in an air conditioned house, drove an air conditioned car to his air conditioned office, and was thus able to spend his entire working days at a constant 70°. For similar reasons his winters were also spent at a rock-steady 70°.

I felt sorry for him.

There is no such thing as unearned comfort: most of the so-called comfort of our civilization is really just a mindless form of numbed neutrality. I was not an incubator baby and have no desire to be an incubator adult. I thrive on variety, yet our whole culture is predicated on the illusion that machines can restructure human psychology.

I had a relative on my mother's side who walked several miles through a blinding snowstorm one night, entered his house, walked over to a fire roaring in the fireplace, held out his hands to it, turned his head around to my eleven-year-old mother, smiled and dropped dead. To my mind his was a horrible death, coming as it did when he was just beginning to enjoy the exquisite reward of comfort.

The thermostat has made such death-states commonplace: if you're always comfortable where do you go to experience the joy of coziness?

Coziness is one of the greatest sensations in the arsenal of happiness, but the genuine article doesn't come cheap. That's one of the things I love about motorcycles: on a bike you become part of the weather. This relationship often makes my day. I once rode through the climax of a Vermont fall foliage extravaganza on a lovely twisty road where one minute black clouds ahead—perhaps to the West—portended a thundershower, but then the road would twist North—perhaps—and the sun would be out. There was a lot of cumulonimbus activity in the area, and I spent several super-intense hours playing a game with the lottery of storms, because I was determined to squeak through the day without having to stop and put my rainsuit on. I have never lost my zest for judging the richness of a motorcycling day by the quality of the suspense around the bends of its twisties, but that afternoon turned out to be special even by those standards, since the uncertainty of comfort was a bonus added to the suspense of lucking on to the next beautiful vista. When the sun went down I was in the Green Mountains and just as I began to suffer from the evening chill, I was caught unaware by a storm I hadn't accounted for which crept up behind a mountain and drenched me to the skin before I could get my rainsuit on. I had planned to camp that night but decided, in one of the great inspirational moments of my life, to cash in on the civilization I am always so ungratefully complaining about, and ended up spending one of the coziest nights of my life in the swankiest motel I could find.

The above mind games suddenly came to a halt as I approached the place on the turnpike where I had had such a memorable experience a few years before that I incorporated it into a feature story I wrote for a special touring issue of "Cycle World" in 1978. Here it is, with their kind permission.

» » » » »

At the tag end of a colorful late fall afternoon in 1971, my Moto Guzzi Ambassador and I were approaching the Somerset exchange on the Pennsylvania Turnpike. Our seemingly endless

and glorious 600-mile day was drawing to a close. What was left of
the sun was directly behind and our shadow was outdistancing us.
The Guzzi was passing the time humming to itself while I was
admiring the shadow-bike's suspension. It was ghosting over the
frost heaves and tar strips without so much as a flicker.

I was faced with one of those enjoyable, you-can't-lose decisions
touring riders often make. Should I stop in Somerset for supper
and then ride to Harrisburg in the refreshing coolness of early
night, or should I keep going and soak up the short-lived, earthy
melancholy of a great day waning imperceptibly into the prospect
of a memorable evening?

Although I was hungry, stopping for food seemed too time
consuming, too rational for my endless-day mood: there is more
than one kind of hunger.

This decision should have been spontaneous, but I was curious
about the time. The older I get the more imagination it takes to
keep moving faster than time, but since 600 miles in the saddle
had reduced me to an extremely mellow but unimaginative lump,
I decided to check my watch.

In the left slash pocket of my jeans I had one of those nickel-
plated dollar watches which at that time sold for $3.95. Like many
enduro riders I used it for timekeeping because it had a big dial
and was rugged and cheap. It had many hard enduro miles under
its case as well as great sentimental value, and so there was no way
I could put a price on it.

As I stood on the pegs to reach in my pocket I remember
thinking I had to be careful because I was moving at 75 miles per
hour and the watch didn't have a lanyard to catch it if it fell.

As I brought it out of my pocket it—unaccountably—slipped
out of my hand.

Instinctively I jerked my left boot upwards to cushion its fall—
as a condemned man might instinctively walk around a puddle in
a wet courtyard on his way to the scaffold.

The watch hit my upcoming boot and bounced into the air.

It glistened in the sun as it sailed along beside the Guzzi.

At this point in time it was a perfectly functioning watch, correct within an unimportant minute or so, with its mainspring energy tight, its escapement ticking precisely to and fro, each little gear jogging according to its size and function and in general paying more attention to the universal laws of physics than the headstrong Guzzi was to the local laws of speed.

You couldn't call this quartzless and digitless timepiece a miracle of technology, but there was no denying it was in a miraculous situation, this piece of time suspended for an instant six inches from the Guzzi's left valve cover and two feet from the whizzing pike—idly ticking away, ticking away, as if it had all the time in the world.

Striking the state of Pennsylvania precisely on edge, my watch bounced three feet above the concrete, its nickel-plating again flashing in the sun.

It was now spinning like the Guzzi's wheels but unlike the Guzzi it was speeding way over its head.

At the second jolt the crystal popped off, glinting everywhichway.

Another ricochet and the backed popped off, whirling away in a shower of sparks.

Then the face went, white as a sheet.

I twisted around in the saddle: if I had been tailgating a semi and its brake lights had just flashed on it wouldn't have mattered.

This I *had* to see.

To my knowledge the watch never stopped bouncing. Its reflections in the evening sun changed from glassy to nickel-bright to white and finally to golden as the brass gears, cogs, wheels and backing plates spilled out on the turnpike at speed. With each diminishing skip the watch got smaller and smaller until suddenly all its remaining parts dissolved in thin air without a trace.

It was beautiful.

» » » » »

On the whole trip to New York with one of mankind's great accomplishments on the back of my bike I only had one crisis.

As I came to the entrance of the tunnel through Tuscarora Mountain on the turnpike, I glanced up to admire the name, which I have always thought was pretty enough for a nation or a girlfriend and didn't see the patch of black ice just ahead in time to avoid it.

I thought I was a goner and froze thinking "Don't accelerate or decelerate."

In the time it takes to say "inertia is the tendency of a body at rest to remain at rest and a body in motion to remain in motion at the same velocity and in the same direction hopefully with the rubber side down," I was bathing in the light at the end of the tunnel.

If I had gone down I'm sure the Remington statue would have been damaged beyond repair, which would have been a greater tragedy than if an insane artist had flung it in the deepest part of an ocean as a protest against the injustice of fate.

» » » » »

The art dealer came to my hotel room.

He hardly looked at the statue. He just turned it upside down and carefully examined its hollow bottom.

Even the greatest art is hollow—if you press your luck with any particular joy too often.

"May I see some identification?" he asked.

I showed him my driver's license.

He held it in front of the inscription on the base of the statue far longer than it seemed necessary—just long enough to give me an uneasy feeling, as if I were an impostor or thief: it was rough.

He cleared his throat.

"I'll give you $6,000 in cold cash right now," he told me, "or if you want me to put it in an auction in about two weeks it will probably bring more."

I asked if he had any idea how much more.

He couldn't say but he thought it would net me considerably more.

"Is there any chance that it would bring less?"

"That's always possible, but it's not likely," he replied matter of factly.

I was elated. Wow! Six grand! Cash. *Now.* A bird in the hand is worth two in the bush—everybody lives by that: why shouldn't I? I had just enough money left to get home, and because that did not include a motel, it meant riding through the cold winter's night. Moreover the cost of the extra oil had to come out of money earmarked for food—but now I could celebrate. I could go to the opera after a fancy meal in a French restaurant. I could get my engine overhauled and ride home in style. Hell, there'd be plenty left over, and besides, I planned to get a full-time job—no sirree!— I was not a third generation loser: hadn't I just taken terrible risks to further my education?

"I'll take the cash."

However, something about his speed in reaching for his wallet bothered me.

He counted out sixty $100 bills on top of the television set.

I picked up the stack of bills, jounced them into a neat stack, and handed them back to him.

"Put the Remington in the auction," I said.

» » » » »

Long before daybreak the next morning I was on my way back to Louisville, packing nine quarts of SAE 10W-40 where the Remington had been, because although I could afford to go hungry, I couldn't afford to be without oil. When the sun came up I turned around to count my blessings and looked at the oil: yup, it was

10W-40 all right. When there were no more cans back there, I'd be home.

Suddenly a wave of melancholia came over me. Why, for God's sake? Wasn't I returning home triumphant? Wasn't I riding a motorcycle? Wasn't the sun shining? Wasn't the temperature in the forties? Why are all of life's great moments tinged with melancholy?

Then I remembered.

When I took my first solo in Ray Devener's 1929 Fleet biplane, I twisted around and looked back at the cockpit where Ray was supposed to be. It was the emptiest sight I had ever seen. It was nothing where something was supposed to be. It was ignorance where knowledge is supposed to be. It was fear where security was supposed to be. All there was in that antique airplane was the "I," and all the "I" could do was guess and hope for the best. Handling the controls was only a stopgap. Sure, if "I" pressed the right rudder pedal and moved the stick to the right the plane banked to the right, and if "I" eased the stick back a little and then neutralized the controls the plane would hang in a perfect bank indefinitely, but not really—*only until it ran out of gas.*

The metaphor created a whole new ballgame: life is simply a matter of levitating whenever possible while getting the most mileage out of the blasted fuel gauge.

My melancholia, I figured, is my greatest asset. *It is my way of intensifying life by turning moments with high potential into brief epiphanies tinged with eternity.* This is what I joyfully settle for when my defense reaction is dead in the water: I have never encountered a facet of conventional life that comes within a country mile of such moments.

I was on a roll. The day was not merely like a dream come true, it was like a coming true that started from an awakening.

When I again passed the early model Gunnison home all by its lonesome in the middle of a lovely field, but now majically on the opposite side of the road, I felt that for once in my life, in my own way, I was the equal of my uncle Foster. He had passed up chances to make a quick buck selling a hundred or more houses to fly-by-night developers, but instead had sold the single house in the middle of a lovely field through a dealer. It was an investment in his future that paid off tens of times over when he sold his business to United States Steel. When I decided to resist the temptation of the phrase "$6,000 in cold cash," and put the Remington's value at risk in an auction, I was simply using the knowledge I had gained from talking to my uncle about how to go about things. I don't think it was any more complicated or profound than that.

» » » » »

THE AFTERMATH

A week later I received a check for $11,000 for the Remington statue.

A few months later a friend of my father's saw it in an art store with a price tag of $17,000. (Today the going price for a Remington is $175,000, which I like to think is more than the going price for a bunch of welded hubcaps.)

My father's friend bought it and donated it to St. Lawrence University. Since Frederick Remington had lived in Canton, New York, where St. Lawrence is, St. Lawrence acquired some Remington paintings and memorabilia and built a small Remington museum on the campus.

Remington's bucking bronco was the centerpiece.

Directly above the statue there was a skylight. One night a person or persons unknown broke the skylight and pulled the statue up through the opening by means of a slip-loop on the end of a rope.

That was many years ago.

As of today, December 15, 1999, the statue has not been recovered.

Perhaps some day it will be, but probably with my name on the base obliterated. If this happens I would be able to tell if it is indeed the stolen Remington because something happened to it while it was bungee strapped on the back of my Triumph, something almost certainly undetectable except by me.

Although my bitter loss is probably irretrievable, something mysterious in that tremendous work of art still belongs to me, not because my name will forever exist beneath the obliteration, but because I took an intensely human journey with that living statue which will never reoccur in the history of a trillion universes.

POSTLUDE

We have now come to the end of the fifth winter in which I have lived cozily and happily amidst word symbols such as these. It is now, as it has been seven days a week for three months, 6:15 A.M. In seven or eight hours on this day I will finish this book and it will become a tangible memory.

In ten or fifteen minutes it will become a memory for you as well, dear reader.

And if I am lucky, in the next ten or fifteen minutes other curious readers will begin it with expectation.

And in a few days they will be where you are now, with ten or fifteen minutes to go.

That is also where I am at this moment.

I am at the end of the book that is my long life, with ten or fifteen minutes to go.

If you understood the first principle of this book, you probably also already knew the secret of packing seven or eight hours into every ten or fifteen minutes of your life.

Seven or eight hours is a deliciously indeterminate length of time—especially today. Goodness!—I've only taken few sips of my first abrosial cup of coffee and Joan is cooking up something mysterious—with that bewitching way of hers—in the way of a celebration. Whatever it is, it will involve food and flowers and a camera, for Joan is not one to leave the heart of anyone she loves untouched by a milestone.

By a striking coincidence a severe blizzard dumped a foot of snow on my world last night and is still doing a beautifully sadistic job of exciting masochists like me. The powerlines are down. (Joan whomped up my coffee on our Svea backpacking stove.)

It is hard to write when my world is in such lovely chaos and begging me to romp in it. Victor Hugo solved the problem of distractions by having his servant take away his clothes so there was nothing he could do but write, but fortunately I get the job done with less extreme measures: the romping will have to wait because I am simply too absorbed in the world of ideas. Besides, I learned early on that if a writer aspires to more than a short story the work schedule must be inflexible; persistence is not only absolutely indispensable but probably is good for a few more points on your I.Q. What I am doing at the moment is not always fun and games, and I'm grateful for the downer moments because they give me a delightful sense of having an edge over the myriads of writers who think this process depends only on inspiration, but whose inspired masterpieces are never finished.

I wish I had more encouraging news, but I know without listening to the radio that our culture has not changed one whit in the past seventy years: children are still not allowed to learn for themselves about the beauty of the earth through snow except on weekends when schools are not in business and therefore cannot prevent such higher educational opportunities.

Don't let anyone tell you luck doesn't play an important part in the creative process: I grab what is dumped in my lap—heck, even a power outage—and shamelessly pretend God inundated my hometown with a foot of snow just so I could establish an honest link between the first and last snowstorms in this book. This is an incurable weakness that comes from staring at blank pieces of yellow paper every morning for three months, and which sometimes leads me to think that I will never really be able to call myself a creative writer until I can notice an ant crawling across a blank page and convert it with my ballpoint pen into a herd of buffaloes, as I have just done in make-believe.

Forgive me for talking shop, but I can't resist a fond glance back at my study as I close the door on it the way I once thought I was closing the door on my life forever at Tucumcari.

As this tender moment suggests, it is not easy to come to the end of a pleasure that begins where words end and self-knowledge begins.

When I left town and headed for Sturgis, I thought I knew everything. It never occurred to me that at the age of 75 I still had a lot to learn, but looking back now at the age of 82, it is clear that such was the case.

Let me quickly summarize what I learned about myself by finishing this book with a short dramatized anecdote because I've suddenly changed my plans for today. I'm quitting early because I'm taking Joan out to brunch, and, for the record, this afternoon we're going to listen to a new recording we've never heard before of Wagner's paean to the creative life, "Die Meistersinger", which we haven't heard for over a year—what a treat that's going to be for this happily married Hans Sachs! Tomorrow we're heading South where we will pick up our winter-stored bikes at Bob's BMW in Maryland and I will start my first ride of the year. Joan's bike will be on a trailer and she will have our canoe on top of her van for our post-Daytona bike week trip down Florida's Peace River. I hope it won't be too peaceful, if you know what I mean. One has to keep the juices, and yes, the *angst*, flowing.

As a last-ditch palliative to offset my cultural irreverences, I don't see how it would be possible to end this book on a more optimistic note than with the following dramatized reminiscence and conclusion.

» » » » »

One evening during Christmas vacation from St. Lawrence, when my family lived in Pawling, New York, I was in the library reading Montaigne's *Essays*. My Uncle Foster was visiting my father and the two brothers were in the bar just an open doorway away. I could tell from the occasional sound of ice cubes clinking in glasses that my father was bartending and my uncle was sitting on a stool facing his brother.

I had yet to discover Henry Adams, so I could not have told

you at that time that his life and mine were lived in roughly parallel years a century apart. Except for the six month's period between Henry Adams's death and my birth, when the world had to struggle along without either of us, our combined lifespans (to date) total 163 years.

At no point in human history has the apparent world changed even 1/10,000th as much—for better or worse—as it has in the 163 years from 1838 to 2002, but this type of often-quoted statistic is meaningless unless you interview the man in the street and discover to your horror that nine times out of ten he views it as an unmitigated blessing.

Anyway, the duration of our combined lives represents the full spectrum of heavy duty scientific activity from the invention of the dynamo, when Henry Adams was 44, to the trip to the moon, when I was 51, from the lethal discovery of radium when he was 60 to my chilling realization at the age of 26 that as the result of what nuclear physics professors had been playing with, there was—in Henry Adams's words regarding radium—"no longer any place to hide."

Henry Adams and I believed, in upward spirals of dread, that although the world we were born into made sense to us when we were children, the world we were about to exit made no sense at all and sooner or later must lead to catastrophic disaster.

The current metaphor for this is a seventeen-year-old kid riding a street-legal sport bike capable of going 194 MPH who assumes he can ride it at that speed on public highways, change his oil behind abandoned schoolhouses, ride without a helmet and with a bald rear tire—all with impunity because he is going to live forever through medical science.

Much as I hate to admit it, especially in the closing stages of my life and this book, the philosophers who oppose my views are in complete control of public opinion.

Stand up and take a bow, Robert of *Zen* fame.

» » » » »

This is the point at which my reflections on contemporary culture in this book end.

» » » » »

However, since my life is not over, let me tie off a few loose ends.

While I was absorbed in Henry Adams's *Education* I was aware of the rising and falling of voices as the two brothers in the bar exchanged confidences.

Occasionally there was a burst of uproarious laughter.

Distracted by one such outburst, I put Montaigne aside and began to eavesdrop on their conversation.

Suddenly, instead of reading about Montaigne's views on the fine points of leading the good life, I was listening to my father's philosophy of business.

He was explaining that the Donnelley Corporation occasionally invested money in new enterprises. The details are unimportant: his point concerned how he went about determining how much money to put at risk for a given venture proposition. He believed in studying the facts and figures and antecedents as thoroughly as possible, thus making an educated guess and setting a value, or specific price, not on the ultimate outcome of the venture, but rather on how much money it would take to get it in the black.

He cited an example and picked a figure at random off the top of his head. The amount was staggering in the world I lived in.

"If the company is not in the black when our money is gone, I figure we're sitting up with a corpse and our money has gone down the rat hole, so we drop the project like a hot potato," he said, adding "no exceptions—I don't believe in flogging a dead horse."

I didn't know which to envy more, the shrewdness of his money-mind, or his haughty contempt for the vice of the mixed metaphor.

There was a short period of silence.

"I don't agree with you at all, Ray," Foster countered. "I believe you should judge a proposition strictly on its potential. Then do your homework, and if you are convinced it makes sense, put at risk every cent you can get your hands on and don't stop at anything until you succeed—even sell your blood as often as they'll let you if it comes to that."

I didn't know which to envy more, the shrewdness of his money-mind or the driven confidence of his imagination.

I had just overheard a conversation between two men who had made themselves rich, one by means of sober, analytical thinking and the other by means of analytical thinking coupled with boundless confidence and imagination. As business philosophies went, despite their major differences, they both worked.

Could it be that there was more to success than what might be learned from a textbook?

I was intrigued, so I went into the bar.

"Want a drink?" my father asked.

"Thanks."

He made me a vodka and tonic.

During the time it took to deplete half the vodka and get a glow on, they asked me questions about my studies at St. Lawrence. Was I taking any business or government courses? Was I making any contacts? Why didn't I quit the tennis team and go out for golf? (Golf was a better game, it turned out, because it was more convivial: many an important business deal has been made on a golf course.)

"But tennis is far more exciting and passionate and I'm good at it," is what I didn't say, despite the vodka, being painfully aware that being a good amateur tennis player doesn't give a guy much scope for impressing millionaires.

I felt so small, as the saying went in those days, that I could sit on the edge of a cigarette paper and dangle my legs over the side.

Perhaps, when you believe yourself to be *that* small, it shows on your face.

The brothers suddenly looked at each other as if they had a common problem.

Then my father said, "Do you think we're trying to run your life?"

"Well, let me put it this way," I said, thanks to a quick gulp of vodka, "I hate government and I love tennis."

"Look," dad said, "I don't care what you do with your life. That's your decision. All I want is a son who does the best he can with what he's got. If all you want to do with your life is pump gas in a filling station, that's fine with me as long as you do it as well as you can."

"Yeah," Uncle Foster said, vitally concerned with the growing tension, "don't spill any!"

Primed by the tension, all three of us laughed uproariously.

» » » » »

Your gas tank is full, sir. As far as I can tell I have crossed all my "t's" and dotted all my "i's." I hope I have cleaned your windshield without leaving streaks that distort your vision. You should check your oil the next time you get gas. Also please remember that I am not completely against technology and that my criticisms of the popular culture resulted from my inability to understand why it isn't obvious that life is not a green screen or a screen peopled with ghosts: my life and your life add up to the one and only bottom line which is that, like it or not, we all have spiritual or abstract needs which have to be taken into account—sometimes forcibly— if we are to live happily within the full range of our potentials. Your tire pressures are all right on the money, sir. Please forgive me if I have mixed any metaphors, haughtily or otherwise. I am proud of what I have finally learned to do for a living. It took me thirty years of hard work to own my own gas station, if you know what I mean, so I hope you'll rejoice with me, dear reader while, having achieved freedom from career stress at the age of 83—and with no regrets, I laugh uproariously all by my lonesome and start packing for Florida.

Before I leave Florida, I plan to spend some time on the beach at Boca Raton where, aeons ago, my father waited for the responses to his expensive full-page ad in "The New York Times". However, unlike my father, I won't be waiting for the offer of an executive position in the business world, but rather for an offer from a publisher for work already accomplished.

My father and I never played on the same team, but it is gratifying to feel that perhaps at long last I may yet be able to claim that at least we played in the same league.

Dear reader for the last time, our collaboration has been a pleasure. And now, if you'll excuse me, I'll take a deep breath and finish this five year enterprise right after this e-c-s-t-a-t-i-c instant goes *poof*!

THE END

If this book does well enough I plan to buy a Remington statue with the proceeds and donate it toSt. Lawrence University with this plaque: Donated to St. Lawrence by the Gunnison family with money earned entirely through Herbert Gunnison's brain and right hand working in unison, with 57 ball point pens for 5 years (with assist from the fraternity of American motorcyclists), so in a sense it may be called a triumph of humanistic education over business and commerce.

God of our fathers, what is man?
So proud, so vain, so great in story!
His fame a blast, his life a span,
A bubble at the height of glory!

From "Samson"
an oratorio by George Frederic Handel,
based on Milton's *Samson Agonistes*,

MOTORCYCLE EVENTS GLOSSARY

For 35 years I entered one or more of these events every weekend.

Enduro: An endurance ride from 50 to 500 miles in which each rider has a starting-time number and must maintain an average speed of 24 mph (2 miles every five minutes). What turns an enduro into a race is that secret time checks must be zeroed. Every contestant starts with 1,000 points and loses one for every minute s/he is late to a check point.

On a 100 mile enduro there are usually about nine secret check points. Swamps and other tests of a contestants ability to maintain a 24 mph average, require that a rider must go as fast as skill will permit until he or she is back on time, but always he or she must be aware that a secret check point might be around the next turn. The penalty for being early at a check point is two points per minute. The extra penalty is designed to discourage speeding on the short stretches of paved road, very dangerous on muddy, knobby, tires and wet brakes.

Hare and Hound Racing: A long race consisting of one loop of 50 miles or more through country terrain.

Hare Scrambles Racing: A race consisting of four to five loops on a course of varied terrain and a length of up to five miles.

Hill Climb: A race up a nearly-impossible steep hill. The object is not just to go over the top, but to do it in the shortest possible time.

Ice Racing: A race on a frozen lake with special studded tires.

Scramble Racing: Forerunner of motocross competition on a track with ruts, swampy sections, steep hills and 90° turns.

GLOSSARY

Chocks: A wedge used for blocking the moment of a wheel.

Graveling: An activity in which birds eat small pebbles in order to aid digestion.

Tank Bag: A leather pouch used for storage when touring on a motocycle.

Get Published, Inc!
Thorofare, NJ 08086
01 September 2009
BA2009244